Canadian Social Welfare Policy

CANADIAN PUBLIC ADMINISTRATION SERIES

COLLECTION ADMINISTRATION PUBLIQUE CANADIENNE

J. E. Hodgetts, *General Editor/Directeur général*
Roch Bolduc, *Directeur associé/Associate Editor*

The Institute of Public Administration of Canada
L'Institut d'administration publique du Canada

This series is sponsored by the Institute of Public Administration of Canada as part of its constitutional commitment to encourage research on contemporary issues in Canadian public administration and public policy, and to foster wider knowledge and understanding amongst practitioners and the concerned citizen. There is no fixed number of volumes planned for the series, but under the supervision of the Research Committee of the Institute, the General Editor, and the Associate Editor, efforts will be made to ensure that significant areas will receive appropriate attention.

L'Institut d'administration publique du Canada commandite cette collection dans le cadre de ses engagements statutaires. Il se doit de promouvoir la recherche sur des problèmes d'actualité portant sur l'administration publique et la détermination des politiques publiques ainsi que d'encourager les praticiens et les citoyens intéressés à les mieux connaître et à les mieux comprendre. Il n'a pas été prévu de nombre de volumes donné pour la collection mais, sous le direction du Comité de recherche de l'Institut, du Directeur général, et du Directeur associé, l'on s'efforce d'accorder l'attention voulue aux questions importantes.

Canada and Immigration: Public Policy and Public Concern
Freda Hawkins

The Biography of an Institution: The Civil Service Commission of Canada, 1908–1967
J. E. Hodgetts, William McCloskey, Reginald Whitaker, V. Seymour Wilson

An edition in French has been published under the title *Histoire d'une institution: La Commission de la Fonction publique du Canada, 1908–1967*, by Les Presses de l'Université Laval

Old Age Pensions and Policy-Making in Canada
Kenneth Bryden

Provincial Governments as Employers: A Survey of Public Personnel Administration in Canada's Provinces
J. E. Hodgetts and O. P. Dwivedi

Transport in Transition: The Reorganization of the Federal Transport Portfolio
John W. Langford

Initiative and Response: The Adaptation of Canadian Federalism to Regional Economic Development
Anthony G. S. Careless

Canada's Salesman to the World: The Department of Trade and Commerce, 1892–1939
O. Mary Hill

Health Insurance and Canadian Public Policy: The Seven Decisions that Created the Canadian Health Insurance System
Malcolm G. Taylor

Conflict over the Columbia:
The Canadian Background to an Historic Treaty
Neil A. Swainson

L'Economiste et la chose publique
Jean-Luc Migué
(Published by Les Presses de l'Université du Québec)

Federalism, Bureaucracy, and Public Policy:
The Politics of Highway Transport Regulation
Richard J. Schultz

Federal-Provincial Collaboration:
The Canada–New Brunswick General Development Agreement
Donald J. Savoie

Judicial Administration in Canada
Perry S. Millar and Carl Baar

The Language of the Skies:
The Bilingual Air Traffic Control Conflict in Canada
Sandford F. Borins

An edition in French has been published under the title
Le français dans les airs: le conflit du bilinguisme dans le contrôle de la circulation aérienne au Canada
by Les Editions Chenelière et Stanké

L'Analyse des politiques gouvernementales: trois monographies
Michel Bellavance, Roland Parenteau et Maurice Patry
(Published by Les Presses de l'Université Laval)

Canadian Social Welfare Policy:
Federal and Provincial Dimensions
Edited by Jacqueline S. Ismael

Canadian Social Welfare Policy

Federal and Provincial Dimensions

Edited by JACQUELINE S. ISMAEL

The Institute of Public Administration of Canada
L'Institut d'administration publique du Canada

McGill-Queen's University Press
Kingston and Montreal

ISBN 0-7735-0579-2 (cloth)
ISBN 0-7735-0612-8 (paper)

Legal deposit 3rd quarter 1985
Bibliothèque nationale du Québec

Printed in Canada

Reprinted 1987
First paperback edition 1987

Canadian Cataloguing in Publication Data
Main entry under title:
Canadian social welfare policy

(Canadian public administration series/Collection administration publique canadienne)

ISBN 0-7735-0579-2 (bound) – ISBN 0-7735-0612-8 (pbk.)

1. Canada – Social policy – Addresses, essays, lectures. I. Ismael, Jacqueline S. II. Institute of Public Administration of Canada. III. Conference on Provincial Social Welfare Policy (1st: 1982: University of Calgary). IV. Series: Canadian public administration series.

HV108.C35 1985 361.6'1'0971 C85-098398-3

Contents

Preface

The first Conference on Provincial Social Welfare Policy, held at the University of Calgary in May 1982, provided evidence of increasing interest among academics, policy-makers, and practitioners in comparative provincial research in the area of social welfare policy, programs, and services. Six of the nine chapters in this volume are revised versions of papers presented at that conference.

I wish to express my appreciation to the authors for their participation in this volume. I also wish to acknowledge the support of the first Conference, the Faculty of Social Welfare of the University of Calgary, and the Institute of Public Administration of Canada in assisting the publication of this volume. In particular, I wish to thank Dean Len Richards whose leadership, encouragement, and confidence inspired this undertaking. I also wish to thank Dr. Ray Thomlison, the current Dean, for his support in bringing this project to fruition.

Jacqueline S. Ismael

Introduction

The provision of assistance to Canadians in need is a hodge-podge of programs that vary across political jurisdictions (federal, provincial, and municipal), categories of people (the unemployed/unemployable, young/old, high risk/low risk, deserving/undeserving), and categories of need (financial assistance/service provision, maintenance/incentive, protection/rehabilitation). The effect of this maze of programs is to fragment and distort the process of providing assistance to the needy at substantial public expense. There is, as a result, increasing disillusionment with the policies of the welfare state that have evolved in Canada during this century.

This disillusionment is reflected in the changing priorities of public policy. The political debate over comprehensive social welfare policy reform, so prominent in the early seventies, was displaced by the end of the decade by debates over the contingencies of federal-provincial relations and the exigencies of fiscal restraint. Correlatively, the focus of political attention on the Canadian social welfare system has shifted from concern with the issues of providing assistance to the needy to concern with issues of public expense. This volume examines the specific reform efforts in a number of social welfare policy areas and identifies the jurisdictional framework of policy making in Canada's federal system as a factor significantly affecting these efforts.

With the demise of a substantial reform focus, the hodge-podge pattern of service provision is likely to remain a principal characteristic of the Canadian social welfare system. In this situation, understanding the patterns of variation within the system is an important part of social welfare policy analysis. This volume addresses one of the principal dimensions of variation—the federal/provincial dimension.

The division of political prerogatives and responsibilities between the federal and provincial governments is established within the constitution. This is the broad framework within which Canadian social welfare policies have evolved.

The first chapter by Leslie Pal serves as an introduction to some of the issues and questions pertaining to federalism and social policy in Canada. Pal examines the definition of the welfare state as a starting point for any analysis of social policy. Using Asa Briggs's classic definition of the welfare state as "modifying the play of market forces," he develops four main categories of transfers which encompass the range of welfare state activities. These are transfers of rights, such as the powers granted to marketing boards; transfers of costs, whereby the state subsidizes certain investment activities; transfers of services, such as health and education; and transfers of monies. He then assesses the current division of responsibilities in Canada between federal and provincial governments in each field, and goes on to examine the constitutional bases for the division of responsibilities, focusing on the most important sections in what used to be known as the BNA Act. Finally, and somewhat more speculatively, he examines the possible implications of the Constitution Act, 1982, on social policy in Canada. Though second-guessing the judiciary is always hazardous, Pal speculates that the implications will be slight, at least insofar as the major spending areas of contemporary social policy (health, education, and social assistance) will go on much as before. Some sections of the Charter of Rights and Freedoms, however, may limit the discretion routinely wielded by social service officers in deciding benefit levels and conditions.

Leonard Shifrin's examination of the "rise and stall" of the federal role in income security focuses more specifically on the national arena. After outlining the half-century of expansion in the federal government's income security programming, he examines the factors which, beginning in the late sixties, caused that process to lose its momentum at a critical juncture, leaving a succession of "missed opportunities and failed initiatives" to mark its subsequent course.

These two chapters examine from different perspectives one of the most salient patterns in the evolution of Canadian social welfare policies—increasing federal involvement, culminating in the seventies with initiatives toward comprehensive social security reform. Derek Hum's chapter on social security reform in the seventies provides a careful examination of these initiatives and their demise. He traces the events leading up to and during the Federal-Provincial Review of Social Security initiated in 1973, the last large-scale attempt to redesign the social security system in Canada and to devise a new method for cost-sharing and delivery. He also outlines the circumstances surrounding the multimillion dollar experiment in negative income taxation conducted during the seventies in Canada, a much-mentioned but little-examined event. While predicting that the issues in the eighties are unlikely to resemble policy debates in the seventies, Hum concludes that social security reform in Canada can never be viewed apart from federal-provincial relations and intergovernmental fiscal squabbles.

The comprehensive social security reform initiative, then, was to a large extent a victim of the changing relationship between the federal and provincial governments, intensified by the changing economic climate. Thus the pattern of federal-provincial relations in social welfare policy seems particularly important in understanding the significant shift in evolutionary direction signalled by the demise of the comprehensive reform initiative. Keith Banting's chapter on pension reform examines the public and private sectors of the existing pension system and describes the division of authority over pensions between the federal and provincial governments. In analysing the conflicting pressures on pensions policy emanating from organized economic and social interests on the one hand and intergovernmental relations on the other, Banting concludes that the institutional conservatism inherent in the federal system is a major barrier to substantive reform of pensions policy. The complex institutional framework within which political decisions are made profoundly alters the balance of forces in pension politics. Banting's central argument is that the large role of the provinces and the complexities of the federal-provincial division of authority have had, and will continue to have, a conservative impact on Canadian pension policy.

Unlike the pension system, unemployment insurance is completely under federal jurisdiction. Leslie Pal's examination of changes in unemployment insurance in the seventies reveals that these changes were significantly influenced by the dynamics of federalism. Pal reviews the evolution of Canadian unemployment insurance during the 1970s in terms of how independent the central government can be from economic and social interests as well as provincial governments. In examining the two dominant models that have been used to explain social policy development, the labour management model and the social control model, he concludes that neither can adequately explain changes in unemployment insurance in the seventies. These changes are more adequately explained by two interrelated dimensions of federalism—fiscal pressures and federal-provincial relations. Pal finds that by the late seventies, although Ottawa's initiatives on unemployment insurance policy were not compromised by federal-provincial negotiations in this area, they were constrained by the dynamics of federalism. This is because the program has become increasingly important in certain regions of the country. Design changes in the unemployment insurance program now explicitly take regional impact into account. Thus federalism is a force of increasing importance in unemployment insurance policy development.

The family allowance program, discussed by Andrew Johnson, is also under federal jurisdiction. The child benefits system, established in 1978, served as the basis for subsequent modifications to the program in 1982. Both sets of programs were intended to cut costs and to shift funds within the system to lower income families. However, without provincial collaboration, these redistributive objectives could not be realized. Nevertheless, based upon available evidence, Johnson concludes that the provinces were not involved in the decision-making process of revamping family allowances. After examining the lack of provincial involvement, he suggests that the federal government has not been entirely successful in attaining its purported goal of a more redistributive child benefits system because of the absence of concerted decision making.

These chapters also demonstrate the way the dimension of political jurisdiction affects the other major dimensions of variation—categories of people and categories of need. While some categories of people in need are served by the social security system, others fall through the safety net of social welfare policies because they do not fit into the categories of provision at any level of political jurisdiction. Derek Hum's chapter on the problems of income supplementation to the working poor focuses on the way the Canada Assistance Plan structures variation in these categories and inhibits initiatives in responding to the needs of the working poor. Closely related to the dimension of political jurisdiction which flows from Canada's peculiar separation of powers as laid down by the constitution is the question of financing social welfare. Canada's formal response is the Canada Assistance Plan, a wide-ranging and flexible arrangement permitting federal cost-sharing of certain provincial expenditures, mainly those on welfare and social services (other than health and education). Clearly the manner by which the federal government transfers monies to the provinces for social welfare expenditures, and the conditions imposed on the provinces by Canada for receipt of these inter-governmental transfers, can have profound implications for what kinds of people and what kinds of needs get served. Consequently, it is not surprising that some Canadians in need, such as the working poor, may be inadvertently or deliberately excluded from provincial assistance programs.

Thus an important aspect of the political jurisdiction dimension and its impact on other dimensions of variation is the issue of patterns of provision across the provinces. Philip Hepworth's chapter on provincial social service departments examines the expenditure patterns that have evolved within and among provinces over the last two decades, noting the limitations of such data for comparative purposes. Utilizing this data cautiously, he attempts to provide the groundwork for a comparison of social assistance and social service expenditures before and after the 1966 Canada Assistance Plan. Federal sharing of the cost of categorical assistance programs was in place before 1966, but the plan represented a consolidation of the existing categorical programs and an extension to include mothers' allowance programs not previously included, as well as the cost-sharing for the first time of social service programs. Quite apart from other changes in governmental activity at the federal and provincial levels, therefore, the 1966 federal legislation might have been expected to lead to some major changes in social assistance and social service programs to cover categories of people and need not previously eligible. That such changes did occur is shown to some extent by the data provided and supported by documentary evidence. The precise impact of the Canada Assistance Plan still awaits evaluation. This chapter sets social service expenditures in the context of other important factors such as total provincial expenditures, unemployment levels, gross provincial product, and so on. Viewed in a wider context, social service department expenditures are a mirror of wider societal changes; they also reflect the persistence of certain resource constraints and patterns of activity already in place prior to 1966. Finally, Hepworth draws attention to the persistence of spending and other differences between provinces which warrant further study.

As Hepworth indicates, the Canada Assistance Plan has been of central significance in the development of social services in the provinces. As a national policy, the role of CAP in the development and growth of provincial social services implies federal leadership in this area. Richard Splane's chapter on the federal-provincial interplay in the development of social welfare programs in Alberta takes issue with this perspective. Focusing on federal-provincial collaboration in the development of CAP, Splane argues that a competitive metaphor of federal-provincial relations leads to generalizations that distort the policy-making dynamic in a federal system. As a major player in developing the plan and in the intergovernmental relations that brought it into being, Splane is able to identify the mechanisms of cooperative federalism operating in that period.

The contributions to this volume examine the issues of Canadian social welfare policy reform from a variety of policy and disciplinary perspectives. Individually, they identify the patterns of social welfare policy jurisdictions that have evolved in Canada's federal system and the problems of reform associated with these patterns. They also reflect the fact that the patterns of political jurisdiction are intrinsically related to other patterns of variation, principally categories of people and categories of need. Together, they suggest that the problems of developing policies for the needy, the focal point of a social welfare system, are increasingly subordinated to the problems of federalism in the Canadian system. This is an area in need of further research if Canadian policy makers are to deal effectively with the problems and potentials of the welfare state in Canada. Greater emphasis on comparative provincial research in this area and other dimensions of social welfare programs and services will contribute to rational decision making in this endeavour.

Contributors

KEITH G. BANTING is Associate Professor of Political Science, University of British Columbia. His recent publications include *Poverty, Politics and Policy: Britain in the 1960's* and *The Welfare State and Canadian Federalism.*

H. PHILIP HEPWORTH is Coordinator, Policy Development, Social Service Directorate, Health and Welfare Canada. Among his recent publications is *Foster Care and Adoption in Canada: A Baseline Study of Child Welfare Services, 1959–1977.*

DEREK P. J. HUM is Professor of Economics and Fellow of St. John's College, University of Manitoba. From 1975 to 1979, he was Director of Research, MINCOME MANITOBA. Among his recent publications is *Federalism and the Poor: A Review of the Canada Assistance Plan.*

JACQUELINE S. ISMAEL is Associate Professor of Social Welfare, The University of Calgary. Among her recent publications are *Kuwait: Social Change in Historical Perspective* and *Juvenile Detention in Calgary: An Analysis of Decision-Making.*

ANDREW F. JOHNSON is Assistant Professor and Chairman of the Department of Political Science at Bishop's University. He is currently conducting research on the relationship of political parties to the development of income security programs in Canada.

LESLIE A. PAL is Assistant Professor of Political Science, The University of Calgary. His current research interests include the influence of bureaucracies on public policy formation.

LEONARD SHIFRIN is a syndicated columnist on social policy and former Executive Director, National Council of Welfare.

RICHARD B. SPLANE is Professor of Social Work, University of British Columbia. He is a former Assistant Deputy Minister, Health and Welfare Canada, and played a leading role in the development of social programs in the 1960s and early 1970s.

Chapter One

Federalism, Social Policy, and the Constitution

LESLIE A. PAL

Few things in Canadian political life have been dissected, debated, deplored, and defended as much as federalism. Federalism, it is argued, defines our national institutions, reflects our history, expresses our genius, echoes our vices, impedes our maturity, and preserves the peace. Any student embarking on a study of federalism will find the terrain well charted but battle-scarred. Canadians have made federalism into a national obsession.

It is rarely possible, in these circumstances, to say anything original or entirely persuasive about Canadian federalism. I shall not try. Instead, this chapter's more modest (and more prudent) task is to introduce and review the relationship between Canadian federalism and social policy. With one recent and notable exception,[1] this relationship has not received from students of social policy the attention or careful analysis that one would expect. The other chapters in this volume address this problem in detail. This chapter serves only to provide an overview of the social security system as it now exists and as it has evolved, of its conventional, constitutional, and rational foundations, and of the possible effects of Canada's new constitution on social policy.

Canada's Social Security System

THE WELFARE STATE AND SOCIAL POLICY

Social policy, in Canada as elsewhere, is usually considered the *sine qua non* of the modern welfare state. Federalism does not alter this identity, it only means that social policy is divided between national and provincial governments. Perhaps the best definition of the welfare state is still the one offered in 1961 by Asa Briggs:

> A "welfare state" is a state in which organized power is deliberately used (through politics and administration) in an effort to modify the play of market forces in at least three directions—first, by guaranteeing individuals

> and families a minimum income irrespective of the market value of their work or their property; second, by narrowing the extent of insecurity by enabling individuals and families to meet certain "social contingencies" (for example, sickness, old age, and unemployment) which lead otherwise to individual and family crises; and third, by ensuring that all citizens without distinction of status or class are offered the best standards available in relation to a certain agreed range of social services.[2]

Even this definition has its problems, however. First, the categories overlap. Canadian health insurance, for example, is a "service" which helps individuals and families deal with the costs of sickness, but also provides the same standard of help to all citizens. Second, the definition seems to exclude policies which help advantaged groups or those with capital and property. Marketing boards, for example, permit agricultural producers to legally restrict output to achieve what is, in effect, a guaranteed income.[3] Moreover, governments may provide tax relief to middle and upper income groups who direct their savings into specific channels such as retirement or home ownership.[4] In most cases, these families or groups are perfectly able to deal unassisted with "social contingencies." Third, if Briggs's general definition of the welfare state is to be taken on its own merits—"an effort to modify the play of market forces"—virtually everything that states do beyond maintaining external defence and domestic order qualifies as "welfare state" policy.

This last point suggests that if we conceive of the political process as a conflict over shares, and policy as the product of this conflict, then many if not most things that governments do will impose costs on some groups and benefits on others, costs and benefits which are different from those which might otherwise result from unbridled market forces. This suggests a view first argued by Richard Titmuss that "social welfare" as commonly understood is only one major mechanism whereby the state distributes benefits; it does so in a host of other ways, such as tax breaks and shelters, subsidies, grants and loans, which while not typically thought of as welfare, serve the same purpose, but different groups.[5]

In order to deal with these conceptual problems and the array of programs and policies which make up the welfare state, I propose the following categories. The modern welfare state "modifies the play of market forces" in four major ways. Each of these ways may be seen as a transfer, thus supporting our intuitive understanding of the welfare state as one which transfers costs and benefits.

The first way is a *transfer of rights,* both positive and negative. In essence, this involves the transfer of small "packages" of sovereignty to groups or individuals, so that they may exercise state powers or enjoy their protection, and benefit thereby. A good example of positive rights is the legal status of marketing boards and professions.[6] Both wield certain state powers which they may use to regulate their goods and services and discipline their members. These powers, *ceteris paribus,* enable these groups to extract higher than market values for their skills or property. Negative rights, or more exactly negative freedoms, reflect the protection the state extends to economic actors to prevent their exploitation. Child labour laws, minimum wages, and anti-discrimination statutes protect classes of people from perceived abuses. Children may not be employees until a certain age; ethnic and religious groups and women may not have their livelihood affected by extra-economic considerations. By transferring rights, the state essentially transfers powers which, when exercised in the marketplace, confer benefits.

The second way is *transfer of costs*. In this transfer, the state offers subsidies, grants, tax shelters, and various other subventions in an effort to alter incentive structures, thereby inducing a particular behaviour. The intent is not to transfer monies or benefits as such to alleviate distress, but to try to get people to do things they might not otherwise do. A rational investor, for example, faces choices and ultimately makes his decisions after calculating the costs and benefits of a range of alternatives. The state, through the various devices mentioned above, can alter this balance of costs and benefits by transferring some or all of the costs of one preferred option to the public purse. A tax break on investments in multiple unit dwellings does precisely this, since it induces behaviour which at least in theory would not otherwise have occurred. Though the efficacy of these techniques has been questioned,[7] they continue to be used. They are distinguished from social welfare transfers by their ad hoc nature, their clear intent to alter behaviour rather than alleviate distress, and by their clientele, who are normally middle and upper income groups with investment resources.

The third category is close to the conventional notion of the welfare state. It involves *transferring services* from the private to the public realm. Health services and education are good examples of activities which were once largely privately organized and funded, but which are now state programs. These services were previously defined by market relations, so that access to and standards of service depended on ability to pay. By transferring these services to the public domain, the state, as Briggs points out, provides all citizens with the same standards, irrespective of income. Market mechanisms may still be employed to a limited degree (e.g., direct charges for books or beds) but allocations within the health and education sectors are made largely on a non-market basis. Not all private services were market ones however, as charities and voluntary aid groups demonstrate. The state has also transferred many of these services to the public domain.

The final technique is *transfers of money*. These transfers symbolize, along with services like health and education, the core of the welfare state. The transfers are not meant primarily to alter behaviour, but to relieve distress which might be the result of loss of income or what Briggs calls "social contingencies." The types of transfers are legion. Money may be transferred as a matter of right, as long as an individual or family has certain characteristics (e.g., family allowances); it may be structured as an insurance scheme, so that payments are tied to contributions; or it may be transferred only as a relief measure to those with low incomes.

These four types of transfers represent a broad range of programs and policies which, though they may overlap slightly, summarize the ways in which the modern welfare state tries to alter market forces. Where does "social policy" fit in these transfers? Conventionally, social policy refers to the last two types of transfers. This suggests that the essence of social policy is "social problems" policy. In this respect then, using the definition of the welfare state offered earlier, social policy is a subset—though a major one—of the welfare state.

CURRENT DIVISION OF RESPONSIBILITIES

The Canadian state engages in all four types of transfer, but federalism has created jurisdictional distinctions in responsibilities and programs. Table 1 gives an idea of the programs in each transfer area by jurisdictional authority (i.e., not by funding source, which is another matter).

Table 1 suggests that the balance of activities in the first two major transfer areas of rights and costs are roughly equal. Within any federal state, sovereignty is divided between national and subnational governments, and so both levels may transfer "packages" of sovereignty to selected groups. In Canada, this transfer may be effected within those jurisdictional areas reserved either for Ottawa or for the provinces. As a result, since powers often overlap, Ottawa and the provinces have both transferred rights to agricultural producer groups (marketing boards) and to labourers (trade union and collective bargaining legislation). Both levels of government have traditionally had some powers in the area of anti-discrimination legislation. Until the Constitution Act, 1982, the balance of powers here favoured the provinces, but Ottawa, at least with respect to federal institutions and federally chartered companies, could and did exercise some powers through the Canadian Human Rights Commission. Most important professional associations, however, such as physicians and lawyers, are provincially licensed, and so in this respect provincial authorities have slightly greater powers in the transfer of rights.

The same rough balance of authority prevails in the next major area of welfare state policy, that of the transfer of costs of certain activities from the private to the public sector. In Canada, both levels of government raise revenues and so both levels may forgo those revenues if they wish to encourage or stimulate certain activities and certain investments. Both levels of government have spending powers, and so may extend subsidies or grants. Because of its greater fiscal resources, in part due to the constitutional right to

TABLE 1

CANADIAN WELFARE STATE
TYPES OF TRANSFER AND JURISDICTION

	Federal	Provincial
Transfers of rights	marketing boards human rights legislation	marketing boards human rights legislation professional associations
Transfers of costs	subsidies grants tax deductions tax credits	subsidies grants tax deductions tax credits
Transfers of services	veterans' services employment services	health education child care
Transfers of money	Family Allowances Canada Pension Plan Unemployment Insurance Guaranteed Income Supp. Spouse's Allowance Old Age Security	worker's compensation Quebec Pension Plan social assistance

certain tax fields, and in part to size, Ottawa uses these transfers more than the provinces.[8]

In the last two types of transfer, of private services to the public domain and monies from governments to individuals, one or the other level of government tends to dominate. These two areas define the social policy field as a subset of the "welfare state." The provinces are responsible for the three major social service areas in Canada: health, education, and social assistance. Social assistance here refers to a wide variety of state-funded or licensed forms of assistance which involve both a transfer of money to individuals, and a range of services, for example, child care programs, alcohol and drug abuse counselling, group homes, senior citizen residences, and recreational facilities. While the federal government pays roughly one-half of the costs of health insurance and post-secondary education through Established Programs Financing (EPF), and a good deal of social assistance expenditures under the Canada Assistance Plan, the provinces are responsible for their delivery and management.[9] Because education is so clearly defined as a provincial jurisdiction, federal assistance in this field has traditionally had fewer strings attached. Health is another matter, though the 1977 EPF arrangements deliberately gave the provinces much greater discretion over spending and management. Social services exclusive of health and education have also been clearly provincial. Ottawa's role has been to help fund provincial services, but the agreements have tended to be flexible.

The picture in the area of money transfers is the reverse of that in services. Here the federal government has responsibility for the major programs in the field: Family Allowances, Canada Pension Plan, Unemployment Insurance, Guaranteed Income Supplement and Spouse's Allowance, and Old Age Security. The provinces each have their own Worker's Compensation programs, Quebec manages the Quebec Pension Plan, and all provinces run social assistance programs which give money to the poor or disabled on a needs basis.[10] Together, these money transfers are sometimes referred to as the "income security" system, since they are designed to support employment income in the face of heavy familial responsibilities, retirement, unemployment, or work-related injuries.

Table 2 summarizes the key features of the Canadian income security and social service system in 1983. Some relatively inexpensive programs, such as Veterans' Allowances and provincial family allowance supplements have not been included.[11] This table does not include transfers in the first two categories discussed in this chapter. The federal government in particular has used the tax system to deliver benefits for child support and encourage savings for home purchase and retirement.[12] There are no satisfactory measures for transfers of rights, though every government in Canada routinely conducts these transfers. Nevertheless, table 2 does give an idea of the division of responsibilities and funding in Canadian social policy, the variety and different types of programs, and their coverage.

Simple addition of program beneficiaries is misleading, since many individuals receive more than one type of benefit. However, discounting this duplication, and adding the numbers who are affected by the transfer of rights or the transfer of costs, it is certain that virtually every Canadian citizen has some direct contact with the welfare state. To use Hugh Heclo's words, "Public income maintenance programs, for example, now interact powerfully with general taxation measures and ostensibly private systems of wage settlement. . . . Minimum subsistence standards, which might ignore arrangements above any given minimum, have yielded to relational standards and concerns with general income distribution—an expansion of perspective by which everyone becomes potentially implicated in government policy."[13]

This complex web of programs and transfers did not emerge overnight. Though steps were taken in various areas before World War II, as in worker's compensation (1920s), old age pensions (1927), and provincial assistance for health care services (1930s), the Canadian welfare state is largely a product of the postwar era. There is no space here to discuss each step along the way; table

TABLE 2

INCOME SECURITY AND SOCIAL SERVICES IN CANADA
1981–82
(Year ending March)

	Program Responsibility		Share of Expenditures			Type of Program	Coverage	Number of Recipients
	Fed	Prov	Fed	Prov	Total			
			(millions of dollars)					(thousands)
Income security								
Family Allowances	X		2,000	—	2,000	Demogrant	Universal for under 18 years old	3,642[1]
Unemp. Insurance	X		5,600	—	5,600	Insurance	Universal for employees	782[2]
CPP/QPP	X	X	2,500	854	3,354	Insurance	Universal for employed/self-employed	1,413/434[3]
Guaranteed Income Supplement	X		2,200	—	2,200	Income-related	Over 65 in need	1,257
Spouse's Allowance	X		203	—	203	Income-related	Spouse between 60 and 64 of OAS recipient; in need	87
Old Age Security	X		6,200	—	6,200	Demogrant	Over 65	2,369
Canada Assistance Plan		X	2,600	1,870	4,520	Income-related	General need	1,503[4]
Worker's Compensation		X	—	1,098	1,098	Insurance	Universal for most employees	n/a
Services								
Health		X	5,911[5]	16,937	—	—	Universal	—
Education		X		15,250	—	—	Universal	—

SOURCES: Statistics Canada, *National Income and Expenditure Accounts*, Cat. 13-001; idem, *Provincial Government Finance*, Cat. 65-205; idem, *Statistical Report on the Operation of the Unemployment Insurance Act*, Cat. 73-001; idem, *Special Security National Programs: Social Allowances and Services*, Cat. 85-510. Department of Finance, *The Fiscal Plan*, April 19, 1983. Régie de Rentes du Québec, *Bulletin*, July 1982.

NOTE: All figures rounded. Expenditures for income security programs are for benefits only.

1 Number of families.
2 Monthly average.
3 Beneficiaries in March 1982.
4 Assistance recipients only.
5 Cash transfers for health and education under EPF.

3 shows key social policy events from 1940 to 1982.[14] A few trends, however, should be noted.

First, despite the jurisdictional tangle in the final product, the postwar Canadian welfare state began with a high degree of unity and purpose. Between 1944 and 1946, the federal government developed a package of proposals which, while not requiring constitutional redistribution of responsibilities, would have given Ottawa exclusive access to major revenue sources in exchange for transfers to the provinces to help fund major social programs such as health insurance and pensions.[15] Ottawa's 1945–46 proposals were rejected by the provinces, but remained a blueprint for federal initiatives over two decades. Health grants in 1948, pensions in 1951, hospital and medical insurance in 1957 and 1968 were all components of the original vision. To be sure, there was often internal resistance to these initiatives within Liberal governments, but the commitment to an extensive welfare state remained at the heart of postwar Canadian Liberalism.

Second, for the first half of the postwar period the federal government was frequently the leader in policy developments. With health grants in 1948, for example, it deliberately set out to build the foundations for national health insurance. It was the main catalyst in the pensions field, in 1950 and again in 1963. It initiated the social security review and led the country into discussions of a guaranteed annual income. The contributions of the provinces and federal opposition parties cannot be discounted: Saskatchewan with hospital and medical insurance,[16] Quebec and the federal New Democratic Party with the Canada Pension Plan,[17] and Alberta with the Canada Assistance Plan[18] come to mind. And yet, until the mid-1960s, federal leadership and dominance prevailed; since then the provinces have asserted themselves markedly.[19]

Third, postwar developments displayed incremental growth in programs and expenditures. In 1947, 38.3 percent of all government spending was made up of social expenditures (i.e., health, education, social assistance, and income security); in 1967 it had risen to 47.5 percent and in 1977 it had reached 50.9 percent.[20] Unlike the United States, which had a "big bang" in 1935 with New Deal initiatives but few changes afterwards, Canadian policy development has been more gradual.[21] This may reflect the insularity of federal/provincial policy making in Canada as well as a parliamentary system which concentrates authority. Whatever the explanation, Canada's welfare state may be a good example of "political learning" in policy making. Programs and policies have often been amended or revised after an initial "test" within an uncertain environment. Some interpretations of the welfare state stress political conflict or the role of the state in suppressing class antagonisms through social policy,[22] but many of the changes listed in table 3 seem also to be rooted in the convictions of experts and politicians that program delivery and integration across programs might be improved.[23]

Finally, overlaying all these trends, there has been a movement away from

TABLE 3

SELECTED DEVELOPMENTS IN CANADIAN SOCIAL POLICY 1940–82

1940–41	Constitutional amendment makes unemployment insurance a federal jurisdiction; Unemployment Insurance Act
1943	*Report on Social Security for Canada* (Marsh Report) published
1944	Family Allowances Act; implemented in 1945
1945–46	White Paper on Employment and Income; Reconstruction Conference and the Green Book Proposals
1947	Saskatchewan introduces hospital insurance
1948	Federal Health Grants to provinces
1951–52	Constitutional amendment gives federal government right to legislate in pensions field; Old Age Security Act; Old Age Assistance Act; Blind Persons Act; federal aid to universities
1954	Disabled Persons Act
1956	Unemployment Assistance Act
1957	Hospital Insurance and Diagnostic Services Act
1961	Quebec introduces allowances for children aged 16 and 17
1962	Saskatchewan Medical Care Insurance Act
1964	Report of the Royal Commission on Health Services; Youth Allowance Act
1965	Canada Pension Plan
1966	Canada Assistance Plan, Guaranteed Income Supplement introduced and implemented in 1967; federal Medical Care Act passed and implemented in 1968
1967	Federal post-secondary education transfers
1970	*Income Security for Canadians* published
1971–72	Report of Special Senate Committee on Poverty; Report of Quebec Commission of Inquiry on Health and Social Welfare; major changes to unemployment insurance; failed attempt to replace family allowances with Family Income Security Plan
1972	British Columbia introduces first provincial supplement to elderly
1973	Major changes to family allowances and Canada and Quebec pension plans
1973–76	Social Security Review
1974–79	Manitoba Basic Annual Income Experimental Project
1975	Spouse's Allowances; unemployment insurance amendments
1977–78	Major unemployment insurance amendments; Established Programs Financing
1978	Federal Refundable Child Tax Credit
1981	Federal budget announces changes to Established Programs Financing and fiscal transfers to provinces
1982	Federal budget limits indexation of family allowances and Old Age Security

building the welfare state towards its reformation and perhaps reduction. A rhetoric of reform has always been central to postwar social policy advocacy, but it was the rest of society, and particularly the market and the economy, which would be reformed and perhaps civilized by the welfare state. Until 1960, social policy advocates were able effectively to claim priority for building and coordinating major new programs. From that point on, reform began to mean something else. It meant not the reform of society by the welfare state, but the reform of welfare state programs themselves. This involved improved coordination, reduced overlap, less complex rules, tighter financial management, and clear priorities. This reflected the impact of recession in the 1970s, but also some aspects of "political learning," in that policy makers were trying to streamline a system constructed piecemeal over two decades. While social policy recently has been overshadowed by the economy, energy, and the constitution, and while some programs have been pared back, the main features of the system remain intact. Reform efforts will continue, as will the introduction of new programs to meet social policy problems such as population aging, child neglect, or youth unemployment.

Federalism and Social Policy

The preceding sketch suggests that Canada has what one writer calls a "bifurcated welfare state."[24] While this usefully describes the division of current programs in the social policy field, it is less true of federal-provincial activities with respect to the transfer of rights or the use of tax expenditures and subventions. Nonetheless, both levels of government are active in all four major areas of welfare state policy, though, as table 1 showed, Ottawa tends to dominate the income security field while the provinces dominate social services.

The reasons for this bifurcation and overlap are too numerous to develop here, though they begin with the constitutional division of powers.[25] They do not end there because of the distinction between what the constitution permits and what it requires. The 1867 BNA Act permitted governments to legislate within the areas listed in section 91 (federal) and sections 92 and 93 (provincial). It did not require that they do so, as it required elections to the House of Commons at least once every five years. Thus the reasons why governments have decided to use certain powers to legislate in certain areas is more complex than a simple delineation of constitutional jurisdictions might suggest. These reasons might include public opinion, elite interaction, ideology, party competition, or class conflict, and in the final analysis will be more telling than simple legal responsibility in explaining policy developments.

The constitution is increasingly restrictive as one moves from transfers of rights to transfers of services. Of all the transfers which characterize the welfare state, limited transfers of rights or sovereignty are rooted in the most basic powers of state. All states in the western tradition are repositories of a general sovereignty or general will. No constitution need belabour this point. All states use this sovereignty to make laws which convey rights to and impose obligations on their citizens. In a federal state, where sovereignty is divided between levels of government, each level may transfer rights to citizens but only within the jurisdictional range assigned to each respective level. The issue is usually whether that transfer is legitimate, or within the competence of that level of government. While the provinces, because of their jurisdiction over property and civil rights (sec. 92[13]), concurrent powers over agriculture (sec. 95), and licensing of most professionals within their boundaries, have been slightly more active than Ottawa in this field, the federal government has also conferred rights on producer groups. In a sense, every area of jurisdiction of either federal or provincial governments is an area where these governments may transfer rights.

The second kind of transfer which defines the welfare state is the transfer of all or part of the costs of certain behaviours from individuals to the public purse. These usually involve either subventions or concessions which serve in one way or another to reduce tax liabilities. Both of these essentially involve the spending and taxation powers of the respective levels of government. The power to spend is held by both Ottawa and the provinces, and while nowhere explicitly discussed in the constitution, it has been defined as permitting expenditures in areas outside the legislative competence of the spending government.[26] Both levels have used this power to extend subsidies, grants, or loans to private companies, though Ottawa has used it for grants to individuals under family allowances.[27] The taxation power is slightly more complex. The constitution gave the provinces power to collect "direct" taxes (sec. 92[2]), license fees (sec. 92[9]) and entitled them to royalties on lands, mines, and minerals (sec.109). At the time, these revenue sources were modest. The Dominion government, on the other hand, received the power to raise money by any means of taxation, direct or indirect (sec. 91[3]). Indirect taxes, consisting of excise and custom duties, were the most lucrative form of taxation in 1867, while direct taxes, such as income or property tax, were rare.[28] Corporate income taxes were not common until the 1930s, and only in 1962 did all provinces levy a personal income tax.[29] Thus, the constitution permits both levels of government to levy income taxes, and since 1941 there have been agreements on how to "share" these tax fields. Ottawa controlled all income tax fields in exchange for payments to the provinces from 1947 to 1962, after which it retreated from the tax fields to permit the provinces to raise their own revenues. If the provinces used the federal tax base, Ottawa collected these taxes free of charge. Thus most tax expenditures are Ottawa's since the provinces levy their rates only on taxable income as defined by federal regulations. The provinces do have their own tax breaks, particularly in the resource field, but Ottawa tends to use the device most frequently.

The constitution speaks more clearly on transfers of services and money. Each province, subject to maintaining the rights of Catholic and Protestant minorities, was given exclusive jurisdiction over education (sec. 93). Health and welfare were assumed to come under the provincial jurisdiction over "hospitals, asylums, charities and eleemosynary institutions" (sec. 92[7]). This was buttressed by powers over "all matters of a merely local or private nature" (sec. 92[16]), since social policy in 1867 was considered such, and by responsibility for municipal institutions (sec. 92[8]). Finally, judicial interpretation in 1937 deemed that compulsory social insurance programs and contributory pensions affected the property and civil rights of employees and employers, a provincial jurisdiction.

The provinces clearly enjoy dominance in the key social policy fields. Federal participation, particularly in the direct transfer of money to individuals, has been secured through constitutional amendment and the use of the spending power, supplemented by responsibility for "peace, order and good government." A 1940 amendment gave Ottawa exclusive jurisdiction over unemployment insurance (sec. 91[2a]), and amendments in 1951 and 1964 allowed it to make laws concurrently with the provinces in relation to old age pensions and supplementary benefits, subject to provincial paramountcy (sec. 94a). The spending power was used to defend the 1944 family allowance program, but is most important for permitting Ottawa to share the costs of health insurance and post-secondary education. Though there is some debate over the term "conditional grant,"[30] the technique has usually involved a grant of money to pay one-half of the costs of a program outside of federal jurisdiction, on certain conditions voluntarily accepted by the grantee. The detail of these conditions has varied, tending to become less specific with each new program. Funding formulae have also evolved from a simple cash transfer, to transfers of cash plus tax room which itself is subject to standardization.

These devices illustrate the differences between what the constitution permits and what it requires, or between the responsibilities and obligations of governments. The provinces are responsible for health insurance and are permitted to legislate for it, but they are not required to do so. The federal government is neither required nor permitted to legislate health insurance. Justifications for a federal role in social policy have thus been needed, and these go beyond the constitution. Apart from considerations of political advantage or ideology, three main arguments have been advanced. First, national standards in provincial programs or national programs run by Ottawa provide a focus for citizenship and national unity. Second, some local and provincial services might not be established or developed to the optimum level because beneficiaries might move elsewhere. This "externalities" problem faces sub-national units but not a national one, and thus Ottawa may have a role in subsidizing local services. Third, regional economic disparities might mean that services in some parts of the country would be greatly inferior to services in other parts. Federal government monies can thus serve to reduce these disparities.

These remarks suggest the care with which we must assess the causal role of the constitution or federalism in Canada. A federal state has divided jurisdictions, and this division is defined by its constitution, but usually in a way which makes the respective orders of government distinct and sovereign within their jurisdiction. If by "federalism" we mean no more than this or perhaps the constitutional division of powers itself, then it is difficult to conclude anything about how "federalism" affects policy making. Knowledge of the rules of a game like hockey or chess does not yield confident predictions on the play, strategy, or outcome of specific contests. Moreover, governments have the option of choosing the type of game or contest they wish to play. This choice rests on a simple distinction between means and ends. Governments may desire a particular end such as increased retirement benefits for citizens, but they may be able to choose among instruments which require differing degrees of federal/provincial cooperation.[31] Intergovernmental conflict is not the inevitable consequence of federalism. Federalism may "mobilize bias" insofar as it defines who the players are; it may have some independent effect on regional perspectives;[32] it certainly will affect the *way* in which decisions are made, but its ultimate effect on such gross aspects of policy as coverage and spending levels may be slight.

The Constitution Act, 1982, and Social Policy

Canada's new constitution, adopted on April 17, 1982, has opened a new but uncertain political future. Important sections, principally the Charter of Rights and Freedoms, contain ambiguous terms and phrases needing judicial interpretation. This will take at least a decade, and any reflections on the new constitution's effects on social policy must be extremely tentative.

A simple but sometimes overlooked point is that while the constitution will indeed change forever the way in which Canadians govern themselves, it will also leave many things untouched. The BNA Act (renamed the Consitution Act, 1867) remains the core of the Canadian constitution, along with a variety of conventions nowhere explicitly written down or defined. A good deal of the process of Canadian government and politics will be unaffected by the constitution. Moreover, in keeping with Canadian tradition, many important decisions and policies may simply continue to circumvent the constitution's loose restrictions on the divisions of powers. Finally, the constitution, and the Charter of Rights and Freedoms in particular, contains some "opting out" and other excepting clauses which may reduce its impact considerably.

A constitution is more than the sum of its parts, since its general function is to order the relations between governments and citizens, and, in a federation, relations between levels of government. One may legitimately ask, therefore, whether the constitution is, on the whole, more or less democratic or more or less centralist than before. In Canada's case these questions can be answered with reference to the process whereby the constitution itself was finally hammered out and accepted. It is possible, in other words, to uncover the original intentions behind the process of constitutional change, and the compromises and agreements made along the way.

As Keith Banting and Richard Simeon have pointed out, different conceptions of democracy were held by the various participants in the constitutional process:

> The federal government appealed to simple national majoritarianism, held to outweigh regional majorities, and to the protection of individual rights from the tyranny of the majority. Opponents of entrenched rights appealed to the rights of legislative majorities, and opposed increasing the authority of non-elected judges. Provincialists argued that when contemplating constitutional change in a federal system, simple majorities were not enough. Concurrent majorities were essential, and those majorities were essential, and those majorities should be legislative ones.[33]

The differences between Ottawa's 1978 constitutional proposals and the final product in 1982 suggest that the federal government's conception of democracy was attenuated in favour of provincial conceptions. The federal government had originally proposed, for example, the limited use of referenda to decide future constitutional amendments, but this was eventually dropped. The Charter of Rights and Freedoms, which in preliminary formulations contained provisions dealing with sex-based discrimination and native claims, and which would have applied universally to all Canadians, was altered in the final accord so that sexual and aboriginal rights were dropped, and governments permitted to exempt legislation from the charter.

The dropping of these provisions angered women and native groups, leading to intense and eventually successful lobbies to reinclude them. While many considered this political horse-trading between governments and pressure groups to be undignified, it did open up the process from an elite, intergovernmental one to include at least some organized members of the public. The charter, compromised though it may be, is still a significant step towards the entrenchment of individual rights in this country. And while regions and provincial legislatures (excepting Quebec) were protected in the amending formulae, it may be that the very existence of a completely domestic means of amending the constitution, which may be initiated by any government in Canada, will stimulate public efforts at constitutional change aimed at legislatures.

The new constitution reflected what Donald Smiley has called the "Third National Policy," a strategy adopted by the federal Liberals in 1980 to increase the stature and power of central institutions, especially in the economic sphere.[34] Ottawa's attempt to unilaterally amend and patriate the constitution in 1980 was the most extreme expression of this impatience with provincialism and its constraints on national policies, but the sentiment was evident in the federal government's concern about mobility rights and the protection of the national economy from balkanization. While the actual centralizing results of the constitution remain to be seen, the process itself was powered by the perception that it was time for the pendulum to swing the other way, from provincial ascendancy to national priorities, from regional protection to national adjustments, from narrow loyalties to national allegiances. The National Energy Program, the Canada Health Act, and Ottawa's tentative international trade strategies all seemed drawn from a political agenda which strives to enhance Ottawa's leadership in critical policy areas.

The two most important features of the constitution are the amending formulae and the Charter of Rights and Freedoms. There are really four amending formulae, covering different aspects of the constitution. Unanimity is required for changes to fundamental features such as the office of the Queen, the size of the Supreme Court, and the amending formula itself; limited changes to the executive government of Canada or the House of Commons and Senate may be made by a simple Act of Parliament; matters which apply to one or a few but not all provinces require their consent and the consent of Parliament.[35] The final amending formula is of the greatest interest to social policy. Section 38 of the Constitution Act, 1982, specifies that "An amendment made under subsection (1) that derogates from the legislative powers, the proprietary rights or any other rights or privileges of the legislature or government of a province" shall not have effect in a province which registers its dissent. The general amending formula requires resolutions of the House of Commons and Senate accompanied by resolutions of the legislative assemblies of at least two-thirds of the provinces with at least 50 percent of the population of all the provinces. Thus, even if this formula were met for a given amendment, a dissenting province could "opt out" of the change. Moreover, according to section 40, if such an amendment involved the transfer of "provincial legislative powers relating to education or other cultural matters from provincial legislatures to Parliament," Canada shall provide "reasonable compensation" to any provinces not party to the agreement.

These amending formulae could affect social policy in various ways. First, amendments may now be made to those sections of the constitution which have traditionally sustained provincial social legislation (such as property and civil rights) without requiring unanimity. While it seems unlikely that the provinces would give up powers in this field, the 1940 unemployment insurance and the 1951 and 1964 pension amendments show it is possible. Without a unanimity requirement, these changes can in theory be made more easily. But the power of any province affected by such an agreement to opt out raises the possibility of "checker board" policies, applying in some parts of the country but not in others. This likelihood may, however, restrain proposals which would generate provincial dissent.

The Charter of Rights and Freedoms holds the greatest potential for affecting Canadian social policy, especially in that area of the welfare state activity consisting of the transfer of rights. Generally speaking, the constitution has little effect on those powers which have supported the transfer of costs, services, or monies as defined earlier in this chapter. The charter, however, attempts to entrench and define certain fundamental rights. The problem is deciding what these rights mean and how far they extend, a problem which will have to be handled by the courts.

The charter possibly extends to every facet of government activity in Canada, since section 32(1) states that it applies to "all matters within the authority of Parliament" and "all matters within the authority of the legislature of each province." Section 33 permits Parliament or provincial legislatures to exempt legislation from the provisions pertaining to fundamental freedoms, legal rights, and equality rights, though such exceptions only apply for five years and must be reenacted to have force. Nonetheless, the charter may apply not only to legislative acts, but to the procedures and decisions of state enterprises, regulatory boards, social service agencies, and perhaps even to quasi-private agencies that receive public funding.

The charter makes explicit reference to social services in section 6, under mobility rights. Any Canadian citizen has the right to move to another province or "pursue the gaining of a livelihood" in any province. These rights are subject to "any laws providing for reasonable residency requirements as a qualification for the receipt of publicly provided social services" and "to any law, program or activity that has as its object the amelioration in a province of conditions of individuals in that province who are socially or economically disadvantaged if the rate of employment in that province is below the rate of employment in Canada." The courts may have to decide what "socially or economically disadvantaged" means. Social assistance programs could be affected by the first clause, while a range of programs and hiring policies may be affected by the second.

The implications of section 7 of the charter are even more ambiguous. It reads: "Everyone has the right to life, liberty, and security of the person and the right not to be deprived thereof except in accordance with the principles of fundamental justice." While the term "due process" has a long history in English jurisprudence, the concept of "fundamental justice" does not, and so the meaning of these rights is obscure. It could have the potential of limiting the discretion of social service agencies in denying, limiting, or otherwise placing conditions upon the receipt of social security payments. In 1982, for example, the termination of a Winnipeg woman's social allowance payments was appealed on the grounds that the process of deciding the termination had contravened section 7 of the charter. The court heard the appeal because of the possibility that the charter (sec. 32[1]) applied to the Social Services Appeal Board in question.[36] Unemployment insurance benefits are routinely reduced or terminated if the recipient has been determined to be violating the regulations, and these decisions are probably subject to whatever procedural safeguards the judges may read into section 7. Section 7 may be further complicated by section 12, which guarantees that "Everyone has the right not to be subjected to any cruel and unusual treatment or punishment." The phrase "unusual treatment," if interpreted broadly, could include innocuous government activities.

Section 15 of the charter presents substantial challenges as well. Subsection 1 assures equality, but subsection 2 goes on to exclude laws, programs, or activities whose purpose is "the amelioration of conditions of disadvantaged individuals or groups." Subsection 1 states that each individual is equal "before and under the law and has the right to equal protection and equal benefit of the law without discrimination" based on race, national or ethnic origin, colour, religion, sex, age, or mental or physical disability. In addition to the "before and under" phrase, the phrase "equal benefit" suggests equality of result or effect. Equal treatment before the law does not mean that different groups will benefit equally in terms of outcomes, but the "equal benefit" clause implies that perhaps they should. Section 15 came into force on April 17, 1985.

The charter will also affect minority language education rights, defined under section 23. French and English minorities and those who received their primary school instruction in Canada in either French or English but are part of the linguistic minority in a province, have the right to educate their children in their language. Families also have the right to have all of their children educated in the same language. These rights apply "wherever in the province the number of children of citizens who have such a right is sufficient to warrant the provision to them out of public funds of minority language instruction." Once again, the courts will have to provide criteria for this qualification, but even so it will probably affect provincial educational policy across the country, particularly in Ontario.

Two other parts of the constitution, outside of the charter, deserve mention. Part II of the Constitution Act, 1982, affirms the "existing aboriginal and treaty rights of the aboriginal peoples of Canada" (defined as Indian, Inuit, and Métis). Native land claims are currently under negotiation, but it is possible that for some groups such as the Métis the clause may be more than a simple affirmation and recognition; it may confer important advantages.[37] Part III of the

Constitution Act, 1982, affirms the commitment of the governments of Canada to equalization and reduction of regional disparities. This is carefully hedged to preclude any alternations of existing powers or authority among the governments, but it does recognize an essential aspect of the Canadian federation, which is the equalization of fiscal capacities across the country to assure "reasonably comparable levels of public services at reasonably comparable levels of taxation."

It is difficult to avoid the conclusion that the Constitution Act, 1982, was an awkward and badly drafted compromise between federal and provincial agendas. The numerous qualifications of important principles and the use of unfamiliar terms will have to be sorted out by the courts, the legislatures, and ultimately the Canadian people over the coming years. The existing edifice of Canadian social policy has hardly been touched by the new constitution, and there is little sign that it will greatly impede or help social policy reform. Rationalization and development of programs will continue to be a matter of intergovernmental bargaining and individual legislative initiative, and these depend on social and political forces more fundamental than a constitution. Insofar as the charter is seen to apply to social policy, it may protect welfare recipients from unbridled bureaucratic discretion, but even this may ultimately depend more on political will than constitutional fiat. It does suggest, however, that an active area of welfare state reform in the coming years will be the transfer of rights and issues related to these rights.

NOTES

I would like to thank my colleagues Neil Nevitte and Ted Morton for their comments on an earlier draft of this paper. Responsibility for any errors of fact or interpretation is mine.

1. Keith G. Banting, *The Welfare State and Canadian Federalism* (Kingston and Montreal: McGill-Queen's University Press and the Institute of Intergovernmental Relations, Queen's University, 1982).

2. Asa Briggs, "The Welfare State in Historical Perspective," *European Journal of Sociology* 2 (1961): 228.

3. In Canada, such boards have been most successful in the marketing of chickens, turkeys, eggs, and milk.

4. These devices are sometimes called "tax expenditures." A good review of the issue is Kenneth Woodside, "The Political Economy of Policy Instruments: Tax Expenditures and Subsidies in Canada," in *The Politics of Canadian Public Policy*, ed. Michael M. Atkinson and Marsha A. Chandler (Toronto: University of Toronto Press, 1983), pp. 173–97.

5. Richard Titmuss, *The Social Division of Welfare* (Liverpool: Liverpool University Press, 1956).

6. On agricultural marketing boards, see J. D. Forbes et al., *Economic Intervention and Regulation in Canadian Agriculture* (Ottawa: Minister of Supply and Services, 1982); on professions see Michael J. Trebilcock et al., *Professional Regulation: A Staff Study of Accountancy, Architecture, Engineering and Law in Ontario Prepared for the Professional Organization Committee* (Toronto: Ministry of the Attorney General, 1979).

7. Richard M. Bird, *Tax Incentives for Investment: The State of the Art* (Toronto: Canadian Tax Foundation, 1980), chap. 6.

8. Woodside, "The Political Economy of Policy Instruments," p. 174.

9. See *Report of the Parliamentary Task Force on Federal-Provincial Fiscal Arrangements* (Ottawa: Minister of Supply and Services, 1981).

10. Social assistance payments are usually combined with counselling services.

11. For a fuller description of the Canadian income security system, see *The Income Security System: Report for the Interprovincial Conference of Ministers Responsible for Social Services* (Ottawa: The Canadian Intergovernmental Conference Secretariat, 1980).

12. On the child tax credit, see National Council of Welfare, *The Refundable Child Tax Credit, What It Is . . . How It Works* (Ottawa, 1978); also Roger S. Smith, *Tax Expenditures: An Examination of Tax Incentives and Tax Preferences in the Canadian Federal Income Tax System* (Toronto: Canadian Tax Foundation, 1979).

13. Hugh Heclo, "Conclusion: Policy Dynamics," in *The Dynamics of Public Policy*, ed. Richard Rose (London: Sage, 1976), p. 256.

14. A detailed history of developments is provided in Dennis Guest, *The Emergence of Social Security in Canada* (Vancouver: University of British Columbia Press, 1981).

15. See Advisory Committee on Reconstruction, *Report on Social Security for Canada* (Ottawa 1943); Department of Reconstruction, *Employment and Income with Specal Reference to the Initial Period of Reconstruction* (Ottawa, 1945); Dominion-Provincial Conference on Reconstruction, *Proposals of the Government of Canada* (Ottawa, 1945).

16. Malcolm G. Taylor, *Health Insurance and Canadian Public Policy: The Seven Decisions that Created the Canadian Health Insurance System* (Montreal: McGill-Queen's University Press and the Institute of Public Administration of Canada, 1978), chaps. 2, 5.

17. Kenneth Bryden, *Old Age Pensions and Policy-Making in Canada* (Montreal: McGill-Queen's University Press and the Institute of Public Administration of Canada, 1974), chap. 8.

18. Leslie Bella, "The Provincial Role in the Canadian Welfare State: The Influence of Provincial Social Policy Initiatives on the Design of the Canada Assistance Plan," *Canadian Public Administration* 22 (Fall 1979): 439–52.

19. Banting, *The Welfare State*, chaps. 5, 6.

20. *The Income Security System*, calculated from table B, p. 117.

21. See Christopher Leman, *The Collapse of Welfare Reform* (Cambridge, Mass.: MIT Press, 1980), chap. 2.

22. See Allan Moscovitch and Glenn Drover, eds. *Inequality: Essays on the Political Economy of Social Welfare* (Toronto: University of Toronto Press, 1981).

23. For example, see Richard Splane, "Social Policy Making in the Government of Canada: Reflections of a Reformist Bureaucrat," in *Canadian Social Policy*, ed. Shankar A. Yelaja (Waterloo: Wilfrid Laurier University Press, 1978), pp. 209–26, and chap. 9 below.

24. Banting, *The Welfare State*, p. 54.

25. In this section, the "constitution" refers to the pre-1982 version unless otherwise indicated.

26. The following relies on Peter W. Hogg, *Constitutional Law of Canada* (Toronto: Carswell, 1977), pp. 68–73.

27. Quebec and Prince Edward Island have similar programs.

28. On the distinction between "direct" and "indirect" taxes, see G. V. La Forest, *The Allocation of Taxing Power Under the Canadian Constitution*, 2nd ed. (Toronto: Canadian Tax Foundation, 1981), chap. 4.

29. Hogg, *Constitutional Law of Canada*, p. 60.

30. Garth Stevenson, *Unfulfilled Union: Canadian Federalism and National Unity*, 2nd ed. (Toronto: Gage, 1982), p. 151.

31. See Michael J. Trebilcock et al., *The Choice of Governing Instrument* (Ottawa: Minister of Supply and Services, 1982).

32. Richard Simeon, "Regionalism and Canadian Political Institutions," *Queen's Quarterly* 82 (Winter 1975): 499– 511.

33. Keith Banting and Richard Simeon, "Federalism, Democracy, and the Future," in *And No One Cheered: Federalism, Democracy, and the Constitution Act,* ed. Keith Banting and Richard Simeon (Toronto: Methuen, 1983), pp. 355–56.

34. Donald Smiley, "A Dangerous Deed: The Constitution Act, 1982," in *And No One Cheered*, ed. Banting and Simeon, pp. 74–95.

35. Sec. 47(1) gives the House of Commons the right to pass resolutions if the Senate has not done so in 180 days.

36. *Charter of Rights Decisions,* 1982, 925–01.

37. Thomas Flanagan "The Case Against Métis Aboriginal Rights," *Canadian Public Policy* 9 (September 1983): 314– 25.

Chapter Two

Income Security: The Rise and Stall of the Federal Role

LEONARD SHIFRIN

It is often said of the Fathers of Confederation that they built better than they knew. And in many respects it is no doubt true. But income security is not one of them. In the case of income security, unfortunately, they built exactly as they knew. They gave jurisdiction over "charities and eleemosynary institutions" to the provinces, and displayed no clairvoyance about a coming era of universal Old Age Security pensions, let alone refundable child tax credits.

The first federal venture into the income security field came in the wake of World War I, when Parliament recognized a need—and an obligation—which it did not feel could simply be left to local charities. The Pension Act of 1919 provided for the payment of pensions to disabled members of the armed forces and to the dependents of deceased members of the armed forces.

Whether or not the conspicuous presence of a great many veterans among the postwar unemployed had anything to do with it, two years later the federal government recognized another need and obligation, though one which it felt constrained from responding to directly. The result was the nation's first income security cost-sharing program. By orders in council authorized under a series of annual appropriation acts, Ottawa began contributing to municipal relief programs on condition that the provinces contributed as well. In the words of the 1922 measure: "It is the expectation of the Federal authorities that the provisions herein will be interpreted broadly and generously by the municipalities so that no resident of Canada willing and able to work and unable to secure employment shall lack food, clothing or shelter for himself or herself and dependents."[1]

It could be argued that the most interesting thing about that statement is the reference to "himself or herself," indicating that sexism in legal drafting had not yet been invented. For present purposes, though, we will say the most interesting thing is that the federal government should so unabashedly have been proclaiming its expectations on the subject. What it reflects is that the public had already come to regard as Ottawa's responsibility what the Fathers of Confederation had deemed to be none of its business.

Through a series of subsequent enactments, the federal government also came to share in provincial and municipal social assistance payments to various other categories of the poor—the aged poor, the disabled poor, and so on. That piecemeal process culminated in 1966 with the passage of the omnibus Canada Assistance Plan, under which Ottawa currently contributes half of the cost of assistance to all persons defined as being in need, irrespective of the category of their neediness. The working poor, however, are not among the groups defined as being in need. As the culmination of a forty-five-year process—meaning the point from which it has subsequently failed to progress further—the Canada Assistance Plan marks one of the three archways into the present era of income security programs in this country.

Descriptions of the direct payments stream of federal government income security initiatives—the set of measures which began with those 1919 pensions to disabled veterans and their dependents—generally focus on the creation of the two big demogrant programs, family allowances in 1944 and the Old Age Security (OAS) pension in 1951. Logically, it should be possible, notwithstanding the lack of foresight on the part of the Fathers of Confederation, to rest the constitutionality of both measures securely on the federal government's spending power—its right to give away money to its citizenry (all those under a certain age in the one case and all those over a certain age in the other). Nonetheless, a constitutional amendment was obtained in 1951 before the federal government's universal pension program was instituted. And in 1957, when the constitutionality of the family allowance program was challenged, the court upheld it on the strength of Ottawa's general power to legislate for "peace, order and good government," rather than its spending power.[2]

Although these two programs continue to loom large in financial terms, the more important guidepost to the current era in direct federal payment programs was the 1966 passage of the income-tested Guaranteed Income Supplement for the Aged (GIS), the world's first negative income tax-style program. But that too, unfortunately, has proven a gateway through which precious little has subsequently passed.

The last of the three streams is social insurance. Here, the great marking event was the judgements of the Supreme Court of Canada and the Judicial Committee of the Privy Council, in 1937, declaring R. B. Bennett's unemployment insurance program ultra vires.[3] Insurance, social or otherwise, said the justices, is a matter of "property and civil rights," and hence a subject of exclusive provincial jurisdiction.

If the question had not gone to the courts until several decades later, the result might well have been different. Today's judges, for instance, would be much more likely to understand that social insurance premiums are a form of taxation, and the chief difference between social insurance and other forms of income security is simply in the nature of the tax used to finance them. The 1937 decision, however, remains a binding part of the constitutional framework of income security. The initiation of unemployment insurance required a 1940 amendment to the BNA Act, and the creation of the Canada Pension Plan, a quarter-century later, with its provisions for disability and dependency benefits, required another. (If the CPP had offered only retirement pensions, it would have been covered by the 1951 amendment which launched Old Age Security demogrants.)

As the most recent mitigation of the effect of the court's 1937 social insurance judgement, the 1964 pre-CPP amendment qualifies as the third entry point to the present. Two things about these three gateways are immediately striking. One is how closely bunched they are: 1964, 1966, and 1966 again. The other is how long ago that was.

The almost two decades since then has not been a blank as far as income security is concerned. Far from it. There have been a multitude of developments at both federal and provincial levels. But its marking events have been missed opportunities and failed initiatives.

From World War II to the mid-sixties, provincial income security programming consisted of small-scale social assistance plans and worker's compensation schemes dating back to the Ontario Act of 1914. Augmentations of the income security system during that half-century were the product of federal initiatives, whether by way of direct payments, social insurance, or cost-sharing provisions. Something changed during the sixties—or, more accurately, a number of things. My list of relevant factors includes Quebec, the coming of Pierre Trudeau, burgeoning bureaucracy, the electoral politics of welfare, and the discovery of tax expenditures.

Until the coming of Quebec's Quiet Revolution in the 1960s, there had never been a provincial government anxious to expand the scope of its welfare system. In fact, with the exception of the CCF in Saskatchewan, there probably had not even been a provincial government sympathetically disposed toward the subject. And Saskatchewan, in those years very much a have-not province, chose to direct its limited social resources into service programs, pioneering such things as hospital insurance and medicare, and leaving income security to the federal government. That is what made it so unprecedented when, in 1964, the Quebec government declared that it would not participate in Ottawa's proposed pay-as-you-go Canada Pension Plan, and threatened instead to establish a funded Quebec plan that would be completely different.

Three years later, after vainly demanding the "repatriation" of Quebec's portion of family allowances (Canada's contribution of the word "patriation" to the English language was yet to come), Quebec abolished the children's exemption in its Income Tax Act and established a universal family allowance program. Four years after that, the Castonguay-Nepveu Commission report appeared, calling for a massive transformation of Quebec's income security system. It proposed a number of new provincial programs, including a two-tiered guaranteed annual income scheme to be financed largely with the money that Ottawa was already spending—less wisely—in the province. When the federal government refused to make such a deal, Quebec refused to accept the 1971 Victoria Charter.

The factors enumerated earlier as having contributed to the change in federal-provincial income security developments in the sixties were certainly not water-tight compartments. Quite to the contrary, they were all very much interrelated. And none more so than the emergent demands of Quebec and the coming of Pierre Trudeau to national power. Eric Kierans, who resigned from the first Trudeau cabinet in disagreement with its economic policies, has observed that when you have a prime minister who cares a great deal more about the recognition of Red China than about tax reform, you get the recognition of Red China and don't get tax reform. Having been special assistant for policy development to the then minister of national health and welfare, John Munro, in 1968–69—Year One of the stillborn Just Society—I can add from my experience that when the prime minister has a similar lack of interest in income security reform, you don't get that either.

The federal government's 1970 White Paper, *Income Security for Canadians,* does not loom large in the perspective of history. Indeed, it didn't even loom large at the time. Proposals framed within the constraint of no additional expenditure were not likely to make a serious dent in the poverty rate.

In 1967, after the Pearson government had installed the senior citizens' portion of a guaranteed income in the form of the guaranteed income supplement for the aged, Mike Pearson asked the father of that measure, deputy welfare minister Joe Willard, to prepare a blueprint for what should follow. The Trudeau government accepted Willard's proposal that the children's portion should come next, but declined to fund it. The result was that the initial version of the Family Income Security Plan (FISP) proposal for income-tested family allowances of up to $20 a month contained such design absurdities as paying full benefits to families with $10,000 income and nothing to those with $10,001.

Eventually the government agreed, grudgingly, to increase total outlays by $150 million (about 20 percent) in order to construct a more reasonable version of FISP, and a March 1971 Gallup poll reported that 66 percent of Canadians supported the measure while only 25 percent were opposed. But because of the Victoria Charter negotiations with Quebec the bill was not proceeded with at that point, and ultimately died on the order paper a few minutes short of third reading when Parliament was dissolved for the 1972 election.

The foundering of the Victoria Charter over income security—of all things—changed Pierre Trudeau's view on the subject. Because it had proven capable of scuttling such truly important matters, it was something which had to be fixed. So he dispatched his former principal secretary, Marc Lalonde, newly elected to Parliament, to be minister of national health and welfare and fix it. Family allowances in those days averaged $7.21, and that was what Quebec wanted to "repatriate." Lalonde's solution was to increase this to $20 and give provinces the option of varying up to 40 percent of that amount according to children's ages and/or family size. In other words, Quebec, which had wanted control of a $7.21 per child federal outlay, got control of $8 worth instead. And the very same keepers of the federal coffers who had so recently insisted that no more money was available for family allowances came up with the extra $1 billion required.

In the same 1973 *Working Paper on Social Security in Canada* (otherwise known as the Orange Paper) in which he presented his solution to the family allowance issue, Lalonde set out proposals for dealing with the real income security problem, on which John Munro and Joe Willard had been rebuffed a few years earlier. His guaranteed income proposal was based on the two-tiered approach of the Castonguay-Nepveu report. And it fell victim to the next of the new factors, burgeoning bureaucracy.

The director of the federal-provincial relations office of one of the provinces once explained that his organization and its counterparts in the other ten capitals are the reason we have so many federal-provincial crises. They have to keep themselves busy, he said, so they have to look for problems. That is part of the new bureaucracy story, but by no means all of it.

There was a time when the people in a welfare department were there because their concern for the subject caused them to choose it. But when the late sixties, early seventies notion of management generalists whose careers take them through a succession of departments came along, it put an end to all that. Increasingly, those in welfare departments came to be the people who had been in finance departments or privy council offices the previous year and would be in employment departments or treasury boards the next. They were well versed in bureaucracy's territorial imperatives and had no consuming passions about improving the welfare system.

The Orange Paper's two-tiered guaranteed income consisted of full income support for those outside the workforce and supplementation for those within it whose earnings were insufficient. The income support tier was just a continuation of provincial social assistance, though perhaps made subject to some modest national standards. But income supplementation was to be a brand new program—which Ottawa wanted to run. In the old days it would certainly have come to pass. In the new world of crisis-making, bloated bureaucracies and musical chairs careers, it didn't. Three years later, after the federal government had backed off and agreed to let the provinces operate the program while it contributed roughly two-thirds of the cost, only three provinces proved even tentatively willing to come up with the remainder. And that was the end of the Orange Paper exercise.

Quebec, Trudeau, and the new bureaucracy were all part of the welfare politics of the early Aquarian Age. But there was an electoral dimension to it as well. In 1968, as a result of the Economic Council of Canada's *Fifth Annual Review*, the country rediscovered poverty. That one Canadian in five in an affluent society should be poor, said the council, was a national disgrace. And the public agreed. Doing something about it—or at least about certain elements of it—became a politically popular thing to do.

In its first term, the Trudeau government squandered its chance to seize the tide. It opted for a major upgrading of unemployment insurance, most of whose beneficiaries are not poor, and tried to avoid putting more money into anything else. The Castonguay proposals were one consequence of that. The precedent-setting advent of a British Columbia pension supplement was another.

In 1972, the NDP, which for three decades had formed the official opposition in British Columbia without ever managing to become the government, campaigned on the promise to establish a provincial supplement to the federal OAS-GIS for senior citizens. It won, and the creation of the program quickly followed. Shortly thereafter, the Liberal opposition in Ontario came out in favour of such a measure, and the governing Conservatives responded by introducing the program themselves. By the time Canada's provincial governments next went to the polls, income-tested senior citizen supplements had come into being in six of the ten provinces. And the attitude of provincial governments toward certain kinds of income security programs had changed accordingly.

On another front, after the federal government abandoned its plan to provide family allowances on an income-tested basis, the Saskatchewan government took over the FISP blueprint, renamed it Family Income Plan (FIP), and instituted it as a provincial family allowance supplement. Manitoba has since followed suit with a similar program, while Quebec introduced a different form of wage-based supplement.

If the Trudeau government had responded vigorously to the revelations of the late sixties about the extent of poverty among Canada's elderly, its working poor families, and so on, provincial income security systems might still consist only of social assistance and worker's compensation. Because it did not, a political vacuum was created, into which various provinces moved to varying degrees.

The last of the factors I referred to was policy makers' discovery of tax expenditures. In its *Sixth Annual Review*, in 1969, the Economic Council observed that the children's exemption in the Income Tax Act was a form of family allowance, in that it provided benefits to taxpayers with children at the treasury's expense.[4] Two years earlier Quebec had anticipated that observation by abolishing the children's exemption in its provincial income tax and distributing the resulting revenues by way of a universal family allowance. Because the size of the benefit from a tax exemption is determined by a person's top tax rate, those with highest incomes lost most from the change, while those with incomes below the tax threshold gained most.

That was a case of a tax expenditure being eliminated in favour of a direct expenditure. In 1972, Ontario did the reverse, replacing a program of senior citizen shelter grants with a refundable shelter tax credit. The following year it added a sales tax credit and pensioners' credit on the same progressive basis, refundable to those below the tax threshold and diminishing with income above it. In the next few years, refundable credits of various sorts came into being in most provinces. Some were designed so narrowly as, for instance, to offset only the school-support portion of property tax for senior citizens. Others, such as cost-of-living tax credits, were small-scale income supplementation schemes for low-income earners.

In 1979, the federal government belatedly joined the club. Financed mainly by a cut in the family allowance and the balance by a reduction in the tax exemption for older children, the refundable child tax credit has become, in effect, the income-tested supplement to the universal allowance—what the GIS is to the universal pension. Its creation means the mechanism is now in place for Ottawa to do what it chose not to do in the late sixties and was blocked by the provinces from doing in the mid-seventies—provide income supplementation to lower-income families. Unfortunately, Ottawa has not built on this base, either by a significant escalation of the value of this credit or by the introduction of companion measures. An energy tax credit, refundable and diminishing in exactly the same manner as the child tax credit, was proposed in John Crosbie's ill-fated budget of December 1979, but it disappeared with the Tory government.

Nonetheless, the refundable tax credit approach may yet prove a route through which Ottawa reasserts itself in the income security field. And an expanded (as opposed to merely increased) Guaranteed Income Supplement could be as well.

Through its spouse's allowance provision, a low-income pensioner's spouse, aged sixty to sixty-five, receives the equivalent of OAS-GIS benefits. There have been many calls for this provision to be extended to cover all the poor in that age group, irrespective of their marital status. Someday it may even happen. And as the 1981 Parliamentary Task Force on Fiscal Federalism (the Breau committee) observed, every time Ottawa extends the ambit of its income security programs, it reduces that required of provincial social assistance.[5]

Recently, the federal government initiated discussions with the provinces of a new national social insurance plan covering income loss from injury and illness. If anything comes of that— and current indications are not very promising—it could either be a relatively modest scheme designed to fill in the gaps between provincial programs of worker's compensation, motor vehicle accident insurance, and so on, or it could be a comprehensive plan subsuming all of its patchwork predecessors.

A long list of maybes could be assembled, but there seems little point. Whether the half-century of growth in the federal income security role ended in the 1960s or merely suffered a temporary interruption is impossible to foretell. Most Canadians, though, probably share the view which underlies the report of the Breau committee, and which is also to be found in the 1979 report of the Pepin-Robarts commission on national unity. Among the essential roles of the central government, said the unity commission, is the pursuit of "equitable benefit sharing for all Canadians." That not only means equalization payments to poorer provinces, it said, but also "redistributing income between individuals."[6]

There is a need in our income security system for programs by which high-cost provinces such as Alberta supplement the benefits provided to their residents by the federal government. But until the panoply of benefits provided by Ottawa constitutes an adequate national base, the federal role will remain conspicuously incomplete.

NOTES

1. P.C. 191, January 25, 1922.
2. *Angers* v. *Minister of National Revenue* (1957) Ex. C.R. 83.
3. *Reference re Employment and Social Insurance Act* (1936) S.C.R. 427 and (1937) 1 D.L.R. 684 respectively.
4. Economic Council of Canada, *Sixth Annual Review, Perspective 1975* (Ottawa: Queen's Printer 1969), p. 110.
5. Canada, Parliamentary Task Force on Federal-Provincial Fiscal Arrangements, *Fiscal Federalism in Canada* (Supply and Services Canada, 1981), p. 151.
6. Task Force on Canadian Unity, *A Future Together* (Supply and Services Canada, 1979), p. 85.

Chapter Three

Social Security Reform during the 1970s

DEREK P. J. HUM

Canadian social policy is in a turmoil. The indignation accompanying the discovery of pervasive poverty and the subsequent optimism connected with the Federal-Provincial Review of Social Security in the early 1970s has largely given way to economic restraint, constitutional frustration, and policy despair. Such hallmarks as the universality principle which underlie our social programs are now being questioned, and ways to change the tax system are also under active discussion. Even more significant are the series of proposals aimed at altering the grants given to the provinces by the federal government for such purposes as education, health care, income assistance, and social services. Fundamental alterations to either the amounts or terms of these transfers would have a profound impact on Canada's social security system. The public agenda promises to be lively and controversial, and this decade will surely mark a new direction in policy development; one quite different from the last.

Federal-provincial relations in social security during the 1970s was symbolized by two major events. One significant event (little publicized) was a jointly funded, multimillion dollar investigation of the economic and social consequences of a guaranteed income for Canadians. This marked the first time in Canada that the social experimentation method was used to assist public policy development. The guaranteed income idea was much discussed in the seventies and was even the basis of official recommendations for reform. Parallel to this extraordinary research effort was another important undertaking—the federal-provincial review of social security (much publicized). This was a politically directed, three-year review which set out to evaluate Canada's entire system of social programs, including financial and jurisdictional responsibilities, with a view towards new federal legislation for cost-sharing.

Neither the guaranteed income experiment nor the social security review proved very satisfying. The experiment remains silent on the work disincentive question, the most contentious of the many issues surrounding a guaranteed income for Canadians. The social security review has now lapsed—and without the hoped-for revisions to the Canada Assistance Plan, or any other jointly agreed basis for cost-sharing social welfare.

This essay describes the background and context to the social security review and the guaranteed income experiment. I begin by outlining the circumstances leading to these two events and go on to consider the social security review itself, outlining its scope and organization, and examining the income maintenance and social services strategies. The fate of Bills C-57 and C-55, which sought to amend the arrangements with respect to federal funding of provincial social services, is also mentioned. I then turn to the guaranteed income experiment and discuss its evolution from idea through implementation to final disposition. The final section contains some general observations.

Prelude to the Review and Experiment

The Canada Assistance Plan (CAP) came into effect in 1967 and remains in force today. The CAP Act attempted a number of goals: better and more comprehensive coverage for those in need of income assistance, including the working poor; increased opportunities for the unemployed; and provincial consolidation of cost-shared social welfare programs. Yet the CAP failed to live up to its original expectations, and by the early 1970s the limitations of the legislation were recognized. Nonetheless, the CAP Act was the high point of the 1960s and the centrepiece of Canada's anti-poverty efforts during that decade.

Canada's concern for poverty was no doubt inspired by the War on Poverty in the United States, but there were also a number of significant reports and events in Canada. In 1968 poverty received its first "official" recognition since the Great Depression when the Economic Council of Canada released its *Fifth Annual Review* and outlined its extent in this country.[1] That same year, Canada established a Senate committee (the Croll Committee) to investigate the entire question of poverty in Canada. Two years later, the Department of National Health and Welfare issued *Income Security for Canadians,*[2] which proposed reforming family allowances and introducing the Family Income Security Plan (FISP)—an income-tested program. The Senate committee report, *Poverty in Canada,* was released in 1971 and called for more major measures, the most important of these being a guaranteed annual income (GAI) to be implemented on a uniform, national basis and financed and administered by the federal government.[3] The recommended program was based on the negative income tax (NIT) principle; that is, delivered on an income-tested or selective basis. Several dissident staff members of the Senate committee wrote their own report but also recommended a guaranteed annual income, though with more generous benefits and to be implemented through the method of demogrants.[4] There were a number of other important reports heralding the seventies. The report of the Quebec Commission of Inquiry on Health and Social Welfare (the Castonguay-Nepveu Commission)[5] was published in 1971; it recommended major restructuring and integration of the health and social service system in Quebec. The income security portion contemplated an innovative two-part guaranteed income program: one plan for those unable to work, and another plan for workers earning low wages. Numerous changes to the Unemployment Insurance Program were also put into effect in 1971. These were made without provincial consultation, and represented a substantial liberalizing of regulations and enhancement of benefits. The federal government, it would appear, was willing to initiate reform and incur additional social spending. Entering the 1970s then, there was a continuing awareness of poverty among Canadians. There was also active discussion of policy reform options, a sincere curiosity concerning the potential role of a guaranteed income, and an emerging suspicion that the CAP provisions would eventually have to be amended or replaced. Economic restraint was not the order of the day.

In 1971, a federal-provincial conference was held in Victoria in an attempt to rewrite and "patriate" the Canadian constitution. The provinces and Canada appeared to reach agreement but Quebec declared that it could not support the "Victoria Charter" because, in part, it "failed to provide for jurisdictional settlement in the field of social policy" and "no patriation of the Constitution would be possible until those concerns were satisfied."[6] There was considerable discontent in federal-provincial relations after the Victoria Conference, and this surfaced in 1972 at the Conference of Provincial Welfare Ministers. Federal disappointment over the failure to patriate the constitution (including an amending formula) was deep. Provincial dissatisfaction was fuelled by the federal government's unilateral changes to unemployment insurance in 1971 and its proposed reform of family allowances.[7] Indeed, several provinces demanded at the conference that the federal government turn over to them the jurisdiction and fiscal resources for family allowances.[8] There was also resentment over federal intrusion into provincial jurisdiction with what provinces felt were ill-conceived and uncoordinated programs. Provincial frustration "had reached an all-time high."[9] Thus, when the Conference of Provincial Welfare Ministers unanimously called for a joint review "to develop better mechanisms for achieving a rationalized social security system in Canada," the federal government quickly and readily agreed.[10]

There were political pressures on the federal government at the time as well. With the New Democratic Party holding the balance of power, the minority Liberal government had to agree informally to reconsider social programs in return for NDP support in Parliament.[11] Furthermore, of all three national parties, it was the NDP that expressed most publicly its commitment to the idea of a guaranteed income.

The Throne Speech on January 4, 1973, opening the twenty-ninth Parliament therefore called for a federal-provincial review of the nation's social security system. This was quickly followed in April 1973 by the federal government's *Working Paper on Social Security in Canada* (the Orange Paper), a document which set the stage for the subsequent discussions.[12] Coinciding with this interest in reviewing social security, policy makers began considering the advantages and disadvantages of the guaranteed income concept. Early attention naturally focused on the possible work disincentive effects of a guaranteed income, and note was made of the income maintenance experiments being conducted in the United States. The White Paper, *Income Security for Canadians,* had called for research into the potential effects of such plans on the Canadian economy, stating:

> An overall guaranteed income program for the whole population that is worthy of consideration is one that offers a substantial level of benefit to people who are normally in the labour market. Therefore, a great deal of further study and investigation, like the experiments now under way in New Jersey and Seattle in the United States, is needed to find out what effects such a program would have on people's motivation, on their incentives to work and save. Until these questions are answered, the fear of its impact on productivity will be the main deterrent to the introduction of a general overall guaranteed income plan.[13]

During 1971, Manitoba showed serious interest in testing the guaranteed income approach, particularly as a demonstration project or administrative test. Edward R. Schreyer, then premier of Manitoba, stated on September 9, 1971: "The Government of Manitoba is committed to launching a pilot project—strictly on an experimental basis, in designated urban and rural areas—to determine if the concept of a GAI can be translated into effective action."[14] In the meantime, research interest was growing in Ottawa, and the minister of national health and welfare announced the establishment of a fund to cover 75 percent of the cost of such experiments. He hoped that collaboration with provinces would develop quickly.

In March 1973, Manitoba submitted a proposal for a guaranteed income project for funding to the Department of National Health and Welfare. The proposal was approved two months later, and on June 4, 1974, Canada and Manitoba formally signed the *Agreement concerning a Basic Annual Income Experiment Project* covering cost-sharing arrangements and the respective roles of the two governments. The Manitoba submission coincided with the release of the Orange Paper and the start of the joint Federal-Provincial Review of Social Security.

The decision to establish the Manitoba Basic Annual Income Experiment (MINCOME MANITOBA) was significant in two respects. First, it sought to evaluate in rigorous manner a guaranteed income program within the broader context of an overall review of the social security system. As such, it responded to the generally recognized need to reform the income security system and to the increasing interest in the concept of guaranteed income. Second, it was the first time Canada employed social experimentation techniques for policy purposes.

The social security review and the guaranteed income experiment are certainly the two most significant events of Canadian social policy during the 1970s. Furthermore, these two events were connected in thought and purpose, in addition to timing. The review is sometimes regarded as an attempt to develop an integrated and coordinated approach to social security,[15] or to supplant certain portions of the CAP legislation,[16] or even as a surrogate for constitutional discussions adjourned at Victoria.[17] But the National Council of Welfare did not fail to see the connection; it bluntly asserted that "the goal of the social security review [was] the establishment of a guaranteed annual income."[18] Similarly, the MINCOME Project was more than just an expensive exercise in econometrics, or a brave new adventure in social experimentation. The joint news release (February 22, 1974) announcing the final approval of the experiment by Canada and Manitoba was quite clear about the role and purpose of the guaranteed income test. It proclaimed (p. 5): "The Manitoba experiment is expected to make an important contribution to the review of Canada's social security system launched last April by all ten provinces and the federal government."

The Social Security Review[19]

The Working Paper on Social Security in Canada (Orange Paper) addressed the broad question of "how best to achieve security of income for all Canadians" (p. 2) and listed five principles for the review to consider: a guaranteed annual income for those unable to work (income support); work incentive programs for those capable of work (income supplementation); a "fair and just relationship" between minimum wages, support, and supplementation; provincial variation; and federal-provincial consensus. The federal government enunciated propositions rather than proposals because it did not wish the working paper to appear definitive; it wanted to facilitate joint review based upon consultation.[20] However, the Orange Paper did contain two specific proposals (which would later be implemented) on family allowances and the Canada and Quebec pension plans.

The Orange Paper suggested five strategies in the form of fourteen propositions for an effective alternative social security system. The five strategies were: an employment strategy, a social insurance strategy, an income support and supplementation strategy, a social and employment services strategy, and a federal-provincial strategy. The employment strategy emphasized jobs as opposed to social assistance. Its orientation was macroeconomic but governments would assist individuals to enter the job market by providing training and skills. The Orange Paper also proposed a community employment program to provide socially useful work for those unemployed for an extended length of time (Propositions 1,2,3). The social insurance strategy would provide for those temporarily unemployed or retired. Social insurance programs would be continued in addition to supplementation of incomes where necessary (Proposition 4). The propositions comprising the income maintenance strategy formed the core of the review. They included a proposal to increase family allowances (Proposition 5), but it was Propositions 6 and 7 that were the central ones. Proposition 6 called for the provision of an income supplement to the working poor; Proposition 7 suggested a guaranteed annual income for those with insufficient income and "unable or not expected to work." Included among those not expected to work were not only the retired or disabled, but also single parent families, and persons "not presently employable by reason of . . . age, lack of skills, or length of time out of the labour force." Old Age Security programs would continue (Proposition 8) as would emergency relief programs "now provided for under the Canada Assistance Plan" (Proposition 9). The social and employment services strategy (Propositions 10 and 11) involved providing individuals with necessary services such as training, counselling, placement, rehabilitation, special work situations, homemaker and child care services, and so on. Finally, the federal-provincial strategy reflected the past failure of constitutional reform efforts as well as the thorny issue of jurisdiction for social policy. It therefore proposed that levels of the income guarantees and supplements, including family allowances, be set by individual provinces (Propositions 12 and 13), and be allowed to vary subject to minimum standards set by the federal government.

The review was to comprise two stages: the first stage would occupy two years and develop policy proposals and program design. The second would be an operational stage between May 1975 and June 1976. In actual fact, only the first stage materialized.

Negotiations and discussions were conducted at three levels: the ministerial level, the continuing committee level, and working parties. The federal and provincial ministers of social welfare would direct the review and make political decisions on proposals. A continuing committee of provincial deputy ministers and the federal deputy minister of welfare would establish and oversee the activities of various working parties and report to the conference of ministers. The ministers met in April 1973 and agreed to establish working parties of technical advisers for three areas: income maintenance, social services, and employment strategy. It was clear at the outset, however, that the working party on income maintenance (WPIM) was to be the major component of the review.

The initial meeting of the WPIM was held in July 1973. Although its terms of reference included identification and analysis of policy and design issues relating to a comprehensive and coordinated income maintenance system, it concentrated initially on design options for family allowances and the Canada Pension Plan. In September 1973 the conference of welfare ministers announced changes to both the Canada/Quebec pension plans and the Family Allowance Program. Thus, two months after the review began, agreement was reached to amend the CPP/QPP and increase substantially the maximum monthly retirement benefits. The payments would also be indexed to the consumer price index. Similarly, family allowance benefits were nearly tripled, indexed, and made subject to taxation. Provinces could vary the level of payments on the basis of age of child or family size so long as the average payment per child in the province was $20 and a minimum of $12 a child was paid. This was quite an innovation, and although consistent with the framework of the Orange Paper (Propositions 5,12,13), it was viewed at the time as a concession to gain the support of Quebec for the review.[21] At this point, many provinces began considering, or introducing, major or minor changes to their social assistance programs. Some provinces even proceeded with totally new income supplementation programs. The changes to family allowances and the two pension plans—both universal programs—had the effect of concentrating further attention on income-tested transfer mechanisms. Additionally, these reforms were costly (about $2 billion annually) and conditioned the subsequent response of the federal cabinet to the later income maintenance proposal and request for further funds.[22]

A second report from the WPIM was presented in February 1974. The ministers now instructed the WPIM to concentrate on an integrated income security program and to focus on support/supplementation options rather than social insurance program changes. At the November 1974 meeting of ministers, six options were presented by the continuing committee on behalf of the WPIM. Three of the six alternatives were income-tested plans (Options 1,2,3), and three were child-related programs (Options 4,5,6). All options would be coordinated with social insurance programs and integrated with the tax system. The ministers rejected the child-related options and requested WPIM to further study the design and cost implications of the income-tested options. The first option was a single guaranteed income system with eligibility based solely on income. The second and third options proposed a two-tier but integrated system; eligibility for the higher level of support would be restricted by an employment availability test. The difference between the second and third options concerned the method of delivery: either through transfer payments or refundable tax credits. The ministers agreed that levels of support could vary across the country; that any work-eligibility test should, if possible, be "objective"; that "Ministers of Finance would have to play a major role within their respective governments"; and "that a modified Canada Assistance Plan could be employed as a vehicle for achieving the reforms Ministers favoured (in particular Options 1 and 2), or entirely new legislation could be introduced."[23]

The November 1974 meeting of the ministers was a turning point and thereafter the review lost momentum. When income maintenance options were presented to a cabinet committee, the two tier system was favoured. The provincial NDP governments of British Columbia, Manitoba, and Saskatchewan, and initially Quebec, favoured a single-tier program. But eventually, in April 1975, the welfare ministers reached an agreement on the basic outline of a new guaranteed income scheme. There would be two components to the program: income support for those "unable to work or for whom employment cannot be found" and income supplementation with "built-in work incentives" for those "who are working but whose income(s) are inadequate." Support levels would be set by the provinces and new cost-sharing arrangements were proposed. The federal government was "prepared to increase substantially its financial contribution—over the 50 percent which now applies to provincial assistance programs—by paying two-thirds of the supplementation component of the guaranteed income system." The "detailed design" of this new guaranteed income system would have to be worked out, and everyone understood that "guidelines relating to the federal sharing of provincial assistance programs under the Canada Assistance Plan . . . [would have to] apply for [this] interim period while the operational design for the income support and supplementation system [was] being developed."[24] Operational details included questions such as work incentives and costs. These could not be easily dismissed[25] but, at least for now, ministers could say that the policy review stage of the review had ended in consensus.[26]

The income support and supplementation proposal had been approved by cabinet committee. However, federal officials were shocked when the full cabinet merely agreed in principle and stated that the program would have to be "delayed," meaning that it was all but dead.[27] The following year the cabinet approved an amended, pared-down version with eligibility restricted to families with children and those aged fifty-five to sixty-five, and costing $240 million instead of the $2 billion price tag of the original program. This was presented to the provinces in February 1976, received general support, but was rejected by Ontario. Only British Columbia appeared enthusiastic and only a few provinces had any hope of implementing the program. Reform of income maintenance in Canada through federal-provincial cooperation ended. Although the social security review devoted most of its time and attention to income security measures, it was to be social services that would emerge as the central agenda item towards the end of the review. The Working Party on Social Services (WPSS) was largely made up of social workers and social service administrators. According to its terms of reference, it was to prepare an inventory of social and employment services, evaluate existing levels of services, and identify methods to improve delivery, coordination and extension.[28] Initially it was thought that social services would merely serve an ancillary function to employment and income maintenance programs; this was the role traditionally assigned social services by economists and public finance experts who dominated the social security review. The analysis of the WPSS was "largely descriptive," "loosely formulated," and evoked little interest when its report was presented in 1975. This was its first and last report and upon its submission the WPSS was officially disbanded.[29]

The original mandate of the working party was to study current cost-sharing arrangements. The WPSS was asked to "develop alternative legislative frameworks for the delivery and financing of social services" and "to examine specifically the question of cost-sharing arrangements for specific kinds of service programs, and to review current problems in the interpretation of the Canada Assistance Plan Act and regulations."[30] But dissatisfaction with the Canada Assistance Plan, particularly the limiting of services to those "in need or likely to become in need," led the federal government to announce "a sweeping change in the approach to the financing and development of social services in Canada."[31] The CAP arrangements for cost-sharing on the basis of "need or likelihood of need" would be replaced; new legislation would be introduced dividing services into five categories according to target groups; sharing would be on a straight 50 percent basis; rehabilitation and support services for the aged and the handicapped would become a priority; and graduated user charges would be introduced. The new legislation would be in place by early 1976.

This was a major departure and both the timing and substance of the initiative deserve to be noted. In 1975 the income maintenance strategy was losing momentum and a new focus was required to salvage the review. According to Van Loon, "early in 1975, the federal deputy minister and his senior advisor on social service programs sat down virtually alone and very rapidly drafted a proposed outline for a new cost-sharing arrangement [for social services]."[32] The previously ignored report of the WPSS had recommended that social services be made available to all, but on a free, subsidized, or full-cost basis according to income. The report addressed the narrow issues of service categories and graduated user charges, but not federal-provincial cost-sharing or administrative arrangements. Consequently, the report was of "extremely limited utility" for designing a new cost-sharing arrangement and led to a "technically inept" and ill-received legislative draft.[33] What followed was a series of negotiations over nearly two years, nine legislative outlines, fourteen federal drafts, but no unusual rancour.

Eventually, a federal ultimatum was issued to "take or leave it," accompanied by a threat to terminate CAP cost-sharing at the end of the legal notice period.[34] The provinces finally agreed to the new proposal, which became Bill C-57, the Social Services Act.

Bill C-57 would have replaced the welfare service portion under Part I of the Canada Assistance Plan Act, repealed those sections of CAP concerning Indian welfare (Part II), and completely repealed the Vocational Rehabilitation of

Disabled Persons Act. The bill received first reading June 20, 1977, but died on the parliamentary order paper. However, it was expected that it would be automatically reintroduced and passed in the next session.

In August 1977 the federal minister of health and welfare announced that Bill C-57 would be replaced by unconditional block-funding. This was a proposal whereby each province would be given a grant in lieu of cost-sharing with no provision that such funds need be spent for social service programs. There had been no federal-provincial consultation. A number of provincial welfare ministers were displeased, but not surprised, by the announcement. Provincial governments had come to resent the fact that cost-sharing might distort their priorities; for its part, the federal government wanted greater predictability and control over its expenditures. Furthermore, the precedent of block-funding had been set when it was introduced for medical insurance;[35] it did not seem unusual to apply it now to social services.

It appeared that Bill C-55, the Social Services Financing Act, would receive certain passage. However, in August 1978 the prime minister announced a series of restraint measures because of the national economic situation. Proposed programs, in contrast to those protected by legislative guarantees, were especially vulnerable. Bill C-55 would have increased federal expenditures in its first year of operation by $61 million over that estimated under the CAP and VRDP programs. The federal contribution under Bill C-55 was projected to rise by $221 million in the second year and reach $1.9 billion in 1987.[36] The federal minsiter of health and welfare finally conceded that Bill C-55 was dead; its death attributable in part to reductions in federal expenditures dictated by events external to the review process[37] and in part to provincial objections and deteriorating federal-provincial relations.[38] Despite numerous negotiations, compromise, and two bills, the welfare services provisions of the Canada Assistance Plan Act remain.

In late 1978, the federal government suddenly introduced the Refundable Child Tax Credit Program. There was little discussion or provincial objection, and the first payments were made in 1979. Though this measure did not fall within the official time period of the social security review, it was symbolic of both the change in economic circumstances as well as the review process. The child tax credit signalled the return to unilateral action by the federal government, the use of the tax system to deliver social benefits, and the shift in emphasis towards selective transfers.[39]

THE GUARANTEED INCOME EXPERIMENT[40]

The first ever large-scale social experiment in Canada was jointly funded by Canada and Manitoba and sought to evaluate the guaranteed income concept. The design of MINCOME MANITOBA was similar to the American experiments in focusing on the question of work disincentives, but there was also strong interest in administrative and operational issues. Indeed, this was the basis for its original support by Manitoba. In June 1971, the minister of health and social development for Manitoba declared at a conference of federal and provincial ministers of welfare that Manitoba was convinced of the validity and justness of the GAI approach. The minister said it was "of vital interest to examine the complexities involved in the administration of guaranteed income programs" and that "much knowledge [could be] gained . . . in a demonstration project." Manitoba saw the "proposed demonstration study project as a federal-provincial responsibility" and requested cost-sharing under the Canada Assistance Plan. The minister's statement concluded by asserting that "Manitoba is prepared to conduct the demonstration without federal participation if it cannot be obtained within a reasonable period of time."[41]

Three months later, in September 1971, Premier Edward Schreyer reiterated this position in a major speech.[42] However, details of Schreyer's thinking can best be gauged through a lengthy interview published by the *Winnipeg Tribune*, July 10, 1971. Premier Schreyer viewed the GAI as essentially involving "income-testing" and observed that it "didn't differ at all [from] a negative income tax." Furthermore, because the GAI "would ... substitute for the Canada Assistance Plan Program," the MINCOME "project would be established under the aegis of the Canada Assistance Plan." He estimated Manitoba's financial involvement at "something over $500,000" and the number of families involved at "possibly 500," but "closer to 300." Shortly after, Canada announced a program to cover 75 percent of the costs of such projects. Manitoba submitted a detailed proposal to Canada in March 1973 but it was an outline for a truly scientific research experiment; it was to cost in excess of $17 million and it contemplated enrolment of well over 1,000 families.[43]

At this point, a clear distinction must be drawn between "demonstrations" or "pilot projects," and "social experiments." The notion of an experiment is exemplified by research procedures commonly employed in the natural or physical sciences. Generally speaking, the method entails formulating special actions to support or falsify hypotheses under controlled conditions, where control is effected by the experimenter either by actually fixing certain variables, or statistically by randomization.[44] The term "experiment" therefore strictly excludes "demonstrations" and "pilot projects." Demonstrations are often employed to dramatize some program already selected on *a priori* considerations as the committed course to follow, while pilot projects are typically feasibility studies of some proposed mechanism to test procedures or detect unforeseen features.[45]

How, then, did the guaranteed income project evolve from a demonstration to a true experiment? There was tremendous interest among federal officials in the American projects, which were designed as research experiments. The idea of a similar endeavour in Canada was tantalizing. Furthermore, given that Manitoba was already committed to a demonstration and sought federal funding, it seemed natural to combine in one project experimental objectives and administrative testing. The relevance of the guaranteed income concept to both the social security review and the Canada Assistance Plan made what seemed logical and useful also opportune. Accordingly, what emerged was not the simple demonstration involving "300 families" and half a million dollars that Manitoba wanted, but an extremely complicated scientific experiment, modelled along the lines of the pioneering American efforts and concentrating on the issue of work responses.

MINCOME's design involved selecting participants and assigning them on a random basis to alternative NIT programs for a three-year period. Families were selected from three sites: the City of Winnipeg, the community of Dauphin, and a number of small rural communities. The sample was stratified by family type and income, and "truncated" at a prespecified income level (approximately $13,000 for a double-headed family of four). Since the primary research objective was work response, the experiment excluded the aged, the disabled, and the institutionalized from participation.

Payments to an initial sample (approximately 1,000) began in 1975. A supplementary sample (approximately 300) was subsequently enrolled and also given payments for a three-year period, but commencing one calendar year after the originally enrolled sample. Three guarantee support levels were tested: $3,800, $4,800, and $5,800 (1975 prices) for a family of four, composed of two adults and two children. Support levels were adjusted for differing family sizes and structure, and increased periodically to maintain approximately constant real value. Three constant benefit reduction tax rates were also specified: .35, .50, and .75. The three support levels and three tax rates gave nine possible combinations. The combination of the highest guarantee and the lowest tax rate was not employed; nor was the combination of the lowest support level with the highest tax rate. Consequently, seven distinct negative income tax plans were tested. A control group was included for comparison purposes.[46]

The unique feature of the MINCOME design was its "saturation" site: every resident in this site was eligible to participate in a single NIT program ($3,800, .50). The Winnipeg portion of the sample was a randomly drawn dispersed sample. Its methodological advantage was the ability to isolate treatment families from one another, thereby making it possible to experimentally vary the NIT program parameters within the same area. However, this very isolation placed treatment families in a highly unrealistic environment—quite unlike the circumstances that would exist under a national NIT whereby all eligible families could receive cash transfers. Therefore MINCOME included the saturation site (Dauphin) in the hope of answering questions about administrative and community issues resulting from a less artificial environment.

The final design of MINCOME may be described then as a compromise or hybrid. It conformed to the format of the "classic" experiment (Winnipeg portion) but it also included "demonstration" aspects (Dauphin).

The organization and conduct of the experiment deserves to be noted. The early design work had been planned jointly by federal and provincial personnel. Once under way, it was announced that while research would be undertaken jointly, the province would be solely responsible for operations. Since MINCOME was ostensibly a research project, this amounted to joint control of all important decisions. There was much to be said for this structure. The joint effort would set a precedent for future endeavours of this type, both governments would receive any credit due, both bureaucracies would become equally committed to the project, both governments would determine the "political" matters, and both administrations would gain expertise and experience. But there were also disadvantages. Decision making might be hesitant or slow, deadlock between the two bureaucracies was a possibility, and opportunities for political interference would be maximized since both governments were involved; conflicts concerning unrelated matters might show up in discussion of experimental decisions. The potential for conflict and confrontation was therefore great. But what were the options? Unilateral action? The federal government probably could not implement the experiment itself because provincial cooperation was required to deliver the "treatment" program. Despite Manitoba's bravado about "going it alone" on a demonstration project, a truly scientific experiment of the magnitude actually proposed was too expensive. For either government to attempt MINCOME by itself on the scale proposed in 1973 was consequently too risky. One possibility might have been to establish an independent crown corporation to conduct the experiment. Although this might assure the research integrity of the project, a crown corporation could also prove cumbersome. Further, it would cost much more because certain overhead expenses associated with activities such as delivering cheques and the like would no longer be available through line departments. A new independent crown corporation might also have difficulty establishing credibility, but more important, social experimentation is the kind of research that necessitates direct government involvement at times. Bearing in mind the cooperative spirit between Canada and Manitoba at the time, joint control of the experiment seemed, therefore, the right and proper choice. Despite auspicious beginnings, dual control of the experiment created many difficulties. Not the least of the problems encountered was distinguishing between research issues, which were to be resolved jointly, and operational concerns, which were a provincial responsibility. The question of an effective organizational structure for MINCOME was never satisfactorily or directly resolved.

The actual conduct of the experiment, of course, had its ups and downs. There were scientific difficulties, political difficulties, management difficulties, operational difficulties—the list goes on. It is not particularly instructive to document all these details. What is significant was the change in "mandate" of the experiment midway through its course. Instead of the implied sequence of design, experimental trial, data collection, analysis, and the production of research results, perhaps culminating in an official report, the experiment was altered in two fundamental ways. First, the research priority was shifted away from the original work disincentive issues towards administrative questions. Second, and more significant, the MINCOME project was to adopt an "archive" strategy. That is, it would collect data but not analyse it.

There were a number of reasons—all interrelated—for this turn of events. The most fundamental and basic was a lack of funds. The experiment had been designed with a total budget of slightly over $17 million in mind. No one really believed that this figure was anything but a wild guess. The number was a convenient one; it had the right "feel" in terms of getting the project approved. As the experiment proceeded, more accurate estimates would be possible and, accordingly, budgets could be redrafted to reflect actual expenditures and resubmitted. Or so it was thought!

The budget total of $17 million soon solidified into a "hard" number. It became the contractual maximum for both governments for a variety of reasons and the problem then became one of spending this total in the best manner possible. At first, the usual cost-cutting measures were taken, including eliminating entire research programs thought to be secondary. When it finally became clear that no additional money would be forthcoming, and that the remaining funds would not be sufficient to conduct a credible investigation of even a scaled-down version of the work disincentive question, there was virtually no alternative but to declare the project a "success" and to close it down gracefully. The project's mandate was therefore redirected towards administrative issues for its remaining life.[47] The project was also told to prepare the data already collected for archival storage and to document whatever work had already been completed. The data, it was hoped, would at least be preserved for analysis at a later date.

The significance of the fixed budget amount established at the beginning of the experiment cannot be overestimated. It must be remembered that guaranteed income payments to the participating families came out of this total amount, and that such payments were adjusted annually by some indexing factor. In other words, the amount allotted for payments was not under the experiment's control; it depended upon such factors as the income of the participants, the rate of inflation in the Canadian economy, and the like. Yet these funds had first claim on the $17 million total because of their "statutory" nature. After these payments, operational costs for data collection, overhead, survey personnel, and so on would have the second claim on funds simply because these bills came next in the normal sequence of activities. Research constituted the last stage of the process and therefore would receive the residual of funds. Given the fixed budget amount and the above expenditure sequence, it is not at all surprising that the experiment was "truncated." With both time and money running out, an archival strategy seemed best for the long run. In the short run, it was also convenient for the experiment to address administration issues with its remaining budget.

In giving prime importance to the initial terms of the funding of the project, I do not wish to imply that there were no other factors. My aim is simply to suggest that there were no villains in the piece, that the project was not shut down for purely political considerations, and that research activities were not "cut off" because any party feared their expected conclusions. The budget total is meant to indicate the logic behind the experiment's change in mandate and its eventual disposition. To be sure, there is a larger story to be told, and obvious questions are raised, such as: Why was the budget not increased? and the like. A complete account of the experiment from start to finish is not possible here.

It must also be remembered that MINCOME's redirection came towards the end of the seventies. The social security review had ended; there was no political support in the country for sweeping reforms of the type promised by a guaranteed income; the GAI concept itself had lost its fashionable patina. Furthermore, the economy's performance was extremely poor and a program of restraint was announced; there had also been a change in government both in Ottawa (with the election of Joe Clark) and in Manitoba (with the election of Sterling Lyon). Given all this, it is understandable why everyone wanted MINCOME to conclude quietly and gracefully.

During the next two years, the fate of the data itself appeared uncertain. The signs were not encouraging. Indeed, the manner in which the data was archived (unpublicized location, unknown means of access, and so on) stirs the imagination to wonder whether those who were arranging its sequestering from the research community were possibly the same individuals who arranged sites for the safe disposal of radioactive waste products. The experiment officially ended in 1979 and in 1981 the Institute for Social and Economic Research (ISER) was created at the University of Manitoba with funding from National Health and Welfare. One of the major aims of the ISER is to prepare the MINCOME data for analysis by qualified researchers. There is therefore some cause for cautious optimism that answers to the questions which the experiment posed in the seventies might just begin to appear in the eighties.

Conclusion

The foregoing examination of the social security review and the guaranteed income experiment reveals that a number of new directions in social policy were pursued during the 1970s. The idea of selective (income-testing) transfers received its broadest discussion and support ever, so that the GAI no longer conjures up the kind of fear that it once did. The idea of tax credits also received wide exposure and serious consideration. The needs-test basis of the Canada

Assistance Plan was definitely on the defensive. There was also a short-lived recognition of the role of social services. But at the end of this decade of reform attempts, the CAP Act remains. Discussions of reforms today focus upon individual areas (such as day care) or programs (family allowances reform). Comprehensive reviews are unlikely and incremental changes are all that can be considered as we face an economy in which the watchword is restraint.

Canada still lacks a consistent and coherent framework for long-run reform of the tax-transfer regime; income security among Canadians remains a major issue. Moreover, the economic context of the eighties is likely to make discussion of social policy initiatives different from those preoccupations of the seventies. Economic attention will turn increasingly to such topics as Canada's low productivity, its lack of capital investment, the need to expand output and employment, and the like. Questions pertaining to income distribution are likely to receive lower priority and, when addressed, will probably focus on "ethical" dimensions such as the universality principle rather than the technical delivery questions which chiefly characterized debate in the seventies. The political context will also be different in the 1980s. There will be greater concern with fiscal federalism issues, particularly attempts to realign federal and provincial funding responsibilities. The central debate will therefore shift to such issues as intergovernmental transfers and away from questions concerning delivering transfers or services to individuals. Tragically perhaps, this discussion will be less accessible and immediate to either the general public or those concerned with social policy. Yet the way Canada conducts its cost-sharing of social welfare expenditures has a pronounced impact on the well-being of individual Canadians in the long run, despite the abstruse nature of intergovernmental arrangements. The significant lesson from the 1970s would also appear to be the prognosis for the future. Social policy reform in Canada is invariably part of a double-feature with federal-provincial relations the main attraction; the 1980s could well be the most severe test of our social welfare ideals and institutions since the Great Depression.

NOTES

I would like to thank Paul Thomas for his comments and suggestions. This research was financed in part by the Social Sciences and Humanities Research Council of Canada, and the Research Grants Committee of the University of Manitoba.

1. Economic Council of Canada, "The Problem of Poverty," *Fifth Annual Review* (Ottawa, 1968), chap. 6.

2. Canada, Department of National Health and Welfare, *Income Security for Canadians* (Ottawa: Queen's Printer, 1970).

3. Canada. *Poverty in Canada: Report of the Special Senate Committee* (Ottawa: Information Canada, 1971).

4. Ian Adams, William Cameron, Brian Hill and Peter Penz, *The Real Poverty Report* (Edmonton: M. G. Hurtig, 1971).

5. Quebec, *Income Security: Report of the Commission of Inquiry on Health and Social Welfare* (Quebec City, 1971).

6. Rick Van Loon, "Reforming Welfare in Canada," *Public Policy* 27 (1979): 469–504 (p. 474 quoted).

7. For a discussion of family allowances, Quebec's position, and federal-provincial relations during this period see John Saywell, ed., *Canadian Annual Review of Politics and Public Affairs 1972* (Toronto: University of Toronto Press, 1974), pp. 88ff.

8. A. W. Johnson, "Canada's Social Security Review 1973–75: The Central Issues," *Canadian Public Policy / Analyse de Politiques* 1, no. 4 (1975): 475.

9. R. Doyle, "Canada's Social Security Review," *Australian Journal of Social Issues* 13, no. 1 (1978): 26.

10. Johnson, "Canada's Social Security Review," p. 457.

11. Van Loon, "Reforming Welfare," p. 475.

12. Canada, Department of National Health and Welfare, *Working Paper on Social Security in Canada* (Ottawa, 1973). This document is commonly referred to as the Orange Paper.

13. *Income Security for Canadians*, p. 41.

14. Edward Schreyer, "A Pilot Project in Manitoba on a Guaranteed Annual Income proposed by the Government of Manitoba," notes for a speech delivered to the Canadian Institute of Chartered Accountants, September 9, 1971.

15. *Working Paper on Social Security*.

16. Communiqué of the social security review, April 30, 1975.

17. Van Loon, "Reforming Welfare," 1979.

18. National Council of Welfare, "Guide to the Guaranteed Income" (Ottawa, 1975), mimeo.

19. A number of individuals have commented on the social security review. Former deputy minister A. W. Johnson gives an account of events up to 1975 in Johnson, "Canada's Social Security Review," Richard Splane, "Social Policy Making in the Government of Canada: Reflections of a Reformist Bureaucrat," in *Canadian Social Policy,* ed. Shankar A. Yelaja (Waterloo: Wilfrid Laurier University Press, 1978), pp. 209–26; and Doyle, "Canada's Social Security Review," describe the review up to the time of Bill C-57. Derek P. J. Hum, "Poverty, Policy and Social Experimentation in Canada: Background and Chronology," in *Reflections on Canadian Incomes* (Ottawa: Economic Council of Canada, 1980) comments on unanswered technical questions raised by the review and its relation to the experimental NIT project. See also J. Ryant, "Federal Provincial Consultation in Social Policy Formulation: A Canadian Example," manuscript, 1980; and C. Rachlis, "A Farewell to Welfare: The Politics of Social Security Reform and Fiscal Federalism in the 1970s," paper presented at annual meeting of the Canadian Political Science Association, Ottawa, 1982. My understanding of events is also taken from technical background papers, the official communiqués of ministers, and conversations with certain individuals involved with the review.

20. Doyle, "Canada's Social Security Review," p. 28.

21. Van Loon, "Reforming Welfare," p. 486.

22. Ibid., p. 493.

23. Communiqué, November 19–20, 1974, p. 13.

24. Communiqué, April 30–May 1, 1975, pp. 4–5.

25. Hum, "Poverty, Policy and Social Experimentation," p. 313.

26. Johnson, "Canada's Social Security Review," p. 462.

27. This account of what went on in the cabinet is drawn entirely from Van Loon, "Reforming Welfare," pp. 493–98.

28. Maurice Kelly, "The New Social Services Legislation—What Next?" *The Social Worker* 45 (1977): 156–60, writes that from the outset WPSS took as its mandate an examination of *all* public social services irrespective of their connection to employment; it wanted to rethink the broad objectives of social services. However, the "descent from ideals to practical realities tended to be difficult for this working party."

29. Ryant, "Federal Provincial Consultation," p. 12.

30. A separate report dealing with possible changes to the federal provincial agreements on the Vocational Rehabilitation of Disabled Persons was also considered at this meeting. The federal government announced that it would extend the existing VRDP agreements for another year, at which time it hoped that "the federal-provincial social security review would have reached agreement on the longer run approach to the social security system, including rehabilitation services." Communiqué, November 19, 20, 1974, p. 5.

31. Communiqué, April 30, 1975, p. 1.

32. Van Loon, "Reforming Welfare," p. 448.

33. Ryant, "Federal Provincial Consultation," p. 14.

34. Van Loon, "Reforming Welfare," p. 489; Johnson, "Canada's Social Security Review," p. 453; Ryant, "Federal Provincial Consultation," pp. 12, 14–16.

35. For a discussion of the politics underlying this initiative see Rick Van Loon, "From Shared Cost to Block Funding and Beyond: The Politics of Health Insurance in Canada," *Journal of Health Politics, Policy and Law* 2 (1978): 469–504.

36. Canada, Department of National Health and Welfare, "Summary of the Principal Components of the Social Services Financing Bill"; "The Federal Legislation on Financing Social Services—1978"; and News Release, May 12, 1978 (Ottawa: Supply and Services).

37. Van Loon, "Reforming Welfare," p. 491.

38. Ryant, "Federal Provincial Consultation," p. 17.

39. The Working Party on Community Employment deserves a brief mention. It was to catalogue programs to assist individuals who had been unemployed for extended periods, and prepare proposals for an employment strategy. The Working Party eventually submitted a "framework for development" and ministers agreed to initiate twenty experimental employment projects across Canada "to gain broader experience." See communiqué, November 19–20, 1974, p. 4. Few projects got beyond the planning stage and all traces of the Community Employment Strategy disappeared with the budget cuts in 1978.

40. The author was research director of MINCOME MANITOBA from 1975 to the project's termination in 1979.

41. R. Toupin, statement delivered at conference of federal and provincial ministers of welfare, June 7–8, 1971.

42. Schreyer, "A Pilot Project," 1971.

43. An appraisal of the welfare system of Manitoba by Professor Clarence Barber was published on December 22, 1972. Barber's report recommended introduction of a guaranteed income. On the day the report was released, Premier Schreyer announced that Manitoba was "on the brink" of concluding a federal-provincial pilot project. It is difficult to tell how much influence Barber's report had.

44. Cf. the following definition given by Henry W. Riecken and Robert F. Boruch, eds., *Social Experimentation: A Method for Planning and Evaluating Social Intervention* (New York: Academic Press, 1974), p. 3: "by experiment is meant that one or more treatment (programs) are administered to some set of persons (or other units) drawn at random from a specified population; and that observations (or measurements) are made to learn how (or how much) some relevant aspect of their behavior following treatment differs from like behavior on the part of an untreated or control group also drawn at random from the same population."

45. No derogatory intent is implied by the distinction between experiments on the one hand and demonstrations and pilot projects on the other. The aim is simply to clarify the term experiment since many policy makers are accustomed to thinking loosely of any trial program as "experimental."

46. The design and sample is discussed in two technical documents. Derek P. J. Hum, Michael E. Laub, and Brian J. Powell, *The Objectives and Design of the Manitoba Basic Annual Income Experiment,* Technical Report No. 1 (Winnipeg: MINCOME MANITOBA, 1979), and Derek P. J. Hum, Michael E. Laub, Charles E. Metcalf, and Donald Sabourin, *The Sample Design and Assignment Model of the Manitoba Basic Annual Income Experiment*, Technical Report No. 2 (Winnipeg: MINCOME MANITOBA, 1979).

47. For a detailed discussion of the project's experience with administering the negative income tax see Derek P. J. Hum, "Canada's Administrative Experience with Negative Income Taxation," *Canadian Taxation* 1, no. 1 (1981): 2–16.

Chapter Four

Institutional Conservatism: Federalism and Pension Reform

KEITH G. BANTING

Pension policy in Canada, as elsewhere in the western world, is under pressure. For almost a decade now, our pension system has been subjected to intensive scrutiny. Numerous advisory commissions have highlighted its deficiencies; representatives of business, labour, pensioners, and others have pressed their views on government; and politicians have argued about the best way forward. While the depth of the recession has slowed the momentum and postponed a final response, important decisions about the future of Canadian pensions will clearly be made during the second half of the 1980s.

At the beginning of the decade, pensions seemed to represent the most tantalizing issue on the social policy agenda, providing at first glance at least a refreshing exception to the pervasive conservatism of contemporary welfare politics. In contrast to the dreary succession of cuts and retrenchment in virtually every other corner of the welfare state, the entire pensions debate was premised on the need for improvement. Intense political controversy certainly surrounded the extent to which, and the way in which, the retirement income system should be enriched. But for defenders of the Canadian welfare state, pensions policy seemed to offer a unique opportunity for advance in an era otherwise dominated by the need to defend the gains of earlier days.

But as always, first appearances can be deceiving. As the decade progressed, the momentum for sweeping reform receded. Debate concentrated on an increasingly narrow set of issues, and increasingly emphasized the importance of the private sector rather than government in meeting the needs of future generations of elderly Canadians.

This ebbing of the reformist impulse reveals much about the essential dynamics of contemporary social policy. It clearly reflects the changing political balance between major economic and social interests with a stake in the welfare state—business, labour, women's organizations, and social groups. But the evolution of "the great pension debate" also points, once again, to the importance of Canadian federalism. As in the past, the complexities of the constitutional process within which pension policy is made constituted a powerful constraint on reform. The central argument of this chapter is that federal-provincial relationships in the pensions field act as a brake on policy change, and as a potent conservative force in Canadian pension politics.[1]

Institutional Fragmentation and Public Policy

Institutions are never neutral. The structure of political institutions inevitably conditions the ability of different interests to shape public policy, smoothing the way for some and raising obstacles to others. In Schattschneider's classic phrase, "organization is the mobilization of bias."[2] One of the most frequently advanced examples of this basic truth concerns the impact of institutional fragmentation on the capacity of the state to introduce new policies. According to this argument, nations in which political authority is highly concentrated in one body are much more capable of major changes in policy direction than nations in which authority is divided up among a number of separate, politically independent institutions. In general terms, the greater the fragmentation of power, the greater the difficulty in securing agreement on policy, and the broader the political consensus required before innovation occurs.

The American congressional system represents the clearest example. Whereas the cabinet system is often seen as facilitating agreement on clear lines of policy, the checks and balances of the congressional system increase the likelihood that reform initiatives will be defeated, delayed, or diluted.[3] Undoubtedly the differences between cabinet and congressional government can be overstated. After all, many cabinet governments also seem immobile in the face of modern pressures; and certainly the congressional system is not the only reason that government plays a smaller role in the United States than in many other countries.[4] But at the very least, the congressional system does seem to require a broader political consensus before major action can be undertaken.

Federalism represents another form of institutional fragmentation, another version of divided power, which has important implications for the expansion of the public sector. The assertion that federal government means limited and even weak government is a long-standing one. Harold Laski, for example, advanced precisely that case in the early decades of this century, and many have followed his lead.[5] Historical studies of the growth of the welfare state, such as that of Anthony Birch, insist that the complications of federalism inhibited the development of social legislation in countries such as Canada, Australia, and the United States; and Heidenheimer's more recent studies continue to point to the importance of institutional complexity in federal systems such as West Germany and the United States in raising obstacles to the extension of social programs.[6]

The proposition that federalism is a conservative factor in the politics of western nations has not received unanimous consent. A revisionist interpretation insists that federalism has actually encouraged the growth of the state. Twenty years ago, for example, Trudeau argued that innovative policies could be introduced more rapidly in federal states than unitary ones. Innovative ideas are always more socially appropriate and politically acceptable in some parts of the country than in others; and the genius of federalism is precisely that innovation can proceed quickly in such regions, with other parts of the country to be convinced later by the example.[7] Another variant of the argument has emerged recently, with some commentators arguing that in an era of activist government, federalism contributes to growth in the public sector by multiplying the number of governments with expansionist tendencies.[8]

What evidence that does exist, however, suggests that such expansionist tendencies have not fully offset the restrictionist impact of federalism. Cross-national studies of public expenditure levels conclude that expenditure as a proportion of the GNP is positively associated with the degree of centralization in government. Cameron discovered that the rate of increase in the public sector as a whole during the period 1960–75 was lower in nations with a federal structure than those with a unitary one, and the findings of Wilensky and of Castles and McKinley agree that, other things being equal, countries with federal systems devote a smaller proportion of their national resources to welfare spending than do those with centralized political systems.[9]

Canadian pension policy provides a classic demonstration of the restrictionist impact of divided jurisdiction. To illustrate this impact and to assess its importance for the future of pension policy, this chapter examines the existing pension system and the complex division of authority between federal and provincial governments in this field. It then analyses the links between the institutional framework and the wider political alignment of economic and social groups which do battle over Canadian pension policy.

The Canadian Pension System

As in other western nations, Canadians have developed two pension systems, a public system consisting of a variety of programs, and a private system based on occupational pensions sponsored by employers. The public pension system is composed of three distinct tiers. The first of these tiers is Old Age Security (OAS), a demogrant program which pays a universal flat-rate pension to everyone aged sixty-five and over, subject only to a qualification based on years of residence in Canada. The second tier is composed of the Canada and Quebec pension plans, which together provide a nationwide contributory pension system that covers all employed persons. The third tier, composed of the Guaranteed Income Supplement (GIS) and similar provincial supplements, constitutes a guaranteed annual income for elderly Canadians. GIS provides a supplementary benefit for those pensioners who have little or no income other

TABLE 1

PUBLIC EXPENDITURE ON PENSIONS AS A PROPORTION OF GDP, 1960–81

	1960		1976		1981	
	Rank	%	Rank	%	Rank	%
Australia	9	3.4	10	5.1	10	5.6[1]
Canada	10	2.8	11	3.8	12	4.6
Denmark	5	4.6	7	7.8	5	9.2
France	2	5.9	3	8.4	3	11.9
Germany	1	9.8	1	12.9	2	12.5
Italy	4	4.8	2	10.4	1	13.0
Japan	12	1.6	12	2.9	11	5.0
Netherlands	3	5.2	5	8.2	6	8.7
Norway	11	2.8	6	7.9	7	7.9
Sweden	6	4.4	4	8.2	4	11.8
United Kingdom	8	4.1	9	6.3	9	7.4
United States	7	4.2	8	6.9	8	7.4
Average		4.5		7.4		8.8

SOURCE: OECD, *Technical and Statistical Annex* (OECD 83.02).
1 1980.

than that provided by OAS, and six provincial governments now have special programs that essentially "top up" the combined OAS-GIS payment for the poorest pensioners.

In comparison with other western democracies, this three-tiered system is relatively small. As table 1 shows, expenditures on public pensions in Canada continue to consume a smaller proportion of the nation's economic resources than in other western democracies.

Part of the reason for this pattern is that in Canada the elderly represent a smaller proportion of the total population than elsewhere. But demography is not the full story. Expenditures are lower also because benefits are lower: public pensions in Canada replace less of preretirement earnings than is the case in most other western democracies, and this pattern will persist even when the Canada and Quebec pension plans are fully matured. Figure 1 shows this relationship for a couple which had average earnings before retirement. The Canadian system is unusual in the importance played by a flat-rate benefit and an income-tested supplement (the OAS-GIS tiers), and as a result low-income earners fare much better here than in most other western nations. But a substantial portion of middle-income Canadians who are dependent primarily on public pensions face a much sharper drop in their living standards when they retire than do their counterparts elsewhere in the western world.[10]

GIS solution

FIGURE 1

PUBLIC PENSIONS AS A PERCENTAGE OF GROSS EARNINGS JUST BEFORE RETIREMENT
One-Earner Couples with Earnings Present throughout Work Years

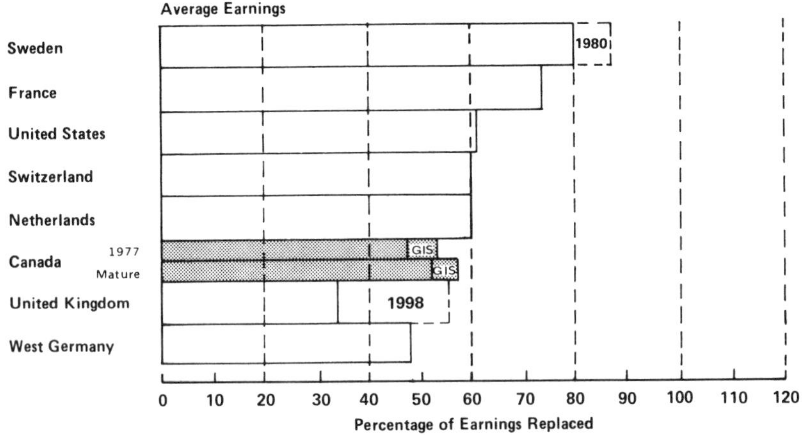

SOURCE: *Report of the Task Force on Retirement Income Policy*, vol. 1 (Ottawa: Minister of Supply and Services, 1980). Reproduced by permission of the Minister of Supply and Services, Canada.

The private pension sector has grown rapidly since World War II. By 1982 over 15,000 occupational pension plans were in operation, covering approximately four and a half million workers. Despite this record of growth, however, private coverage remains partial at best: about 44 percent of paid workers enjoy the protection of a private pension, a figure that has increased only marginally over the last decade. The extent of coverage varies enormously from industry to industry, with only public administration providing anything close to comprehensive coverage; and high income groups enjoy substantially better protection than the poorly paid (see table 2). Personal savings do supplement the private retirement income system and are subsidized through the device of Registered Retirement Savings Plans, a tax-deferral technique. But participation in this program is also confined largely to tax payers in the upper income levels.

Once again, by international standards, the private system is limited. Among western democracies, only the United States has less complete private protection, as figure 2 demonstrates. In addition, at the outset of the contemporary debate both vesting and locking-in of employee contributions came later in Canada, and increases in pensions-in-pay to compensate for inflation appeared to be less common than in many other countries.[11] As a consequence, private pensions represented a small sector of the full retirement

TABLE 2

OCCUPATIONAL PENSION PLAN COVERAGE BY EARNINGS LEVEL, 1979*

Earnings ($)	Private Sector (%)	Public Sector (%)	Total (%)
Up to 7,499	9.4	25.0	10.8
7,500–14,999	43.8	82.5	48.3
15,000–22,499	64.3	94.7	72.5
22,500–29,999	70.2	97.8	84.2
30,000 or over	76.4	97.7	83.7

SOURCE: Health and Welfare Canada, *Rapport*, vol. 4, no. 3 (1981).

*As measured by the percentage of Canada/Quebec Pension Plan contributors also covered by occupational pension plans.

FIGURE 2

PROPORTION OF PAID WORKERS IN CANADA AND SEVEN OTHER COUNTRIES COVERED BY EMPLOYER-SPONSORED PENSION PLANS, 1976

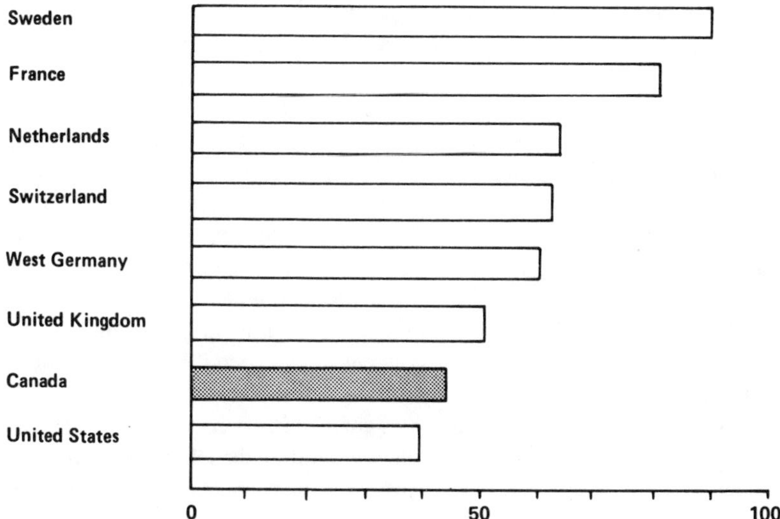

Approximate

SOURCE: *Report of the Task Force on Retirement Income Policy*, vol. 1 (Ottawa: Minister of Supply and Services, 1980). Reproduced by permission of the Minister of Supply and Services, Canada.

income system. Whereas public pensions provided more than half of the income of the elderly in 1975, occupational pensions and annuities accounted for only 12 percent.[12]

Political controversy over the Canadian retirement income system has been fuelled by the same forces that have swept through other western industrial nations: demographic change, low economic growth, and inflation. The proportion of the Canadian population represented by those sixty-five and over will rise steadily over the next fifty years, perhaps even doubling by 2030, putting major pressure on the pension system. By international standards, this demographic bulge should prove reasonably manageable, since our population is still young. At the turn of the century, the aged will still represent a smaller proportion of the population than they do in many European countries right now; only in the third decade of the coming century will such levels be exceeded. Policy adjustments in anticipation of this trend are important, but policy makers have perhaps a decade in which to make necessary changes, an unusual luxury for governments today.

As in other nations, demographic trends pose the greatest problem for the public sector of the retirement income system. Since OAS and GIS are financed exclusively out of general tax revenues, they are, in effect, purely pay-go programs, and their cost will mount steadily over the next half century. The Canada and Quebec pension plans are partially funded; contributions and the interest earned by the accumulated reserves have so far always exceeded benefits paid out, and as of mid-1984, the Canada Pension Plan had a surplus of over $26 billion. But by the early 1990s the flow of benefits will begin to exceed revenues, and by the early years of the twenty-first century the two funds will be exhausted, unless changes are made before then. While demographic change thus represents a long-term problem for the public sector, inflation represents an immediate challenge for the private sector. With the important exception of the occupational pensions provided for public servants, few private pension plans have made adequate increases in payments to those now retired and, not surprisingly, one of the most burning issues in contemporary pension politics has been whether the private sector could provide sufficient inflation protection. This—even more than coverage—has been the political Achilles' heel of the private pension industry.

Thus by international standards, the Canadian pension system is limited, and many Canadians face an even more uncertain future than that facing the retired in many other countries. It is hardly surprising therefore that pension reform has been a major issue on the social policy agenda of the nation. But as in the past, potential responses to these concerns are heavily conditioned by the complex institutional framework within which Canadian pension policy is formulated. The institutional barriers to change are formidable, and deserve careful attention.

The Conservatism of Divided Authority

The division of authority over pensions between the federal and provincial governments is exceedingly complex, even by Canadian standards. In the first place, regulation of private pensions is primarily a provincial responsibility. By 1979, six provinces had enacted legislation governing vesting, solvency, investment and disclosure requirements; and the legislature of a seventh province, New Brunswick, began consideration of similar legislation during its 1981–82 session. The federal government, however, also has a role in this area. The federal Pension Benefits Standards Act governs sectors of the economy subject to direct federal jurisdiction, such as banking, shipping, railways, and communications; and Revenue Canada establishes guidelines for plans seeking to qualify for deduction of contributions and exemption of investment income under the federal Income Tax Act. Thus both levels of government are involved in the regulation of the private pension sector.[13]

This system of divided jurisdiction complicates the process of achieving major reforms in occupational pensions on a nation-wide basis, as is clearly illustrated by the debate over mandatory pensions. Most analysts accept that private plan coverage is unlikely to spread significantly on a voluntary basis, and that—paradoxically perhaps—only compulsion by the state could ensure a major expansion of the private sector. Proposals to require all employers to sponsor pensions meeting specified standards have been a recurring feature of pensions discussions, but the idea always becomes ensnared in jurisdictional complexity. The federal task force on pensions—to take one example—argued that

> mandatory standard plans would require a highly detailed federal-provincial consensus—a consensus that would be very difficult to achieve. Without such a consensus, however, some jurisdictions might require standard plans while others might not. Moreover, standard plans might vary among the provinces and between the federal government and the provinces. In that event a large administrative burden would be thrust on employers with plans in several jurisdictions. The situation could become unworkable.[14]

Representatives of business organizations and provincial pensions officials have emphasized the same problems, often in virtually identical language.[15] None of this means that reform of private pensions or even mandatory pensions in one province is impossible. But divided jurisdiction does complicate the process, affording extra arguments and opportunities to opponents of change, and reducing the prospects for major reform on a nation-wide basis.

Authority over contributory public pensions is also divided, with even more striking consequences. A 1935 judicial ruling clearly established that social insurance was a provincial responsibility, and constitutional amendment was required before the federal government could enter the contributory pensions field. The provincial governments agreed to the necessary amendments in 1951 and 1964, but only on terms which guaranteed them a continuing role in pension politics. The addition to the constitution, Section 94A of the Constitution Act, retained provincial paramountcy by stipulating that no federal pension plan "shall affect the operation of any law present or future of a provincial legislature in relation to any such matter." From the outset, however, there was substantial uncertainty about the precise meaning of this constitutional clause, and the provincial governments therefore also sought much more specific powers over the Canada Pension Plan itself. In return for provincial agreement to the 1964 amendment, the federal government had to agree to write provincial rights into the proposed Canada Pension Plan Act. Accordingly, the act provides that amendments to the plan must be approved by two-thirds of the provincial governments representing at least two-thirds of the population. In addition, the act states that any province may opt out and establish its own plan, in which case the CPP ceases to operate generally in that province. This provision was exercised at the outset by Quebec, but it remains an option for other provinces in the future.

These rules have created a system of multiple vetoes over changes to the Canada Pension Plan. First, the federal government has the authority to block any change of which it disapproves. Second, the requirement that two-thirds of the provincial governments must agree means that any four provinces can, in concert, block a change. Third and more important, the requirement that the assenting provinces represent two-thirds of the total population gives special weight to the largest provinces. Ontario has a veto in its own right, and will retain that power as long as more than one-third of Canadians live within its borders. In addition, the formula contains one of the most fascinating anomalies in Canadian federalism: Quebec is included in the two-thirds rule governing changes to the CPP, despite the fact that it operates its own Quebec Pension Plan. Quebec's share of the population does not entitle it to a veto in its own right, but certainly Quebec and one other province could conceivably block a CPP amendment desired by every other Canadian government.

These complexities are compounded further by the relationship between the Canada Pension Plan and the Quebec Pension Plan. Legally the two plans are separate, but in practice strong pressures bind them together. If the two plans diverged sharply, a host of administrative and political headaches would quickly ensue: transfer arrangements between the plans for contributors moving into or out of Quebec would be greatly complicated, and might simply collapse; large employers would need separate pension arrangements in the two parts of the country, since payments from the Canada and Quebec plans are normally taken into account in the design of private plans; and the public plan providing the lower benefits would soon be subject to public pressure to match its more generous partner. To avoid all of these headaches, pension planners in both Ottawa and Quebec City accept that the Canada and Quebec plans should remain broadly parallel, with neither side making significant changes alone. These pressures are not absolute, and minor differences between the two do exist. Nevertheless, major changes are undoubtedly much easier if initiated simultaneously.

In effect then, the CPP rules and the pressure for parallelism between the CPP and the QPP create a set of vetoes: the federal government, Ontario, Quebec, or several combinations of other provinces can all stop change. These veto points slow the pace of change and insulate pensions from contemporary political pressures. While advocates of expansion must carry the day in Ottawa and in Toronto, Quebec City, and at least five additional provincial capitals, opponents of expansion need win in only one of the three major sites, and so far at least the Ontario government has proven particularly receptive to their cause, for reasons considered more fully below.

The particular opposition of Ontario has been reinforced by a more general provincial interest in resisting a major liberalization of CPP benefits. In many countries, including the United States, political pressures shifted pension plans increasingly to a pay-go basis, as politicians increased benefits without making comparable increases in contribution rates. In Canada, however, federal dynamics restrain such pressures. In order to gain provincial agreement to the constitutional amendment needed to establish the Canada Pension Plan, the federal government also had to abandon its initial preference for a purely pay-go system, and adopt a partially funded one, with the large surpluses that would build up in the early years to be loaned to the provincial governments on favourable terms. As the CPP Advisory Committee noted as early as 1975, "the CPP has become the backbone of provincial debt financing," contributing more than 30 percent of total provincial borrowing.[16] As table 3 indicates, Ontario in particular has made heavy use of the fund, drawing over $14 billion by mid-1984. But the day of reckoning draws near. With the number of beneficiaries now growing rapidly, the amount available for loans to the provinces is dwindling. Current projections suggest that after 1985 the provinces will have to repay more to the CPP Investment Fund than they can take out in fresh loans, establishing a negative cash flow that will accelerate rapidly after 1992. In this situation, provinces have a vested interest in opposing any major liberalization of CPP benefits that would speed up the repayment timetable.

These institutional barriers to expansion tend to deflect the impact of electoral competition at the national level away from the Canada Pension Plan. Federal parties simply cannot make election promises to increase CPP benefits; at best they can promise to try. In contrast to British parties, which made reform

TABLE 3

PROVINCIAL AND FEDERAL SECURITIES PURCHASED BY THE CANADA PENSION PLAN INVESTMENT FUND, AS OF JUNE 30, 1984

Issuer of Securities	Total to Date ($ millions)
Newfoundland	548.2
P.E.I.	114.8
Nova Scotia	1,038.3
New Brunswick	787.8
Quebec*	107.4
Ontario	14,104.8
Manitoba	1,503.1
Saskatchewan	1,191.3
Alberta	2,909.6
British Columbia	4,000.3
Canada	197.5
Total	26,503.0

SOURCE: Health and Welfare Canada, *Canada Pension Plan Statistical Bulletin*, vol. 16, no. 2 (June 1984).

*Amounts available to Quebec relate only to the contribution of some federal employees in that province (e.g., armed forces personnel and RCMP officers).

of contributory pensions a central issue in every election between 1959 and 1974, Canadian parties are virtually silent. "Without the various vetoes," one federal official concurred, "we would certainly see more federal election platforms with CPP items." Electioneering is thus focused even more intensely on exclusively federal retirement programs such as the Guaranteed Income Supplement, as the 1980 election demonstrated. A $35 increase in the monthly supplement was almost the only concrete election promise made by the Liberal party, and the increase was actually being paid out within months of its victory, something that simply could not happen with the Canada Pension Plan. But growth in the income-tested supplement is less significant than a similar rate of growth in the much broader CPP.

Federalism is thus a decidedly conservative force in Canadian pension politics. Provincial responsibility for regulating private pensions militates against nation-wide standards and would certainly complicate any attempt to mandate universal private coverage. And the system of multiple veto points insulates contributory public pensions from the expansionist pressures inherent in democratic politics. This does not mean that the role of private pensions is protected in perpetuity. Institutional obstacles, however real, can be overcome if the political pressures are great enough. But this institutional framework clearly affords the private sector more protection than it would otherwise enjoy. At a minimum, the complex division of authority slows the pace of decision making, giving the private sector more time to marshal its defences against challengers. But in addition, the pension rules ensure that, more so than in most policy areas, reform can only proceed on the basis of broad consensus, a system which inevitably benefits those least interested in change.

To illustrate the weight of these institutional factors, it is essential to turn to an examination of the wider political alignments that dominate this field, and the ways in which federalism influences the balance between them.

Pension Politics

Canadian pension politics flow through two overlapping conflict systems. The first consists of organized economic and social interests, which tend at critical moments to coalesce into two broad lobbies, one supporting private sector plans and the other demanding expansion of public plans. In this, our pensions politics closely resemble those of many other western industrial nations. But in Canada these battles are overlaid by a second conflict system, an intergovernmental one, characterized by frequently intense conflict and bargaining between federal and provincial authorities. The key to understanding the forces that shape pension policies lies in the links between the two systems of conflict.

THE SOCIAL CONFLICT

Not surprisingly, financial and business elites make up the core of the private sector lobby. Financial spokesmen invariably insist that the individual, not the state, is primarily responsible for retirement planning, and that private pension plans maximize freedom of choice, since they can be tailored to differing needs and aspirations through the collective bargaining process. But the preference for private plans reflects powerful economic concerns as well. By the mid-1970s pension contributions represented nearly 20 percent of gross savings, and the accumulated assets of pension funds were equivalent to one third of the GNP, a figure that will rise steadily over the next decades (see figure 3). Pools of capital of such magnitude represent tremendous power. The battle over control of pensions is essentially a battle over one of the commanding heights of the Canadian economy.

Business elites consistently seek to preserve maximum room for private plans. They resisted the establishment of contributory public pensions in the 1960s, and sought to minimize their scope when some kind of plan became inevitable.[17] In the early 1980s, they again mobilized against expansion of the

FIGURE 3

BOOK VALUE OF PENSION FUND ASSETS AS A PROPORTION OF GNP, BY TYPE OF PLAN, 1962–77

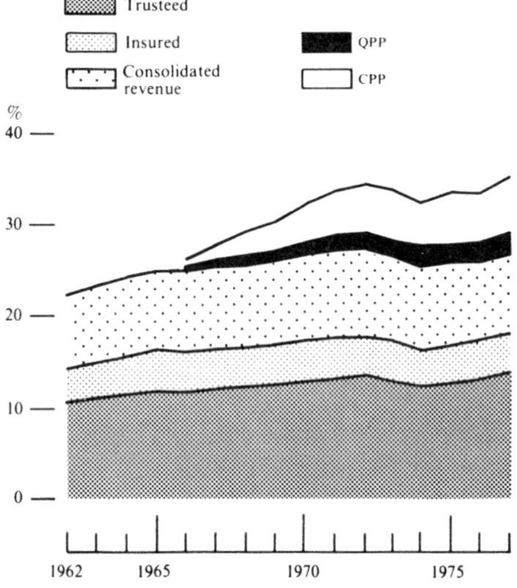

SOURCE: Economic Council of Canada, *One in Three: Pensions for Canadians to 2030* (Ottawa: Minister of Supply and Services, 1979). Reproduced by permission of the Minister of Supply and Services, Canada.

public sector. But while the private sector is united in its opposition to any expansion of the Canada Pension Plan, it has greater difficulty in achieving consensus on a package of significant improvements in private plans. Financial intermediaries, such as trust companies and insurance companies, which derive much of their economic importance from the management of pension funds, strongly support the extension and enrichment of private plans, compulsorily if necessary. Not surprisingly, however, the businesses which actually sponsor private plans are much more cautious about increasing their pension costs, especially during a recession. Equally important, agreement within the private sector is complicated by a major gulf between the interests of large and small business that opens up whenever pension issues arise. Criss-crossed as it is by these fundamental divisions, the private sector has had difficulty in agreeing on a common response to demands for pension reform.

Disagreement reigned, for example, on the two most fundamental proposals for reform of private pensions, mandatory coverage and excess interest. Financial organizations tended to advocate mandatory private pensions in order to solve the coverage problem, and large corporations were prepared to consider such an option, especially if it were the only alternative to an expanded CPP. Thus, in a quintessentially Canadian stance, the Business Council on National Issues came out in favour of "mandatory pensions if necessary, but not necessarily mandatory pensions."[18] The small business sector, however, was implacably opposed, and their own organizations—as well as the Canadian Chamber of Commerce and the Canadian Manufacturers' Association—reflected their concerns.[19] Similar conflicts diluted a commitment to inflation protection. Financial spokesmen advocated that "excess interest" earned in periods of high interest rates be used to improve benefit levels rather than reduce employers' contributions to their plans, as is often the case now.[20] But major industrial organizations remained hostile to any legislated requirement for inflation protection, preferring to continue to rely on voluntary, *ad hoc* adjustments.[21]

In order to avoid open disarray during the pension battle, nine business organizations—representing all major sectors of industry—agreed to a common position on pensions in August 1982.[22] Given the divisions, the consensus was limited to a package of marginal improvements in existing private plans: earlier vesting, compulsory benefits for spouses, improvements in portability. While these changes are not unimportant, the private sector consensus still represented a minimal response to the pressures for major pension reform, and no effective response at all to concerns about coverage and automatic indexing. From the point of view of the private sector, the political danger of this position was that it passed the initiative to the public sector lobby, which claimed to have a comprehensive solution to the central problems of the pension system.

The public sector lobby is really a loose amalgam of groups with similar views on pensions: labour, pensioner associations, welfare organizations, and women's rights groups. In contrast to the private pension lobby, the public lobby has the advantage of relatively broad agreement on the basic approach to pensions reform. Differences in priorities do exist among the various elements within the public lobby, but everyone is agreed that the central strategy is a significant expansion of the Canada and Quebec pension plans. Labour is clearly the most important element in this broad grouping. Canadian unions have been strong advocates of public pensions since the interwar years, and during the battle over the introduction of the CPP, the strong support of the Canadian Labour Congress was critical in helping to offset a strident campaign against it by the Canadian Life Insurance Officers' Association and the Canadian Chamber of Commerce.[23] In the late 1970s, the CLC initiated the present round of debate by proposing that public pensions be increased so that, in combination, they provide 75 percent of preretirement earnings for those who received the average industrial wage. The main element in the proposal was a doubling of CPP benefit levels, which would make it the basic retirement income vehicle for the bulk of the working population. The private sector would then be left with only a supplementary role, providing for early retirement and for the additional needs of those with above average wages.[24]

These views have been largely shared by pensioner groups and welfare organizations, such as the National Welfare Council and the Canadian Council on Social Development. Spokesmen from both of these interests tend to give more attention to the needs of the current elderly than does labour, for obvious reasons; but in general, they share the same commitment to meeting retirement income needs through public sector programs.[25] Women's rights groups have also established an increasingly active presence in the pensions debate, and they too generally argue that the Canada and Quebec pension plans should become the basic retirement income vehicle for Canadians.[26] Representatives of women's groups complained occasionally that the CLC's detailed proposals concentrated on improving the benefits of male workers, and did not give sufficient attention to the particular needs of women.[27] But the broad approach to pension reform is similar.

The battle lines over pensions reform thus assumed their classic pattern once again. During the early 1980s, the public sector lobby took the offensive, armed with a relatively agreed policy, while the private sector lobby remained on the defensive, scrambling to improve occupational pensions but unable to agree on solutions to their weakest points. The public sector lobby therefore seemed to have the advantage. But as the decade wore on, the momentum ebbed away, in part because the deepening recession pushed social policy initiatives of all kinds further down the political agenda. In addition, however, the public sector lobby was confronted with the logic of federalism. The complexities of the process protected the private sector from the full force of the attack, and provided it with more time and greater political opportunities to adjust to an increasingly hostile environment.

THE GOVERNMENTAL CONFLICT

Given divided authority over pensions, final policy decisions are hammered out in a familiar process of federal-provincial bargaining. To understand the institutional dynamics of the process, it is essential to look at the orientations of the key governments at the table, especially Quebec, Ontario, and the federal government, and the nature of their linkages with the two external lobbies.

Quebec governments have proven to be champions of public sector expansion ever since the establishment of contributory public pensions in the 1960s. Quebec was the only province firmly committed to introducing its own plan at that time, and it exercised an expansionist pressure on the design of the plans that came into effect.[28] Since then, Quebec has often pressed for enrichment. Despite the pressures for parallelism between the two plans, it proceeded first with expansion in the early 1970s, and the Quebec benefits for survivors and the disabled are significantly higher than those paid by the Canada Pension Plan. This broad orientation persisted as the new round of negotiations approached. In 1978 the report of the province's own expert commission—known as the *Cofirentes Report*—recommended an expansion of the Quebec Pension Plan sufficient to make it the basic pension vehicle for the working population, together with a financing formula that would achieve greater redistribution from high- to low-income earners.[29] The basic thrust of the report was well received within Quebec political circles.

Both politics and economics conspired in pointing to such a response. On the political front, the Quebec Pension Plan plays an important role in Quebec nationalism. Essentially the QPP is seen as an instrument for reducing Quebecers' dependence on the "foreign" financiers of English Canada and the United States. It was Quebec that insisted on partial funding at the outset, so as to generate a pool of public capital for economic development in the province. The agency that manages the fund, the Caisse de dépôt et de placement du Québec, has emerged as a critical purchaser of Quebec government bonds and the owner of the largest portfolio of common stocks in Canada. For Quebec nationalists, the Caisse is a symbol of the growing French-Canadian role in the world of finance, a world hitherto dominated by anglophones, and any expansion of pensions should definitely come through the QPP, which channels funds into the Caisse, rather than through private plans, which channel capital into private financial institutions. Economics have reinforced this political preference. Pension contributions channelled through the private sector often leave the province in order to seek a higher rate of return elsewhere. Funds channelled through the Caisse, on the other hand, can be reserved for investment in the province.

The governing Parti Québécois is naturally responsive to this logic. As a critical and stable purchaser of Quebec government and Hydro-Quebec bond issues, the Caisse can act as a moderating influence in the market during times of political tension, as in the period following the election of the Parti Québécois in November 1976.[30] Such a financial cushion would be important in any renewed drive towards independence. In addition, an expanded QPP would also fit the party's broad leanings in social policy. While the economic recession has increasingly narrowed the government's freedom for manoeuvre and led to cuts in public services, the Parti Québécois is broadly supportive of public pensions. In the summer of 1982 both the minister of finance and the minister of social development indicated that legislation to expand the Quebec Pension Plan, by enriching benefits and strengthening the financial base, was imminent.[31]

Internal political dynamics thus incline Quebec towards a public sector response to retirement income needs. But the province's external links to the wider Canadian pension system constrain such expansionist instincts. While Quebec does have the authority to act unilaterally, the pressures to proceed in concert with the CPP have grown stronger. Throughout 1982 and 1983, the minister of finance, Jacques Parizeau, repeatedly emphasized the need for "une certaine harmonisation des deux régimes" to preserve labour mobility between provinces.[32] Moreover, the pervasive effects of economic recession have raised the dangers of unilateralism significantly. Income tax levels and overall production costs are already higher in Quebec than in the rest of the country, and even the Parti Québécois would be nervous about a major expansion of the Quebec Pension Plan unless coordinated with comparable changes in the Canada Pension Plan. Thus Parizeau insisted that "il y aura negotiation, et dans les negotiations, il y aura partiellement un compromis."[33] Nevertheless, the Quebec regime would enter such negotiations instinctively inclined towards a public sector response to retirement income needs.

Ontario, on the other hand, instinctively leans in the opposite direction. The conservative ideology of the Progressive Conservative party, which has formed the government continuously since 1943, reinforced by the influence of the private pension industry which is largely headquartered in that province and has close connections with provincial officials, has made Ontario a persistent champion of the private sector. During the 1960s, Ontario would have preferred to mandate an expansion of private plans rather than establish the Canada Pension Plan. When that option failed, it argued that any public plan should provide only minimum benefit levels in order to leave ample scope for private plans, and that the benefits should be closely tied to actual contributions, since too generous a benefit-contribution ratio might also discourage the growth of private plans.[34] While the Ontario government was not particularly happy with the form which the CPP finally took in 1965, its success in gaining a veto over future amendments to the plan has left it in a much stronger position to guard against any major expansion of public contributory pensions.

Ontario did accept enrichment of CPP benefits in the early 1970s, but since then its opposition has stiffened. As we have seen, the province has by far the biggest CPP debt, and the prospect of repayment is daunting, especially given the province's serious and seemingly intractable deficit. As the Ontario Treasury pointed out sternly in 1976, the earlier round of benefit improvements meant that the fund would run down earlier than anticipated, accelerating the point at which Ontario would have to repay.[35] The government's initial response was a campaign for a fully funded CPP[36] but this drive was quickly impaled on the horns of a classic dilemma for pension conservatives. A fully funded CPP would take trillions of dollars out of the economy and put them in government hands, creating a potent instrument of political control over the economy. Ontario officials sought to avoid the problem by devising mechanisms to channel the money into private investment institutions. The Ontario financial community, however, was not reassured. Investment spokesmen, the Toronto Stock Exchange, and others expressed grave reservations, and their fears were later echoed by the province's own Royal Commission on pensions.[37] In light of the opposition, Ontario backed off, and began to support operating the Canada Pension Plan largely on a pay-go basis, but with a contingency fund equal to twice the estimated annual benefit and administration cost. The official purpose of such a "contingency fund" would be to absorb any unanticipated costs and smooth the escalation of contribution rates. Conveniently, however, the fund would also mean that the provinces would perhaps never have to repay the borrowed capital.[38]

In addition, Ontario continues to oppose an enrichment of CPP benefits. To drive its point home, it vetoed a benefit change proposed by the federal government in 1977. Known inelegantly as the "child-rearing drop-out clause," the provision would have benefited people who withdrew temporarily from the labour force to raise children, by allowing them to disregard that period in the calculation of average lifetime earnings. Ontario argued that the proposal would generate unacceptable redistribution among groups of beneficiaries, but the veto was also a warning to the federal government about the evolution of the CPP generally. The provincial treasurer of the day sternly warned that "Ontario will . . . not let the CPP degenerate into another federally-administered welfare plan."[39] The response from women's groups to the 1977 veto was so overwhelmingly hostile that Ontario dropped its opposition in 1983 and the clause came into effect. But the basic approach has not changed: the CPP should not be a tool of income redistribution, and the private sector should be the primary vehicle of retirement saving. During the 1980s the province has focused its proposals on improvements in existing private pensions, and its recommendations have been largely congruent with the broad consensus within the private pension industry.[40] Ontario has been more supportive of a legal requirement for partial inflation protection than industry. But with this exception, the historic alliance between the Ontario government and the private sector remains intact. As an internal document prepared by the province's own pension officials summarized the situation: "*Ontario: Champion of the Private Sector*. Ontario, through its treasurer, has been the principal government voice supporting the private pension system. The private sector looks to Ontario for support on pivotal pension issues which could determine the balance of government private sector pensions."[41]

As the champion of a private sector policy, Ontario is armed with the impressive power of an absolute veto over any expansion of the Canada Pension Plan. Yet, as in the case of Quebec, a host of pressures constrain Ontario's capacity to invoke its clear legal powers. In the first place, public opinion in the province often appears sympathetic to the public lobby. As the former treasurer lamented when addressing an audience of financiers, "one's flexibility (in federal-provincial negotiations) is influenced far less by one's peers around the table than by your constituents back home"; and on mainstreet Ontario, "there is little knowledge that there is an alternative solution to expanding the CPP."[42] Vetoing better public pensions could be politically tricky, even in Ontario. Furthermore, the provincial government's room for manoeuvre has been reduced by its indebtedness to the CPP. If other governments were to make expansion of the plan a precondition of a financing formula which would postpone repayment, Ontario would face a trilogy of unpalatable choices: to acquiesce; to veto the changes and repay the debts; or to withdraw from the CPP altogether. To avoid such a dangerous situation, Ontario does not want to be left politically isolated and exposed. The support of three or four other provinces would provide much greater political flexibility, and in June 1981, the Ontario treasurer accordingly launched a drive to build a broader interprovincial coalition in favour of his approach. He persuaded his provincial counterparts to establish a joint working party on pension reform, arguing that unless they could establish an interprovincial consensus, Ottawa might employ "the old divide-and-conquer method" and impose its views.[43]

The initial response of the other provinces to the Ontario message was reasonably sympathetic. The electoral defeat of the New Democratic government of Saskatchewan in 1982 removed Ontario's major provincial opponent, although Manitoba has filled the void in part. British Columbia—the only other province to oppose the child-rearing provision in 1977—soon came out against expansion of the CPP, other than perhaps the minor step of completing the increase in maximum pensionable earnings to the average industrial wage more quickly than had been planned; and Alberta seemed similarly inclined.[44] The Atlantic provinces are usually cross-pressured in this area. Private pension coverage is particularly low in that region, and only the CPP can readily respond to pension needs there; yet the provincial governments in eastern Canada are decidedly nervous about any acceleration of the debt repayment. While these provinces have traditionally not played an active role in national pension politics, they began to develop a more independent position in the 1980s. New Brunswick initiated standards for private pensions for the first time, and Nova Scotia set up its own royal commission on pensions. The Atlantic provinces thus remain important swing elements in the struggle for allies in the intergovernmental forum.

The final key player at the bargaining table is the federal government. Since the 1940s the federal government has tended to play an expansionist role in welfare politics. Indeed, most federal officials are convinced that many of the important social advances of the last forty years would not have occurred without federal intervention, and they regard a continuing social role for Ottawa as critical to the federation. First, the federal government sees itself as the ultimate guarantor of broadly equal treatment of Canadians in all parts of the country: without various federal measures, standards of social services would diverge much more dramatically in rich and poor regions. Second, the federal government regards income security as an instrument for sustaining its own political legitimacy and power within the federal system. Virtually every other community and social service is provincially delivered, making income security the only direct link between Ottawa and individual citizens—besides taxation, that is. Ottawa, therefore, has a clear incentive to maintain a vigorous role in income security, one of its major weapons in the continuing struggle for the loyalties of Canadians.

These dimensions of the federal role incline it instinctively towards a public sector response to pension needs. Relying on private pensions passes the key decisions to the provincial governments, forcing Canadians to look once again for provincial solutions to their most important personal problems. Moreover, such an approach would almost certainly fail to provide broadly equal protection across the country. Because private pension coverage varies sharply between rich and poor regions, only a mandatory system would provide anything like comparable standards across the country. But, as noted earlier, federal officials tend to be sceptical about the prospects of obtaining a sufficiently broad federal-provincial consensus to make such a policy effective on a nation-wide basis. In addition, the federal government is not deeply in debt to the CPP fund, and can therefore be more sanguine about a liberalization of benefits and a gradual transition to a purely pay-go basis for the plan. In 1973, for example, Ottawa took the lead in enriching the program, with its own proposals on indexation going much further even than the earlier initiatives of Quebec.

Federal expansionist instincts are counterbalanced, however, by intergovernmental and economic pressures, both of which became increasingly severe in the early 1980s. Ottawa must cope with the reality of provincial vetoes, and certainly any federal decision to press for a major expansion of CPP would have precipitated a dramatic federal-provincial battle. In the pension politics of the 1960s and 1970s, the federal government tended to side with Quebec and stare down Ontario's objections politically, but the latter's 1977 veto suggests that this has become more difficult. As one senior federal official mused privately early in the 1980s, "Ontario would be a tough nut to crack." And after the resolution of the intense intergovernmental wars over the constitution and energy policy, Ottawa seemed less and less interested in mounting another campaign, especially against Ontario, the province which had provided critical support in those other battles.

Equally important were economic constraints. In the early 1980s, recession and a swollen public debt shifted federal priorities from social policy to economic development, and the government's public expenditure plans for the decade called for a decline in the proportion of federal spending allocated to social programs.[45] Periods of economic crisis catch pension reformers within the federal government in a deadly cross-fire. On one side, proposals for rapid expansion of the CPP or enrichment of private plans confront redoubled industry opposition to increased labour costs and an insistence that reforms be phased in slowly over a decade or more. On the other side, fiscal restraint precludes immediate increases in Old Age Security and the Guaranteed Income Supplement. During 1982 and 1983, for example, the minister of national health and welfare repeatedly argued that a $750 million increase in GIS spending needed to raise single pensioners above the poverty line, a step supported by virtually everyone, would simply have to wait "until the economy is a little better."[46] And when an increase was finally announced in the 1984 budget, it was only half as large as expected.

These intergovernmental and economic pressures steadily tempered federal enthusiasm for pension reform, even under the Liberal government. In the heady days after the 1980 election, Prime Minister Trudeau declared that pension reform would be the major social priority of that Parliament, and the minister of national health and welfare launched a campaign in favour of major reform, focusing public attention on the issue and mobilizing groups with pension concerns. A National Pension Conference, held in March 1981, was a microcosm of all the forces in the pensions debate and attracted tremendous media attention;[47] a series of regional conferences financed by the department and focused mainly on "women and pensions" sustained the drive; the department also commissioned public opinion surveys to demonstrate public concern; and the minister even mounted the rostrum at the United Nations during debate on the International Year of the Disabled to call for increased CPP disability protection, and then met with provincial welfare ministers in February 1982 to demand support for such an amendment, support that was not immediately forthcoming.[48]

But the rest of 1982 and 1983 saw the momentum ebb away, sapped by the continuing tension between Health and Welfare Canada and the Department of Finance. The minister of national health and welfare campaigned strenuously for enrichment of the pension system, putting particular emphasis on the problem of coverage. Formally the minister simply argued for a mandatory approach, leaving open the question of whether to rely on the CPP or mandatory private coverage for all employees.[49] But the complications facing mandatory private coverage make the CPP route much simpler, and Health and Welfare clearly favoured a significant expansion of the CPP, together with a number of improvements in private plans. On the other hand, the Department of Finance, which is much more concerned about the impact of pension reform on economic recovery in general and capital formation in particular, appeared to favour relying almost exclusively on improvements in occupational plans and expanded tax incentives for private savings.

This subterranean conflict continued unabated for several years, despite the mediation efforts of the Privy Council Office. The eventual outcome was foreshadowed, however, when the government's Green Paper emerged—after many delays—at the end of 1982.[50] The paper advanced specific proposals for the reform of existing private plans but made no similar commitment to expansion of the CPP, and the minister of national health and welfare was soon complaining publicly that the paper was "a conservative statement of the real extent of pension problems in the country."[51] A parliamentary committee which subsequently examined the paper largely endorsed this private sector orientation, although it did propose that housewives be eligible for participation in the CPP, an idea advanced by segments of the women's movement.[52] Even this proposal was deferred, however, when the minister of finance finally announced the federal position in his 1984 budget: existing private plans would be improved, personal savings for retirement would be further encouraged by tax changes; reforms of the CPP, however, would simply be postponed for "further discussion with the provinces and interested groups."[53]

By 1984—after eight years of elaborate analysis and discussion—the complex pattern of governmental alliances was slowly settling into a new form. In the 1960s and 1970s, the federal authorities had allied themselves with the expansionist aims of Quebec; in the 1980s, Ottawa was clearly accommodating itself to a different set of intergovernmental and economic pressures and moving towards Ontario, its old pension adversary. Indeed, by early 1984, the positions of the federal Liberals and Ontario Conservatives were virtually identical on many specific points.[54] The national election victory of the Progressive Conservatives in September was unlikely to upset this emerging *entente cordiale*.

Conclusions

At the time of writing, the final bargaining among the eleven governments of Canada has yet to commence. But the preceding analysis of the retirement income system and the major political alignments that have shaped it in the recent past does point firmly to important conclusions.

First, the structure of political institutions is a key influence on the politics of pensions. As in other nations, the potent forces of political ideology and economic interest constitute the primary lines of division, and shape the major lobbies that do battle over the future shape of the retirement income system. But in Canada, conflict between economic interests is overlaid by a second system of intergovernmental conflict, in which different governments not only ally themselves with specific economic groups but also advance distinct financial and political interests of their own.

Second, the politics of Canadian pensions confirm the proposition that the fragmentation of authority constrains the pace of change. Federalism remains a conservative force in Canadian pensions. The complexities of this system simultaneously reduce the feasibility of mandatory private coverage and raise the obstacles confronting advocates of the expansion of public plans. Institutions are never the only factor shaping public policy, and in the 1980s economic recession proved equally important in tempering the reformist impulses of governments. But while one can hope that recessions prove temporary, the institutional barriers to changes in pension policy will remain.

In the longer term, there is no doubt that federalism affords the private sector greater protection than it would otherwise enjoy, providing it with more time and opportunities to cope in a more demanding world.

Finally, the system of formal checks and balances in the pensions field represents a clear deviation from the essentially majoritarian conception of democracy inherent in the tradition of parliamentary government. The rules require a much higher level of agreement before change can take place than in other areas of public policy, higher even than that required by the new amending formula for most aspects of the Canadian constitution.[55] This institutional framework undoubtedly contributes to stability in one element of the increasingly unstable world of social policy. But the danger is that we have created an inflexible system that is incapable of adapting to changes in the economic and social needs of Canadians.

NOTES

1. This paper represents the development of a theme introduced briefly in my *The Welfare State and Canadian Federalism* (Kingston and Montreal: McGill-Queen's University Press and the Institute of Intergovernmental Relations, Queen's University, 1982). An earlier version of part of this chapter appeared as "The Decision Rules: Federalism and Pension Reform," in *Pensions Today and Tomorrow: Background Studies* (Toronto: Ontario Economic Council, 1984).

2. Elmer Eric Schattschneider, *The Semi-Sovereign People* (New York: Holt, Rinehart and Winston, 1960), p. 71.

3. Ibid.; also J. MacGregor Burns, *The Deadlock of Democracy* (Englewood Cliffs, N.J.: Prentice-Hall, 1963); Arnold J. Heidenheimer, Hugh Heclo, and Carolyn T. Adams, *Comparative Public Policy: The Politics of Social Choice in Europe and America* (New York: St. Martin's Press, 1975); Christopher Leman, *The Collapse of Welfare Reform* (Cambridge: MIT Press, 1980).

4. On these qualifications, see Richard Neustadt, "White House and Whitehall," in *Policy-Making in Britain,* ed. Richard Rose (London: Macmillan, 1969), pp. 291–306; Anthony King, "Ideas, Institutions and Policies of Government," *British Journal of Political Science* 3 (1973): 291–313 and 409–23.

5. See for example, Harold J. Laski, "The Obsolescence of Federalism," in *The People, Politics and the Politician*, ed. A. N. Christensen and E. M. Kirkpatrick (New York: Holt, 1941): pp. 111–17.

6. Anthony Harold Birch, *Federalism, Finance and Social Legislation in Canada, Australia and the United States* (Oxford: Clarendon Press, 1955); Heidenheimer et al., *Comparative Public Policy*, and Arnold J. Heidenheimer, "The Politics of Public Education, Health and Welfare in the U.S.A. and Western Europe: How Growth and Reform Potentials Have Differed," *British Journal of Political Science* 3 (1973): 315–40.

7. Pierre Elliott Trudeau, "The Practice and Theory of Federalism," in *Social Purpose for Canada*, ed. M. Oliver (Toronto: University of Toronto Press, 1967): pp. 371–93.

8. For Canadian examples of this argument, see Alan Cairns, "The Governments and Societies of Canadian Federalism," *Canadian Journal of Political Science* 19 (1977): 695–725; and "The Other Crisis of Canadian Federalism," *Canadian Public Administration* 22 (1979): 175–95.

9. David R. Cameron, "The Expansion of the Public Economy: A Comparative Analysis," *American Political Science Review* 72 (1978): 1243–61; Harold Wilensky, *The Welfare State and Equality* (Berkeley, Calif.: University of California Press, 1975), pp. 52–54; F. Castles and R. D. McKinlay, "The Importance of Politics: An Analysis of the Public Welfare Commitment in Advanced Democratic States," in *Social and Educational Research in Action*, ed. Michael Wilson (London: Longmans, 1978), pp. 329–48; and F. Castles and R. D. McKinlay, *Democratic Politics and Policy Outcomes* (Milton Keynes: Open University, 1979), chaps. 4 and 5.

10. See especially Canada, Task Force on Retirement Income Policy, *The Retirement Income System in Canada* (Ottawa: Minister of Supply and Services, 1980), vol. 2, app. 2. For other appraisals of the Canadian pension system, see Economic Council of Canada, *One in Three: Pensions for Canadians to 2030* (Ottawa: Minister of Supply and Services, 1979); Royal Commission on the Status of Pensions in Ontario, *Report*, 9 vols. (Toronto: Queen's Printer, 1981); Quebec, *La securité financière des personnes agées au Québec* (Quebec: Editeur Officiel, 1978); Special Senate Committee on Retirement Age Policies, *Retirement without Tears* (Ottawa: Minister of Supply and Services, 1979), pt. 3.

11. Task Force, *The Retirement Income System,* vol. 2, app. 2; Keith H. Cooper and Colin C. Mills, *Canada at the Pension Crossroads* (New York: Financial Executives Research Foundation, 1978), app. 1.

12. Task Force on Retirement Income Policy, *Summary Report*, table 2.

13. For discussions of the evolution of pension standards legislation, see Frank M. Kleiler, *Canadian Regulation of Pension Plans* (Washington: United States Department of Labor, 1970); and Royal Commission on the Status of Pensions in Ontario, *Report,* vol. 3, chap. 18.

14. Task Force, *The Retirement Income System,* 1: 217.

15. See, for example, the testimony of L. E. Cloward of William M. Mercer Ltd. on behalf of the Board of Trade of Metropolitan Toronto before the Ontario Select Committee on Pensions, *Proceedings*, August 20, 1981, p. 5; also the testimony of D. Stouffer, senior budget adviser, Ontario Ministry of Treasury and Economics, *Proceedings,* January 7, 1982, p. 16. Similar comments were made by George Ford, director of pensions, Government of Saskatchewan, in Canadian Centre for Policy Alternatives, *Policy Alternatives* (Summer 1981), p. 4.

16. Canada Pension Plan Advisory Committee, *The Rate of Return on the Investment Fund of the Canada Pension Plan* (Ottawa, 1975), pp. 7–8 and app. 4.

17. For a history of this battle, see Kenneth Bryden, *Old Age Pensions and Policy-Making in Canada* (Montreal: McGill-Queen's University Press and the Institute of Public Administration of Canada, 1974).

18. Testimony before the Ontario Select Committee on Pensions, *Proceedings*, January 21, 1982, p. 23.

19. See J. F. Bullock, president of the Canadian Federation of Independent Business, "Presentation to the National Pension Conference," March 31, 1981; Canadian Chamber of Commerce, "Canada's Pension System, Submission to the Minister of National Health and Welfare" (March 1981); and Canadian Manufacturers' Association, "Submission to the Honourable Monique Bégin, Minister of National Health and Welfare, on Pension Policies" (May 1981).

20. Canadian Life and Health Insurance Association, "Discussion Paper on a National Pension System," submitted to the National Pensions Conference (March 1981), and "Submission to the Nova Scotia Royal Commission on Pensions" (December 1981); and the testimony of the Trust Companies Association of Canada before the Ontario Select Committee on Pensions, *Proceedings*, August 27, 1981.

21. Testimony of the Business Council on National Issues before the Ontario Select Committee on Pensions, *Proceedings*, January 21, 1982 (p. 25); Association of Canadian Pension Management, "Draft for Discussion, Pension Background Paper" (June 1981); Canadian Chamber of Commerce, "Presentation to the Ontario Select Committee on Pensions" (January 20, 1982); Canadian Manufacturers' Association, "Policy Statement on Protection of Pensions Against Inflation, Including the Excess Interest Approach" (November 1981).

22. "Pension Policy–Issues and Positions: Consensus of the Business Committee on Pension Policy" (August 1982).

23. Bryden, *Old Age Pensions*, p. 162.

24. Canadian Labour Congress, *Pension Policy Statement* (1978) reprinted in *Canadian Labour* (June 1978): 23–24; "Statement on Pension Policy to the National Pension Conference" (March 1981); and *The CLC Proposal for Pension Reform* (June 1982).

25. See, for example, the comments of Charles MacDonald, president of the National Pensioners and Senior Citizens Federation, *Montreal Gazette*, April 2, 1981. For an assessment of the role of welfare organizations, see Ken Battle, "They Also Serve Who Stand and Complain: Social Welfare Groups and the Politics of Pension Reform," paper presented at the Pensions Conference organized by the Canadian Centre for Policy Alternatives (Montreal, March 1981).

26. Louise Dulude, *Pension Reform with Women in Mind* (Ottawa: Canadian Advisory Council on the Status of Women, 1981); National Action Committee on the Status of Women, Pension Committee, "Women and Pensions" (January 1982).

27. See, for example, Dulude, *Pension Reform*, pp. 81–82. For a discussion of the gap between labour and women's representatives at the National Pensions Conference, see *Pension Digest* 2, no. 2 (May 1981): 6–7.

28. Bryden, *Old Age Pensions*; and Richard Simeon, *Federal-Provincial Diplomacy: The Making of Recent Policy in Canada* (Toronto: University of Toronto Press, 1972).

29. *La securité financière des personnes agées*. The report was particularly critical of private plans and gave great weight to "les avantages fondamentaux d'universalité et de securité" of the Quebec Pension Plan (p. 25).

30. See *Globe and Mail*, April 11 and 13, 1981.

31. "Transcription du Discours de l'Honourable Jacques Parizeau," l'Université Laval, le 20 avril 1982; "Notes Pour Une Allocation de Monsieur Denis Lazure,

Ministre d'Etat au Développement Social du Québec à L'Assemblée Annuelle 1982 de l'Institut Canadien de la Retraite," 11 mai 1982.

32. Ibid., p. 8.

33. Ibid. See also the comments by Lazure, *Globe and Mail*, May 12, 1982. In May 1983, Parizeau simply observed that "we don't yet know what Ontario is willing to accept." *Globe and Mail*, May 30, 1983.

34. Bryden, *Old Age Pensions*.

35. Ontario, Ministry of Treasury, Economics and Intergovernmental Affairs, "Review of Issues in Financing the Canada Pension Plan" (April 1976).

36. Ontario, Ministry of Treasury, Economics and Intergovernmental Affairs, "The Economics of Financing National Pension Plans," paper presented to the Royal Commission on the Status of Pensions in Ontario (Toronto, 1977).

37. Royal Commission on the Status of Pensions in Ontario, *Report* vol. 5. chap. 7.

38. See ibid., 5: 102–3; also testimony of the senior pensions adviser to the treasurer before the Ontario Select Committee on Pensions, *Proceedings*, January 7, 1982, especially pp. 28–37; and the Select Committee on Pensions, *First Report* (October 19, 1981), p. 3.

39. Hon. Darcy McKeough, "Remarks to the International Pensions Conference," Grey Rocks Inn, June 13, 1977, p. 9. For a general analysis of Ontario's objections, see the Royal Commission on the Status of Pensions in Ontario, *Report* 5: 115–18.

40. Hon. Frank Miller, *Ontario Budget 1981* (May 19, 1981); Ontario Select Committee on Pensions, *Final Report* (March 1982); Hon. William Davis, "Address to the Joint Meeting of the Toronto Society of Financial Analysts and the Toronto Association of Business Economists" (April 22, 1982); also Hon. Larry Grossman, as reported in *Globe and Mail*, Dec. 3, 1983, and Feb. 14, 1984.

41. Pension Policy Unit, Office of the Budget and Intergovernmental Financc, Ministry of Treasury and Economics, "Pension Reform: Present Strategies and Pivotal Issues" (April 7, 1982), p. 7.

42. Hon. Frank Miller, "Remarks to the Financial Executives' Institute Pension Conference" (November 17, 1982). The most thorough survey of public attitudes towards pension issues in Ontario, which was conducted for the Royal Commission on the Status of Pensions in Ontario, tends to support this view. See *Report* 8, chap. 2: 19–96.

43. *Globe and Mail*, July 16, 1981.

44. British Columbia, *Developing a Pension Policy for the Future* (June 1982); on Alberta, see the *Financial Post*, November 7, 1981.

45. *The Budget* (Ottawa: Department of Finance, 1980), pp. 32–33.

46. *Hansard*, November 24, 1981, p. 13159.

47. See National Pensions Conference, *Proceedings* (Ottawa: Minister of Supply and Services, 1981), and *Summary of Submissions* (Ottawa: Minister of Supply and Services, 1981).

48. Ministers of Social Services, Communiqué, February 23, 1982.

49. See, for example, "Coverage: The Key Issue of Pension Reform," presentation by the Honourable Monique Bégin, Minister of National Health and Welfare to the Special Parliamentary Committee on Pension Reform (April 21, 1983).

50. *Better Pensions for Canadians* (Ottawa: Minister of Supply and Services, 1982).

51. "Coverage: The Key Issue in Pension Reform."

52. Special Committee on Pension Reform, *Report of the Parliamentary Task Force on Pension Reform* (Ottawa: Supply and Services Canada, 1983).

53. Hon. Marc Lalonde, *Action Plan for Pension Reform* (Ottawa: Department of Finance, 1984), p. 14; also *Building Better Pensions for Canadians: Improved Tax Assistance for Retirement Saving* (Ottawa: Department of Finance, 1984).

54. For example, the Ontario treasurer proposed in a speech on February 12, 1984, that the private pension plans be required to index benefits to the extent of 60 percent of increases in the consumer price index. Precisely the same position was included in the federal budget of February 15, 1984. See *Globe and Mail*, February 14, 1984, and *Action Plan for Pension Reform*.

55. Except for a short list of provisions for which unanimity is needed, constitutional change requires agreement of two-thirds of the provinces representing only *half* of the population, so no individual province has a veto. Dissenting provinces can opt out of changes which they dislike, but then they can also opt out of the Canada Pension Plan if they object to its evolution.

Chapter Five

Revision and Retreat: Canadian Unemployment Insurance 1971–1981

LESLIE A. PAL

Modern political analysis of social security programs has tended recently to emphasize two explanatory models. The first is a model of social control, which explains major social security measures as responses either to vocal working class demands or to the potential political instability created by tough economic circumstances (typically recessions or depressions). The labour management model on the other hand argues that the state implements certain programs in order to assist the accumulation process. Thus worker's compensation, education, and even health insurance do for the accumulation process what it cannot do for itself: they maintain a relatively efficient labour force and labour market. This model may be easily extended to encompass standards legislation, training programs, urban transport, and so on.[1]

Conceptually at least, the models are markedly different. Policies made in order to enhance labour market efficiency and increase profits could, if they are punitive or coercive, generate unrest. Policies made with an eye to social peace could undermine efficiency and profits. In actual practice of course, policies may try to address both goals simultaneously, and so one model will not be clearly superior to the other. Despite this problem, authors do tend to hold one or the other view, and focus on the rationales applied by policy-makers themselves to support the model.

Both of these approaches have recently been applied to analyses of the Canadian unemployment insurance (UI) program. Alvin Finkel,[2] Carl Cuneo,[3] and James Struthers,[4] have each examined the political forces leading to the passage of the 1940 Unemployment Insurance Act. Cuneo and Finkel emphasize in varying degrees the social control model of explanation. Finkel argues that the 1935 Employment and Social Insurance Act, Prime Minister Bennett's aborted attempt to introduce UI in Canada, was partly a response to business interests which recognized the "threat posed by the discontent of unemployed workers."[5] Cuneo asserts that the 1935 act was "a mediating response to the conflict over unemployment between the capitalist class and the working class,"[6] while the 1940 act "reflected the greater weight of the state's interest in social control than in the efficacy of labour's interest in wage subsistence or of capitalists' interest in accumulation."[7] Struthers, on the other hand, emphasizes the labour management dimension. Comparing Bennett's 1935 legislation with proposed UI amendments in 1978, he argues that both sought to coerce the unemployed and enhance their incentive to work.[8]

While Cuneo and Finkel do highlight some labour-management aspects of the early UI program, the weight of their explanation is borne by the federal government's need to introduce some ameliorative measures in a period of severe social tension. This is plausible, when one considers the times and the fact that the program was indeed new. But how should we assess subsequent changes in the program, once it was routinized and accepted? Do the models discussed above, and the social control one in particular, still apply with the same force? Probably not, for the following reasons.

First, routinization, especially in a program with such a powerful regulatory dimension as UI, implies the establishment and development of an administrative apparatus. The social control model, even though it implies relative autonomy for the state in dealing with vested interests, still assumes that the agenda over which this autonomy is exercised is determined directly by the clash of social forces. But bureaucratic logic may be independent from, even while interacting with, the logic of social forces. Hence, the politics of an established program may be very different from the politics of a new one.[9]

Second, there is the problem of explaining substantial liberalization of a program in the absence of crisis. The social control model presumes an extraordinary social crisis as the basis for program initiation. But substantial liberalization can occur through the accumulation of unremarkable changes, or in one massive revision, as was the case for UI in 1971. Some other model is needed to deal with these changes.

Third, the social control model, at least as presented by Finkel and Cuneo, assumes a wide range of conflicting class and interest group positions. The state's relative autonomy arises from this confusion. While intuitively appealing, it may be that unanimity of views and interests provides an equally strong basis for relative autonomy. Organized labour and business certainly had opposing views on UI in the 1970s, but their respective stances had not changed in years. State officials often know exactly what the responses of the Canadian Labour Congress or the Canadian Chamber of Commerce will be to any given set of proposed amendments. Hence these associations (and indeed most others) are largely ignored at the policy formulation stage.

Finally, the social control model fails to capture the nuance of the Canadian federal system. Does a decrease in the coercive dimension of the program at the federal level mean that coercion declines or increases at the provincial level? Do spending increases at the federal level mean a net increase in overall social security expenditures, no net change, or an actual decrease? Federal attempts to respond to unrest can conflict with provincial ones, as can attempts to manage labour.

This chapter approaches some of these general issues and questions by examining changes to the Canadian UI program in the 1970s.[10] By 1970 the program had been in place for thirty years, and was solidly part of the social security system. It was substantially liberalized in 1971 and then, in a period of recession and social tension, substantially cut back. A close examination of the rationale for these changes reveals few of the features one would expect from the social control model. Instead, two other forces or logics determined events. One was the growing concern with the effective management of labour across the country. This led to important differences with some of the provinces, and indeed reveals that political conflict over UI in the 1970s was at least as much, if not more, a matter of intergovernmental relations than relations between Ottawa and private interests. The other force or logic was what we shall term "fiscal constraint." It is a factor internal to political logic, and not one that is immediately governed by social forces. Most modern western governments accept it as a key decision rule, though to varying degrees.

In combination, these forces suggest a substantial autonomy for policy makers, at least in the UI field. The emphasis on these forces is not intended to exclude the occasionally decisive influence of elections, such as those in 1971 and 1974, or other variables such as party ideology. This chapter is concerned with changes in the "deep structure" of policy over a decade, and consequently explores a deeper level of explanation.

The 1970-71 Revisions

Canada's first successful UI program was launched on August 7, 1940.[11] Twenty-one specific forms of employment were exempted from coverage, the most prominent among them being agriculture, horticulture and forestry, fishing, most lumbering and logging, transportation by water or by air, domestic service, hospital employees, teachers, Government of Canada employees appointed under the Civil Service Act or certified as permanent, municipal and provincial employees unless their employers agreed, and generally any employment earning more than $2,000 a year.[12] Roughly 42 percent of the labour force was covered. To be eligible for benefits, workers were required to make proper contributions in insured employment for at least 180 days during the two years immediately preceding the claim, in addition to demonstrating that they were indeed unemployed and capable and available for work.[13] Employers and employees contributed equally to the plan, and Ottawa contributed 20 percent of the total private sector premiums. The government also paid administrative costs.[14] The benefit rate ranged as high as 63.3 percent for the lowest-earning class, to 37 percent for the highest class.[15] The maximum benefit duration was one day of benefits for each five daily contributions in the last five years, or one year for someone with five years of continuous employment.

The original act was amended many times and was completely overhauled in 1955.[16] There were a host of technical changes in the program, some restrictive and some expansive. Supplementary benefits (introduced in a 1950 amendment to assist seasonal workers) were integrated as seasonal benefits;[17] the entrance requirement was slightly relaxed, as were requalifying conditions. The maximum benefit duration was reduced from one year to thirty-six weeks, but the minimum benefit period was increased from six to fifteen weeks. The benefit rate averaged 50 percent across all earnings categories, with higher rates applying to lower categories. By 1955, slightly more than 75 percent of wage and salary earners in Canada were covered by UI.[18]

The 1955 act represented, on the whole, a modest liberalization of the program. Passed in a period of relatively low unemployment (average annual rates since the war had been 3 percent), it was consequently strained during the 1957–62 recession (when average annual unemployment rates reached 7 percent). High unemployment and more liberal provisions eventually reduced the UI Fund to a slim reserve of $874,881 in 1964.[19] The government made advances to the fund to keep it solvent, and in 1961 appointed a Committee of Inquiry into the Unemployment Insurance Act, chaired by E. C. Gill, an insurance executive. Its report raised the curtain on almost a decade of investigation into the program. An interdepartmental review, including Finance, Labour, and Health and Welfare, submitted a report to the minister of labour on March 25, 1966.[20] Some of its recommendations were incorporated into the commission's 1968 report on the program.[21]

Though there had been business and labour representations to the Gill Committee, for the most part the reviews of the program conducted in the 1960s were internal to the federal government and took place largely within the context of developing an appropriate manpower policy. "Supply-side" economics, increasingly popular after the 1957–62 recession, suggested that manpower training and placement had to be given a higher priority in economic management.[22] Accordingly, the employment services administered by the commission were transferred in 1966 to the newly created Department of Manpower and Immigration. By 1970, however, policy makers were coming to see UI more within the context of social than economic policy.

According to Johnson,[23] there was increasing ministerial dissatisfaction in 1968 and 1969 with the Trudeau government's failure to meet its stirring election promise of a "Just Society." Three major social policy proposals were being considered at the time: a guaranteed annual income plan sponsored by the Department of Health and Welfare; a negative income tax scheme, favoured by Finance and the Treasury Board; and an enhanced and expanded UI program. The guaranteed annual income scheme was rejected, primarily because of cost, but also because it would have required provincial acceptance. This left a new

UI program, the general features of which had been in the planning stage since 1968, as the best alternative.

The proposed revisions were announced on June 17, 1970 in a White Paper entitled *Unemployment Insurance in the 70's*. It was referred to the Commons Standing Committee on Labour, Manpower, and Immigration, which held thirty meetings between September 15 and November 3, 1970, received fifty-three submissions, and heard evidence from thirty-three organizations. Typically, the 1971 UI Act differed only slightly from the White Paper. But the White Paper, together with the committee hearings and Commons debates, provides evidence of the concerns which were uppermost in policy makers' minds.

The White Paper's proposals rested on the premise of affluence. Canada was about to savour the fruits of the "post-industrial era with a spiralling gross national product and a rising standard of living."[24] Affluence carried the responsibility of equitable distribution, and a modern social policy demanded the provision of a wide array of services rather than the simple transfer of income. The White Paper clearly characterized the new UI program by pointing out that it was meant to be in "keeping with a more realistic approach to social policy."[25] The economic or labour management component of the scheme was not ignored, however, in that "a new reoriented program must provide an efficient pipeline to vocational counselling, job opportunities, and other manpower programs in order to help the unemployed requalify for jobs under changing technological conditions. In addition to increased financial payments during unemployment, the complementary battery of services provided by other government agencies designed to assist workers will be used to ensure the success of a reoriented unemployment insurance program for the 70's."[26]

Enhanced services clearly had a policing function as well. In view of substantially increased benefits, universal coverage, and greatly relaxed entrance requirements, the White Paper argued that the two mandatory personal interviews for all claimants would, while primarily helping the individual, "also serve to identify people who should not be receiving benefits. The effect will be to reduce to a minimum abuses in the present plan due to the lack of personal contact."[27]

A crucial feature of the White Paper was its view of imminent labour market changes. It argued that the rapid technological changes associated with post-industrialism would threaten previously secure employment. Automation would increase the incidence of unexpected, temporary layoffs. Public servants, teachers, skilled and semi-skilled alike would be threatened. Unemployment would not, in aggregate, rise much at all, but turnover would increase. A new UI scheme could respond to these developments and yet remain solvent. Part of the response was contained in the "service" component of the program. In a key passage, the White Paper argued that "A reoriented unemployment insurance program, however, can keep the door to the mainstream of society open. The combination of financial aid, plus complementary services provided by other government agencies designed to assist the worker to be absorbed quickly into the labour force, will help to save him from sinking into the quicksands of chronic unemployment."[28]

The UI program has traditionally been defended on grounds something like these. It is a program which permits people either to search longer for a job commensurate with their abilities or to wait until economic conditions improve enough to supply such jobs.[29] But the White Paper also implied that without a revised scheme, many unemployed workers in the 1970s would become discouraged and drop out of the labour market. The normal functions of that market, wherein unemployed workers eventually seek the best available job, would be thwarted. In an important sense therefore, the liberality of the program was designed to enhance work incentives.

Thus the program, while presented primarily as a social security measure to help combat poverty and to redistribute income, at the same time had an important labour management component. Was this component important? Can it explain the expansion of the program, or its liberality? A review of the Standing Committee proceedings and Commons debates suggests not. This may seem surprising in an era when the economic, and especially labour market, effects of social programs are so prominent in policy debate. There certainly were questions about the effect of the new program on incentives, virtually all of them coming from the Progressive Conservatives. In the course of second reading debate on Bill C-229, Lincoln Alexander put the issue pointedly: "We feel that it is a disincentive, that it will stifle initiative and, most important and lasting, it will encourage people to take the attitude: why should we work, when the government will look after us? This is an attitude taken, not by the majority of people but too many of the minority."[30]

Bryce Mackasey, minister of labour and in charge of the legislation, rebutted this charge by arguing that the major thrust of the program was to lessen the relation between past weeks worked and future benefits, to ensure that those who most needed help would receive it; that most people would still be better off working than not; that most people were honest; and that surveillance by the commission would catch most offenders.[31] The question of abuse had been raised earlier in the Standing Committee examination of the White Paper. There Mackasey had admitted that in "all probability conditions will be a little more rigid under the future plan because we will see these people at least twice."[32]

Apart from partisan jousting, the largest number of questions in Commons debate were technical ones. The proposals themselves appeared to respond to the public's wishes,[33] and the opposition was reluctant to press vigorously. As well, Bill C-229 was quite complex, and much time was spent discussing points of information and minor disagreements (e.g., why was the cut-off for government contributions 4 percent unemployment, rather than 5 percent or 6 percent).

The most important reason for the absence of significant debate was that all participants believed the proposals would add little if anything to the costs of the existing program. The question of costs had arisen at the Cabinet Social Policy Committee discussions of the plan before the release of the White Paper, and potential Finance and Treasury Board objections were silenced with the argument that though there might be fluctuations in the government's share under the scheme, there would not be a net increase.[34] In committee review of the White Paper, Mackasey argued that more generous UI benefits would not increase the net costs of the program because of the extended coverage provisions. The contributions of people less likely to become unemployed would pay for increased benefits for the entire insured population.[35] Six months later, during committee review of Bill C-229, D. Alan, director of policy analysis and formulation for the commission, commented that the $800 million limit on government advances to the UI Account "represented, as an upper limit on the amount of advances, presumably the worst possible case we could think of in terms of a deficit."[36] A few days after this statement, Mackasey agreed that he could say, without equivocation or even hesitation, that the program was actuarially sound.[37]

It is difficult to overestimate the impact of this unanimity of expert opinion. It forestalled criticism in cabinet, in the House, and in the Standing Committee. Some opposition and government members probed the submitted figures, but the very complexity of the act and the confidence of officials soon persuaded everyone that considered the matter. Table 1 shows how inaccurate the White Paper's cost estimates were. The commission projected an increase in benefit payments under the new plan of about 4.03 percent in its first full year of operation (assuming an annual unemployment rate of 5.3 percent in 1972—the actual rate was 6.3 percent). The actual increase was 110.17 percent between 1971 and 1972, though annual increases thereafter were only 7.07 and 5.74 percent. To be fair, the commission did project the costs of the program for different unemployment rates, preferring that approach to forecasting what it thought actual unemployment rates would be.[38] The commission forecast a total of $1.017 billion in benefit costs for 1972, assuming an unemployment rate of 6.5 percent. This was $854.8 million less than actual costs for that year.[39]

The Unemployment Insurance Act, 1971, was passed by the House of Commons of June 14, 1971, and received royal assent on June 23, 1971 (*S.C.*, 1970–72, c.48). Benefit provisions took effect June 27, 1971, while coverage was extended as of January 2, 1972. A review of the key elements of the new legislation suggests that it substantially liberalized UI in Canada (items in parentheses refer to the relevant sections of the 1971 act):

Coverage. It was made universal, from approximately 80 percent of the wage/salary earning labour force to 96 percent. (secs. 3; 4)

Entrance Requirements. For those without a previous claim it was

TABLE 1

ESTIMATED AND ACTUAL BENEFIT PAYMENTS, 1970–75

Year	(1) Total Est. Benefits ($ millions)	(2) Actual Benefits ($ millions)	(3) (2) − (1) ($ millions)	(2)/(1)	% Increase over Previous Year (1)	% Increase over Previous Year (2)
1970	810	695.2	−114.8	0.86	—	—
1971	843	890.6	47.6	1.06	4.07	28.11
1972	877	1871.8	994.8	2.13	4.03	110.17
1973	936	2004.2	1068.2	2.14	6.73	7.07
1974	997	2119.2	1122.2	2.13	6.52	5.74
1975	1062	3144.0	2082.0	2.96	6.52	48.36

SOURCES: Canada, House of Commons, Standing Committee on Labour, Manpower and Immigration, 2nd sess., 28th Parl., September 16, 1970, app. "M," *Facts and Figures Unemployment Insurance in the 70*'s, p. 142, table entitled "Estimated Yearly Benefit and Administrative Costs for the Proposed System Compared with Projected Present System Costs." Statistics Canada, Cat. 86-201, 1976, p. 136, table 5. Statistics Canada, Cat. 86-201, 1978, p. 152, table 5.

eight insurable weeks in the last fifty-two; for those with a previous claim, eight insurable weeks since the beginning of the benefit week. This contrasted with the 1955 requirement of thirty insurable weeks in the last two years, eight being in the year preceding the claim. (secs. 17; 18)
Benefits. These were increased from an average of 43 percent of earnings with an upper limit of $53/week to 66.6 percent of earnings up to $100/week. Benefits were made taxable, and contributions tax deductible. Minimum benefits of $20/week were instituted, and a dependents' rate of 75 percent was paid to all claimants in extended benefit phases and to low-income earners in the initial phases. (sec.24)
Special Benefits. Sickness, maternity, and retirement benefits were payable to claimants with twenty weeks of insurable employment in the qualifying period. (secs. 24[2]; 29; 31[2])
Duration. The act instituted a complex five-phase benefit structure. In the initial benefit period a maximum of eight weeks benefit was available for claimants with eight to fifteen weeks insurable employment, those ranging up to nineteen weeks receiving additional benefit weeks, and those with twenty or more weeks eligible for a maximum of fifteen weeks' benefits. If still unemployed at this point, a second reestablishment phase of ten benefit weeks automatically applied. The other three phases depended on labour force attachment, the regional unemployment rate, and the national unemployment rate. The maximum benefit duration was fifty-one weeks. (secs. 20[2]; 32; 34; 37; 38)
Financing. The old formula wherein the government paid 20 percent of combined employer/employee contributions into a fund was abandoned in favour of establishing an Unemployment Insurance Account. Private sector contributions were to pay for administrative costs, sickness, maternity and retirement benefits, and regular benefits in the first two phases up to a national unemployment rate of 4 percent. The federal government was to pay, out of the Consolidated Revenue Fund, for all extended benefits and regular benefits in the first two phases for national unemployment rates over 4 percent. The act authorized the government to make advances of up to $800 million to the account. (secs. 131–37)

The preceding summary ignores many of the baroque nuances of the act, but nevertheless sufficiently establishes the point that UI was made more liberal. Entrance requirements were relaxed, redistribution across income classes and regions was explicitly fostered, and various "welfare" provisions (e.g., the dependents' rate and special benefits) were included, reducing the strict insurance aspects of the program. This liberalization, it was argued, could be achieved at little or no extra cost to the government. There were no fiscal constraints and thus the central agencies responsible for holding the line on expenditures were neutralized.

Labour management concerns were not, as pointed out earlier, absent from the act. The waiting period was increased from one to two weeks (sec. 23) and UI's function of fragmenting the labour forces was preserved through the distinction made between minor attachment claimants (with eight to nineteen weeks of insurable employment) and major attachment claimants (with at least twenty weeks).[40] Only major attachment claimants for example were eligible for special benefits, some extended benefits, and advance benefit payments (a lump sum payment of three weeks which the claimant could keep regardless of how quickly he found employment). And as mentioned earlier, the mandatory interviews could serve a policing function.

Despite these features, the coercive components of the 1971 legislation were not the prominent ones. The disqualification for voluntary quits, misconduct, job refusals, and other infractions was lowered from a maximum of six weeks to three (though benefits were deemed to have been paid for any weeks of disqualification). More fundamentally, the philosophy of the White Paper and the act was that the market itself creates disincentives by discouraging workers; UI could, through better benefits and services, keep the work ethic flickering. The new scheme was intended to have a positive and encouraging effect on the labour market, not a coercive one. Thus, insofar as it was concerned with work incentives at all, it took a generous view.

Post-1971 Changes

The 1971 expansion of the UI program was the product, not of social tension, but of long bureaucratic gestation over the 1960s, a "service" philosophy, and the absence of fiscal constraints. The latter was as much the offspring of faulty forecasts as it was of a confidence in government revenue-generating capacities.

This balance of circumstances changed dramatically over the next eight years. Cost became a primary concern, though it combined in complex ways with the question of incentives and the growing priority of managing labour. Actions taken on these fronts were in strong measure internal to "political logic" and had only indirect links to any agenda set by outside interests or classes. A surprising aspect of this "political logic" was the salience of federal-provincial relations, even in a policy field ostensibly entirely within Ottawa's jurisdiction.

The 1971 program was in trouble almost immediately upon implementation. The act received some criticism in the fall of 1971, the *Globe and Mail* (September 6) going so far as to call it "immoral and stupid."[41] As evidence of cost miscalculations began to accumulate in the late summer and fall of 1972 however, the tone of public criticism sharpened considerably. It was intensified

TABLE 2

UNEMPLOYMENT INSURANCE DISQUALIFICATIONS AND DISENTITLEMENTS, 1972–76

Year	(1) Average Monthly Total Disqualifications and Disentitlements	(2) Average Monthly Total Claims	(3) (1) as % of (2)
1972	73,875	803,794	9.1
1973	101,129	828,287	12.2
1974	119,991	827,740	14.5
1975	130,888	1,048,984	12.4
1976	146,721	1,006,119	14.5

SOURCE: Statistics Canada, Cat. 86-201, 1978, table 3, p. 148; and table 2, p. 145.

by the federal election campaign that was under way at about the same time, the prime minister himself denouncing "freeloading" in one of his speeches. All through September and October 1972 Mackasey defended UI in the papers and on the platform.[42] The Liberals were badly punished at the polls, and some of them partly blamed the UI fiasco.[43]

Legislative action had to be taken almost immediately. Because the House was not sitting, Mackasey in October 1972 obtained a governor general's warrant for $234 million for the UI Account. On January 17, 1973, Robert Andras, the new minister of manpower and immigration, introduced Bill C-124 to remove the $800 million ceiling on government advances to the account. He also introduced Bill C-125, with the aim of tightening up program administration, curbing abuse, and raising entrance requirements for voluntary quits, misconduct firings, and job refusals. Bill C-125 was withdrawn on October 29, 1973 because it was unlikely to receive NDP support.

Its parliamentary weakness and reliance on the NDP limited the government's power to tighten the program through legislation. This was accomplished instead by the commission through its regulatory powers. The 1973 replacement of the Separation Certificate by the Record of Employment was one technique to this end,[44] as was the doubling of benefit control officers in the same year.[45] The other technique was a jump in the disqualification rate. Table 2 shows this clearly.

In 1975 the commission intensified its control procedures through the addition of the Special Job Finding and Placement Drive (calling for mandatory interviews with claimants in occupations in high demand), mandatory preregistration with Canada Manpower offices to receive benefits, a new Record of Employment, and extended employer audits.[46]

Between 1975 and 1978, with its parliamentary strength restored, the government introduced and passed three major revisions to the 1971 act. The first was Bill C-69, introduced in the House by Robert Andras on July 8, 1975, and given royal assent on December 20, 1975. Its key features were the elimination of the 75 percent dependency benefit rate in favour of a standard benefit rate of 66.6 percent; the discontinuation of the advance benefit payment; a doubling of the maximum disqualification rate to six weeks; and a new financing formula whereby the threshold for government contributions was set at a moving average of monthly national unemployment rates over the previous eight years.

The next major legislative revision was Bill C-27, introduced by Bud Cullen, the new minister of manpower and immigration, on December 9, 1976, and finally passed by the House, under closure, on July 19, 1977, receiving royal assent on August 5, 1977. This was a complex and far-reaching bill which not only sought to amend UI, but proposed the creation of a new Department of Employment and Immigration out of the former Unemployment Insurance Commission and Department of Manpower and Immigration. Commission and Manpower offices were combined into Canada Employment Centres, and the Unemployment Insurance Commission was replaced with the Canada Employment and Immigration Commission. The major UI amendments were the introduction of the variable entrance requirement, whereby the minimum period of insurable weeks needed to qualify for benefits was raised to a range of ten to fourteen, depending on the regional unemployment rate; the reduction of the five-phase benefit structure to three, with the third extended phase now tied entirely to regional unemployment rates; a reduction in the maximum entitlement of minor attachment claimants; and the "developmental" use of the UI Account for work-sharing and job creation.

Bill C-14 was the last of the major amendments in the 1970s. Introduced by Bud Cullen in his new capacity as minister of employment and immigration on November 2, 1978, it was passed by the House on December 22, 1978 (again, under closure) and received royal assent on the same day. Its major amendments were as follows: a change in the minimum insurability formula to an hours basis rather than an income basis—thus reducing claims from people working few hours but at high rates; higher entrance requirements for repeaters, new entrants, and reentrants; a reduction in the benefit rate from 66.6 to 60 percent; a portion of extended benefit costs would now be borne by employer and employee contributions; and a provision whereby high-income earners would pay back a portion of UI benefits received in the previous year.

There were various other UI amendments after 1975, in addition to the ones mentioned above, which tended to improve program equity and flexibility, but the overwhelming effect of the 1975–78 changes was restrictive. Moreover, these changes were made in a period when national unemployment rates were climbing up to 7 or 8 percent and beyond. Why? What political dynamics underlay these amendments?

One force behind the changes, especially Bill C-69, was the desire to rationalize and coordinate UI with other social programs. Andras argued, for example, that the 1973 increase in family allowances made the old 75 percent dependency benefit rate unnecessary. Similarly, the improvements to the guaranteed Income Supplement, old age security, and full operation of the Canada and Quebec pension plans made it possible, in the government's view, to reduce the maximum age of UI coverage from seventy to sixty-five.[47] Coordination of UI with other programs had been one of the aims of the Federal-Provincial Social Security Review.[48] Federal officials had been working since 1973 on a plan which would shift some of the program's welfare features (e.g., dependents' benefits, sickness benefits) on to one of the "tiers" of the proposed income supplementation/support scheme. By 1975 the review had all but expired, and Ottawa decided to proceed with rationalization itself.[49]

The desire to coordinate UI with other social programs was nonetheless the least important impetus behind the 1975–78 changes. Two others were more prominent. The first of these was the management of labour. The issue resolved itself into the question of program abuse and UI's effects on work incentives. The large unanticipated increase in benefit payments after 1971 was difficult to explain in the sense that the total number of claims did not themselves rise dramatically (see table 2). In the fall of 1972 the press seized upon abuse and misuse as the culprit. The program was too lenient, too permissive—or so the argument ran—and provided malingerers ample opportunity to collect benefits while skiing in the Rockies or sunning in Florida. This problem could be, and was, met through the commission's control procedures mentioned earlier.[50] But while enhanced control procedures could attack some alleged abuses, they could not deal effectively with the larger problem of work disincentives. This was left to legislation.

It is important to recall that UI intentionally has a "disincentive" effect, in that it provides temporary income while a claimant searches for employment best suited to his skills and experience. Problems arise when claimants are drawn out of employment because UI appears as an attractive alternative (clearly possible for people working at minimum wage or in bad conditions), or when they are induced to remain on benefits longer than they need to, by contriving to refuse suitable or available employment, or are able to move in and out of the program, working only long enough to qualify. Each of these responses to an overly generous program will, *ceteris paribus*, increase the measured unemployment rate. Paradoxically, therefore, it appears theoretically possible for UI to exacerbate the very problem it was designed to combat. While a good deal of academic ink has been spilled on the subject, the unemployment effect of UI is still a moot point. This is because, while there does appear to be some disincentive effect, no one really knows its magnitude. More importantly, the broader questions of whether this has increased labour market efficiency, or indeed whether UI expenditures have raised aggregate demand (thereby increasing employment), have not been addressed.[51] The inconclusive evidence on this question makes the cognitive framework used by policy-makers crucial to an understanding of the 1975–78 changes.

Robert Andras, introducing Bill C-69 in 1975, argued that they were "directed toward improving the influence of the act on the relationship between supply and demand for labour . . . . However, we intend to make certain that Canadians who are working . . . do not have to carry the added burden of supporting able-bodied people who do not want to work."[52] Andras pointed to the rising trend in voluntary quits (an annual average of 250,000) as a major problem, and indicated in committee testimony that the department had considered complete disqualification as a means of dealing with it.[53]

Bud Cullen, Andras's successor in Manpower and Immigration, held the same views on UI disincentive effects. The 1977 legislation was clearly aimed at the work incentives of those with "an intermittent or unstable attachment to the active work force."[54] The new simplified benefit structure would "curtail benefit entitlement to those with a relatively short labour force attachment living in regions of low unemployment."[55] "Developmental" use of UI funds was designed for those cases where "the role of the UI program to facilitate job searches has, inevitably, a diminished applicability."[56] The intent of the 1978 changes was identical:

> The essence of the changes we propose to the unemployment insurance program is two-fold. First, we want to reduce some of the disincentives to work which are present in the program. Second, we want to encourage workers to establish more stable work patterns and develop longer attachments to the active work force, thereby reducing their dependency on unemployment insurance. . . . The new emphasis will be on encouraging all Canadian workers to look for, accept and remain at work.[57]

It is clear from these remarks that a completely different set of priorities was motivating UI policy. The encouraging effect of UI on potentially discouraged workers in a rapidly changing labour market—a notion behind the 1971 act—was replaced by a determination to use the program to induce more strenuous job search. This was to be done by reducing eligibility for benefits and the income support provided by UI. From a kind of cocoon, partially shielding workers from the harsh law of the market, the program was turned into something like a whip to drive them into that market.[58]

Seen in this light, the 1975–78 program changes fit the labour management model of the functions of social security. The program was progressively tightened to remove impediments to the flow of the reserve army of unemployed into low-paying or unpleasant labour, dead-end jobs, or seasonal work. Workers would have to more willingly mould themselves to what was available. By reducing the scope of UI assistance, the state was widening the scope of coercive forces exercised through the labour market. But the UI reductions were a passive mode of policy implementation; their necessary complement was an active mode seen in more vigorous manpower and employment policies wherein people could be induced to work, rather than collect benefits, or be drawn into training programs in greater numbers.[59]

Fiscal constraint was another factor, along with rationalization and labour management, which explains some major policy developments. This factor operated in three ways. The first, and crudest, was in the sense of an overall "ceiling" on gross benefit expenditures. It was not a clearly or coherently defined limit, but both Andras and Cullen, after the 1972 jump in total benefit payments, cavilled against the large sums being spent. As politicians, they were unconcerned with the subtleties of the contra-cyclical effects of the program; they worried about dollars and cents. Cullen was especially worried, since he felt that he had been misled as a committee member reviewing the White Paper figures. As minister, he held the view that there should be an overall cap or ceiling on benefit payments of around $4 billion.[60] This sort of fiscal caution is a much ignored feature of the policy-making process—it certainly does not inhere in all policy makers to the same degree, but it has been a powerful restraint, especially in the social policy field.

The second aspect of fiscal constraint was that each of the three changes in 1975, 1977, and 1978 was made within the context of the general expenditure reductions. The changes were not of course made reluctantly, indeed some of the eventual amendments were less far-reaching than the original proposals had been.[61] They expressed a post-1975 shift towards expenditure reduction. The Bill C-69 changes, for example, were first outlined in John Turner's 1975 budget.[62] They were to produce $660 million in savings for the government when fully implemented on January 1, 1976 (assuming a 7 percent unemployment rate). The 1977 budgetary stance was also contractionary and the $275 million annual savings from Bill C-27 reflected this.[63] The 1978 amendments were expected to produce $935 million in reductions, and were themselves the result of desires to carry forward the less-than-successful 1977 cuts.[64] The prime minister's austerity statement upon returning from the Bonn Summit simply provided the occasion for previously planned cuts.[65] Program changes therefore were motivated as much by a visceral sense that UI expenditures were too high, as they were by more general austerity measures being taken throughout the federal government.

The last dimension to the fiscal constraint factor is perhaps the most subtle and interesting of the three. A corollary of the government's post-1975 austerity program was increased difficulty in obtaining approval for new departmental programs. In January 1972 the responsibility for the UI Act passed to Manpower and Immigration, even though the commission remained autonomous. This autonomy was removed in 1977 with the amalgamation of the commission and the department into the new Department of Employment and Immigration. UI, in other words, increasingly came under the supervision and control of officials whose primary interest was manpower policy. They now had some control over the UI Account, which consisted of employer and employee contributions intended to cover certain program costs up to an unemployment rate of 4 percent. The government portion consisted of advances from the Consolidated Revenue Fund to cover temporary deficits in the account, and also the handling of other benefits. The account's early financial difficulties were remedied through premium increases and possibly through the elimination of subsidized rates for newly covered occupations. By 1976 the account was in surplus, even though the government's portion of benefit costs was still very high. The government took two steps. First, it reduced its share of UI costs by altering the financing formula after 1975, making private contributions take up larger and larger responsibilities. So, from paying 50 percent of total UI program costs in 1975, the government's share decreased to approximately 20 percent in 1980.[66]

The second step was to dip into the account's surplus in order to fund new manpower programs. As Cullen put it:

> There's a fund there and it was constantly in surplus . . . a hundred million or two hundred million dollars could go a long way on job creation, job training, cooperative education, work sharing, and had all kinds of potential. Everybody says "I don't want to be on unemployment, I want to work." Well, why not put them to work and use the money to help them work . . . ?
>
> It was getting to be very difficult to fund, to find the money to do the things we wanted to do. Here was another possible source . . . and it was the kind of money that could be available on a regular basis. In other words, the agreement we entered into with New Brunswick was a three-year program—that's damn tough to do with job creation when every year you have to go to Treasury Board and make your pitch. . . . So this gave us an extra source. We had programs that we wanted to work but we couldn't make them work with the limited amount of money that was available to us, especially of course with the announcement of the one billion dollar cut.[67]

As Cullen suggests in the last part of this statement, the shift in funding sources and the fiscal constraints within the department reflected the larger imperatives of the austerity program, and yet they had a logic of their own within this framework. It is quite probable that surplus UI funds would have been appropriated even without the stimulus of general restraint, since it was the path of least resistance compared to dealing with central agencies. Moreover, the ploy also reflected the belief that it was better to have people working than leave them idle on UI. As a social philosophy this is unobjectionable; as an item of government policy, however, it echoes the distrust of "free handouts."

Labour management goals and differing varieties of fiscal constraints thus combined to determine the major changes in the UI program in the 1970s. They may be distinguished analytically, and even empirically, but they worked in close combination. Does this mean that "in reality" fiscal constraint factors may be reduced to concerns with managing and disciplining labour? Not at all—the logic of constraints provided its own dynamics in the unfolding of policies, reinforcing and complicating the logic of managing labour.

Intergovernmental Relations and UI

The relative autonomy of the logic of constraints may be seen quite clearly in its effects on intergovernmental relations. In many respects UI is an interesting case for the study of Canadian federalism. Ostensibly a program completely within federal jurisdiction, it should be a policy area containing relatively little intergovernmental activity. Moreover, the program should be heavily influenced by employer and employee interests. Employers and employees sit on the commission; as an insurance program it requires private sector contributions; and finally it deals directly with a key problem for both capital and labour—unemployment. Therefore UI should be largely a matter of consultation and negotiation between economic associations and the federal government.

This has not, however, been the case. The 1970 White Paper, for example, was invented by a cluster of officials largely outside the commission's normal authority structure.[68] Private interests responded to the White Paper and the legislation during the proceedings of the Standing Committee on Labour, Manpower, and Immigration, but despite voluminous testimony and some strong objections from employer groups, they made hardly a wrinkle in the act. Some groups did raise special problems. Mackasey faced strong opposition from teachers, who after a decade of burgeoning demand for their services, did not see the need for coverage. The construction associations lobbied hard against experiencc rating because of the characteristic employment instability in their industry.[69] On the whole, however, Mackasey and his advisers tended to view the private interest representations, especially from employers, with some amusement, since in essentials these representations have remained the same since 1940. Officials themselves know which technical changes will be considered "pro-labour" or "pro-business," and consequently how employer and employee associations will react.[70] Consultation is still pursued, but from the government's viewpoint probably more for legitimation than for real dialogue.

In the early 1970s, by contrast, the provinces were not preoccupied with UI. The 1971 revisions did not raise serious problems for three reasons. First, since the intent was to make UI payments sufficient on their own to sustain an unemployed person, provincial welfare expenditures would be reduced.[71]

TABLE 3

TRANSFER AS A PERCENTAGE OF UI EXPENDITURES

	1975	1976	1977	1978	1979
Newfoundland	+72.8	+72.8	+74.5	+75.7	+75.5
Prince Edward Island	+66.1	+67.4	+69.7	+70.0	+71.7
Nova Scotia	+31.4	+37.4	+43.0	+41.5	+41.0
New Brunswick	+56.7	+58.9	+62.5	+61.9	+61.9
Quebec	+30.5	+34.1	+35.6	+35.9	+34.9
Ontario	−32.3	−46.4	−57.2	−55.2	−56.8
Manitoba	−108.5	−86.2	−51.5	−28.6	−44.4
Saskatchewan	−92.7	−88.8	−65.3	−46.3	−56.7
Alberta	−268.9	−251.1	−225.5	−208.0	−205.0
British Columbia	+18.8	+6.8	+0.5	+10.0	+0.4

SOURCE: Canada, Employment and Immigration Canada, *Unemployment Insurance: Interprovincial Transfers*, Technical Study 9, Task Force on Unemployment Insurance (Ottawa, 1981), p. 8.

Second, provincial governments were not compelled to bring their own employees into the program. If they did decide to do so, then all employees would have to be covered, to prevent placing only "bad risks" (e.g., seasonal employees) under the federal plan. The third reason arose from the solution to Quebec's objection that sickness and maternity benefits were within provincial jurisdiction. The legislation provided an "opting out" clause, whereby UI special benefits would be reduced or eliminated upon the implementation of provincial plans.

Expenditure reductions create different political dynamics from expenditure increases. UI expenditures are vital to the economies of the high unemployment provinces, principally the Atlantic region and Quebec. Table 3 shows the interprovincial transfers of UI monies, and demonstrates their importance to the eastern provinces. For every four benefit dollars spent in Newfoundland, three came from other provinces; for every benefit dollar spent in Alberta, over two dollars were sent out of province in contributions. Bill C-14 reduced UI expenditures in the eastern provinces by 9.6 percent in 1979.[72] Predictably therefore, the greatest resistance to the 1975–78 changes came from these regions.

This resistance was expressed on a number of levels. The first was the cabinet. Cullen tried in 1977, for example, to drop fishermen from the program. As self-employed workers, they should not have been eligible for coverage, but had been left in the 1971 Act until the Department of Fisheries could arrive at a plan to help them.[73] Romeo LeBlanc, minister of fisheries and New Brunswick's spokesman in the cabinet, rejected the proposal. Consequently, Cullen never took this idea to the public.[74] The second level was the Liberal caucus. Cullen brought Bill C-27 forward without having had extensive caucus discussions, and found himself facing strong objections from Atlantic MPs. The variable entrance requirement, originally an opposition suggestion, provided one way out of the impasse, since it permitted a general increase in entrance requirements while responding to the objections of MPs from high unemployment regions.

The third level of resistance came from the provinces themselves, primarily over the greater welfare costs they expected due to tighter UI provisions. Three of the provinces—Newfoundland, Nova Scotia, and Ontario—took the rare step of appearing before the Standing Committee on Labour, Manpower, and Immigration during its examination of Bill C-14.[75] Ottawa agreed that provincial welfare costs would increase. It simply argued that they would be small, and in any case were cost-shared.[76] The provinces disputed these figures, claiming that they would be higher.[77]

It became clear to federal policy makers by 1978 that substantial program changes reducing costs and emphasizing manpower goals would raise vociferous complaints, not primarily from private interests, but from provincial and regional ones. Employers supported most of the changes, usually calling for even tighter restrictions, and the Canadian Labour Congress, perhaps still smarting from the wage controls episode, raised only passive resistance. Despite UI's substantial redistributive effects among income classes,[78] resistance to the retreat from the 1971 legislation was not organized primarily along class lines, but along regional and governmental lines.

The impact of these regional and governmental pressures has been felt primarily in two ways. First, Ottawa's readiness to consult has increased greatly since 1975. Somewhat disillusioned with the fortunes of the social security review, and determined to guard its full powers in one of the few social programs over which it has full constitutional control, Ottawa was less than enthusiastic and open in its consultations with the provinces on the 1975–78 UI changes. However, with the need, toward the end of the controls program, to coordinate federal and provincial economic policies, the willingness to consult increased.[79] But the specific willingness to deal more openly on UI probably had as much to do with the strong regional representations that had been made previously. The Clark government tried to have discussions with the provinces about proposed UI changes well in advance of legislation. There were also intensive intergovernmental consultations over the 1981 report of the Task Force on Unemployment Insurance.

The second result has been the way that UI policy changes themselves are designed. In 1975, program changes were made without prolonged consideration of their regional impact. By 1980, partly as a result of the growth in UI expenditures themselves, and partly as a result of the 1975–78 regional responses to program changes, policy makers favoured modifications which had the least detrimental impact in the east.[80] From simply having regional impact, the program had acquired a regional intent, even in its most pedestrian features.

The intergovernmental clash over UI in the 1970s, and the recent increase in consultations, have affected the program's evolution profoundly. Neither the labour management nor the social control models can fully capture the political dynamics that were contained in the intergovernmental dimension of UI. The peculiar meshing of federal and provincial programs that comprises the Canadian social security system creates delicate checks and balances. If Ottawa decreases its spending in one program, provincial spending in other programs is likely to increase. Regardless of goals of labour management or social control, this leads provincial governments to oppose federal expenditure restraint. And so while employers dwell on disincentives, and unions threaten social unrest, governments talk of compensating expenditures, cost-sharing, and revenue balance.

CONCLUSIONS

This chapter has argued that two popular models used to explain social security programs—the social control model and the labour management model—are perhaps most helpful when dealing with the politics of new programs. Established programs are likely to have different dynamics and forces, ones which are, at any rate, difficult to encompass completely within either or both of the models.

The social control model did not appear to have any purchase on the nature of the 1971 revisions. There were traces of the features associated with the labour management model, but they had a different complexion from what one would expect. Concern about the disincentive effects of the new program was not prominent, and approving remarks were made about the insulation that claimants would have from labour market forces while on benefits. There is nothing in the labour management model that says that social policies have to be coercive, but it does imply some short- or long-term benefit to the accumulation process, either through a better labour force or a more efficient labour market. While these were indeed the stated goals of the White Paper, employers themselves disagreed.

The labour management model did, however, have a strong bearing on the retreat from the White Paper contained in Bills C-69, C-27, and C-14. Clearly, social control concerns were not uppermost, since the reductions to the program came at times of record high unemployment. Rather, changes were motivated by a pervasive distrust of claimants, a desire to put them to work, to in effect reduce their range of choices and force them to respond more quickly to labour market signals.

As useful as the labour management model was in understanding developments in the 1970s, it revealed only part of the story. A vital aspect, first in its absence and then in its extreme visibility, was that of "fiscal constraint." It refers to the flexibility of resource allocation within the state and across its agencies. Contrary to the myth that Canadian governments spend recklessly, it appears that strong fiscal constraints—a sense of the finitude of resources—have been present for most of postwar budgetary history.[81] The dynamics that arise from these constraints are specific to the political level, they do not simply reflect external social forces. To be sure, they combine and coalesce with these forces, but they retain a scope of explanation which contributes substantially to our understanding of policy development.

With respect to UI in the 1970s, the absence of constraints, due to forecasts which underestimated the real costs of the program, was decisive in neutralizing resistance by central agencies. It protected the bill in House examination, and allowed its sponsors to ignore the displeasure of employers. Subsequently, it was the high costs of the program that stimulated suspicion of widespread abuse. Moreover, fiscal constraints, combined with the unique features of the UI Account, gave employment policy in the mid-1970s its peculiar shell-game qualities.

The concept of fiscal constraint and its resultant dynamics helped in understanding the pattern of intergovernmental disagreements over the 1975–78 UI amendments. What disagreement there was focused on the fiscal effects of UI reductions: provincial treasuries would have to take up the slack. This kind of argument has been a perennial feature of Canadian federalism. It is a function of the fact that when there are two programs, both addressing some given problem, and one program is reduced, the demand for the other one rises. The manner in which provincial concerns were articulated suggests that social control/labour management goals, at least with respect to UI changes in this period, were easily eclipsed by revenue or resource goals.

An examination of UI in the 1970s, the process of its revision in 1971, and the subsequent retreats, suggest some tentative conclusions about the Canadian state in the 1980s. The changes confirm the view that the specific weight of the state in Canadian society is greater than in some other countries.[82] Changes to UI, a program which should be of vital concern to private interests, were initiated almost completely within or between governments. Consultations with the private sector appear more as public relations exercises than real dialogues. Contrary to most of the thinking on the subject, however, it is possible that the state's "relative autonomy" in this case derived not from a confused fragmentation of private interests, all divided one against the other, but from their predictable and tiresome cohesion. On few other issues are the respective positions of labour and capital so firm, so clear, and so traditional as on UI.

The post-1971 changes to UI seem to fit an emerging pattern of reductions in social security expenditures. Critics of the welfare state who welcome these reductions often support the notion of a "smaller" state and a wider consequent scope for individual freedom. But is this equation of "welfare reductions" with "greater freedom" valid? At least with respect to UI, it can be questioned on three grounds. First, reductions in the program were intended to increase the coercive force of the market on individuals. This is an old argument, but it bears repeating. Markets sometimes simply substitute the rule of harsh and blind laws for the rule of weak or imperfect men. But more importantly, and this is the second point, "markets" have to be created and sustained. The "developmental" uses of UI funds, the benefit control mechanisms, the proliferation of mandatory interviews and registrations, make it almost pointless to speak of "reductions" in UI: the program is just as complex now as before the changes. The third point is that these program alterations, which in one sense implied reductions in expenditures and scope, fostered an increase in intergovernmental consultation and activity. Consulting governments are not necessarily big or overpowering governments, but the main point is that in a federal system such as Canada's, moving toward social security "reductions" may mean, at least in the short term, a pronounced increase in executive interaction.

The worrisome implication of these speculations is that we may indeed in the 1980s face reductions in state spending, particularly on social security, but at the same time will have to cope with even bigger and more distant government.

EPILOGUE

The preceding account was written before the most recent UI program changes. These changes cast further light on the dynamics suggested in this chapter. Unemployment insurance and manpower policy have recently been eclipsed by energy negotiations and the constitution as matters of intergovernmental bargaining and public concern, but the first two years of the new Liberal government saw interesting and intricate manoeuvres over UI.

The guiding framework for Ottawa's decision making in 1980–82 assumed that Canada would enjoy an economic boom based on megaproject development, high technology, and increased exports. Foreshadowed in the NEP, and then more clearly articulated in the 1981 federal budget, this vision suggested a radical transformation in the structure of the Canadian economy, perhaps its most important transformation in the postwar period. Massive investments would be required for resource development, and some of the money would have to come from the public sector. New skills would be demanded, in new parts of the country. Retraining and more concerted manpower policies were needed, as well as very large labour force migrations across occupations and across the nation. The world demand for certain commodities in the next decade would increase, and Canada's potential in these areas (e.g., communications and agriculture) was promising, but intensified public efforts would be needed to meet this potential. The emphasis on trade led, for example, to the proposal of CANAGREX, a crown corporation designed to market agricultural products abroad, and the reorganization of the departments of External Affairs and Industry, Trade and Commerce.

The effect of this vision on UI was expressed in the report of a special task force established to examine the program and its role in the 1980s. The report, entitled *Unemployment Insurance in the 1980s*, was released in July 1981. Its analysis of the Canadian labour market in the 1980s suggested that there would be an increase in female participation rates; the overall rate of growth in the labour force would be low, lower indeed than increases in available employment over the decade, leading to a secular decline in unemployment rates; and the strongest employment expansion would come in the energy-related industries, primarily in the west. The adjustments contingent on these developments suggested to the task force that UI would have to reassert labour market objectives and deemphasize income security objectives. Mobility would have to be enhanced, and the program would have to be mindful of its regional impacts, in order to facilitate, not impede, desired changes.

The report's recommendations were complex, but may be roughly divided into three categories. First, there were various recommendations to streamline the program and make it less cumbersome and opaque. Different entrance requirements, the three-phase benefit structure, annoying maternity benefit provisions, along with some other items were to be changed to make the program more comprehensible. A second category of changes dealt with equity. These were revisions to remove anomalies in the act which permitted some categories of claimants to receive more than others might fairly expect. The task force recommended several measures, such as an increased entrance requirement and doubled period of disqualification for voluntary quitting, which would have reduced the generosity of the program and forced more people out into the labour market. It should be noted, however, that one of the recommendations in this category, the streamlined benefit structure, actually increased benefits for working women. That the overall impact of the task force's recommendations was to restrict the program can be clearly seen from its own estimates of the financial implications of its proposals: private sector contributions to UI would increase by $75 million, government contributions would decrease by $295 million, for a net reduction of $220 million in benefits.

Like most of the major changes made to the UI program since 1940, these suggestions came from within the bureaucracy. Consultation was to come after their release, and the minister did indeed make relatively vigorous efforts to meet with employer and employee representatives across the country through the fall of 1981. Consultations also proceeded with provincial governments. The reaction from peak organizations in the private sector was distinctly negative. Though the government had taken the view that the task force recommendations were open for negotiation and revision, both labour and business objected to what they perceived as a *fait accompli*. Moreover, they were upset with those recommendations shifting program costs onto the private sector and away from the government. Trade unions in particular saw the report as the worst in a long series of attempts since 1975 to eviscerate the program. The provinces were easier to deal with for a number of reasons. First, unlike Bill C-14, the proposed benefit reductions were not large. Second, negotiations over the Bill C-14 cuts had been conducted by provincial ministers of welfare, and their natural concern had been with the effect of UI reductions on their own assistance payments. In 1981, because the recommendations were part of a larger package dealing with labour market policies and economic development, not to mention transfer payments, treasury ministers were in charge. Their view was that what mattered to a province was the net fiscal effect of federal program expenditures, so that if UI cuts were balanced by increases in other expenditures, there would be no great problem.[83]

The task force report was obsolete almost from the day it was published. Rather than decreasing, unemployment spiralled alarmingly in December 1981. Instead of labour market adjustments from declining industries to new, growing industries, there seemed only decline. The task force report had assumed an "upside" coinciding with the "downside" of economic change in the 1980s; UI would smooth the shift from one to the other. Without the shift, the rationale for program changes evaporated. Furthermore, reductions of the nature contemplated in the report, if implemented while thousands were facing unemployment, would seem heartless and be politically suicidal. Apart from some minor increases in premiums, the revival of "developmental uses" of UI (i.e., worksharing, job creation, and training), and relaxed maternity benefit requirements, politicians have decided to leave the program alone.

These developments since 1980 suggest the following. First, the emphasis on labour management goals has continued, as the task force report clearly shows. At the same time, the details of contemplated program changes suggest the continued prevalence of fiscal constraints as a force in policy making. Second, the government has continued to discount the views of employer and employee groups. The irony of this is that while the private sector appears to be losing its "ownership" of UI (an "ownership" implied in the original 1940 legislation), it is being made to shoulder a greater proportion of the costs. Third, provinces continue to be central actors in UI program evolution and reform. Indeed, insofar as future UI changes will try to enhance its labour market impact, it is inevitable that provincial interests will insist on being consulted. Flows of labour and capital across the country are of vital importance to provincial jurisdictions, and any program which affects these flows will be analysed carefully. As the economy improves, it is likely that UI changes along the lines suggested by the task force will once again be considered. Intergovernmental bargaining will strongly influence this process.

NOTES

Research for this paper was conducted at the University of Waterloo, and I gratefully acknowledge the financial assistance extended by the university's Research Grants program. I would also like to thank Dale Holland for searching out and compiling materials, and Mary Pal for comments on the manuscript.

1. Versions of these models may be found in Suzanne de Brunhoff, *State, Capital and Economic Policy* (London: Pluto Press, 1978), Laurence Harris, "The State and Economy: Some Theoretical Problems," in *The Socialist Register 1980*, ed. Ralph Miliband and John Saville (London: The Merlin Press, 1980), pp. 243–62, John Holloway and Sol Picciotto, eds., *State and Capital: A Marxist Debate* (London: Edward Arnold, 1978), and Frances Fox Piven and Richard A. Cloward, *Regulating the Poor: The Functions of Public Welfare* (New York: Pantheon Books, 1971). These models do not of course exhaust the explanatory possibilities; see for example David R. Cameron, "The Expansion of the Public Economy: A Comparative Analysis," *American Political Science Review* 72 (1978): 1243–61, Francis G. Castles, "How Does Politics Matter? Structure or Agency in the Determination of Public Policy Outcomes," *European Journal of Political Research* 9 (1981): 119–32, and Ramesh Mishra, *Society and Social Policy*, 2nd ed. (London: Macmillan, 1981).

2. Alvin Finkel, "Origins of the Welfare State in Canada," in *The Canadian State*, ed. Leo Panitch (Toronto: University of Toronto Press, 1977), chap. 12, and Alvin Finkel, *Business and Social Reform* (Toronto: James Lorimer, 1979).

3. Carl J. Cuneo, "State, Class, and Reserve Labour: The Case of the 1941 Canadian Unemployment Insurance Act," *The Canadian Review of Sociology and Anthropology* 16 (1979): 147–70, and Carl J. Cuneo, "State Mediation of Class Contradictions in Canadian Unemployment Insurance, 1930–1935," *Studies in Political Economy* 3 (Spring 1980): 37–63.

4. James Struthers, "Two Depressions: Bennett, Trudeau and the Unemployed," *Journal of Canadian Studies* 14 (1979): 70–80, and James Struthers, *No Fault of Their Own: Unemployment and the Canadian Welfare State, 1914–1941* (Toronto: University of Toronto Press, 1983).

5. Finkel, *Business and Social Reform*, p. 98.

6. Cuneo, "State Mediation," pp. 37–38.

7. Cuneo, "State, Class, and Reserve Labour," p. 149.

8. Struthers, "Two Depressions," p. 79.

9. Arguments for a distinct though interdependent "political logic" may be found in André Blais and Philippe Faucher, "La politique industrielle dans les économies capitalistes avancées," *Canadian Journal of Political Science* 14 (1981): 3–35; Fred Block, "Beyond Relative Autonomy: State Managers as Historical Subjects," in *The Socialist Register 1980*, ed. Ralph Miliband and John Saville (London: The Merlin Press, 1980), pp. 227–42; C. Crouch, "The State, Capital and Liberal Democracy," in *State and Economy in Contemporary Capitalism*, ed. Colin Crouch (London: Croom Helm, 1979), pp. 13–54; and Charles E. Lindblom, *Politics and Markets* (New York: Basic Books, 1977).

10. Only the important changes will be dealt with here. Most of the administrative and regulatory changes will have to be ignored, as will court decisions and the following acts:
1. Statute Law (Status of Women) Amendment Act, 1975, *Statutes of Canada*, 1974–76, c. 66. This provided for a more liberal maternity benefit.
2. Unemployment Insurance Entitlements Adjustment Act, 1977, *Statutes of Canada*, 1976–77, c. 11. This reinstated benefits for people adversely affected by Bill C-69.
3. Unemployment Insurance Amendment Act, 1980, *Statutes of Canada*, , 1980, c. 35. This extended the variable entrance requirement to June 1982 and shifted more of the costs of the program to the private sector.

11. *Statutes of Canada*, 1940, c. 44. A constitutional amendment required to bring UI within the federal jurisdiction (sec. 91[2a] of the British North America Act) was passed July 10, 1940 (3–4 George VI, c. 36 [UK]). Contributions became payable on July 1, 1941, and benefits could be collected as of January 27, 1942.

12. *Statutes of Canada*, 1940, c. 44, First Schedule, pt. 2.

13. Ibid., secs. 28(i)–(iv).

14. Ibid., secs. 11 and 17(1).

15. Statistics Canada, *Catalogue 86-201* (Ottawa, 1978), p. 124, table A. Eligible employees were divided into seven earnings classes. These benefit rates applied to the midpoint of thc earnings range as of July 1, 1941.

16. A good review of these amendments, and of the program's postwar history, may be found in Gary Dingledine, *A Chronology of Response: The Evolution of Unemployment Insurance from 1940 to 1980* (Ottawa: Minister of Supply and Services, 1981).

17. *Statutes of Canada*, 1955, c. 50, secs. 49–53. For the 1950 amendment see ibid., 1950, c. 1.

18. Dingledine, *Chronology of Response*, p. 37.

19. Unemployment Insurance Commission, *Annual Report 1964* (Ottawa, 1965), p. 50, app. 10. One crude measure of the fund's solvency is the ratio of reserves to total benefits paid. This ratio declined from 4.7 in 1954 to 0.0024 in 1964. The recession was not the sole cause of insolvency; according to Laurence Alexander Kelly, "Unemployment Insurance in Canada: Economic, Social and Financial Aspects" (Ph.D. thesis, Queen's University, 1967), p. 164, the erosion of the fund really began in 1948.

20. Dingledine, *Chronology of Response*, pp. 45–46.

21. Unemployment Insurance Commission, *Report of the Study for Updating the Unemployment Insurance Programme* (Ottawa, 1968).

22. For discussions of this shift, see G. P. A. McDonald, "Labour, Manpower and Government Reorganization," *Canadian Public Administration* 10 (1967): 471–98, and Richard W. Phidd and G. Bruce Doern, *The Politics and Management of Canadian Economic Policy* (Toronto: Macmillan, 1978), chap. 10.

23. Andrew F. Johnson, "A Minister as an Agent of Policy Change: The Case of Unemployment Insurance in the Seventies," *Canadian Public Administration* 24 (1981): 612–33.

24. Department of Labour, *Unemployment Insurance in the 70's* (Ottawa, 1970), p. 3.

25. Ibid., p. 5.

26. Ibid.

27. Ibid., p. 11.

28. Ibid., p. 6.

29. See Saul J. Blaustein, *Unemployment Insurance: Objectives and Issues* (Kalamazoo, Mich.: The W. E. Upjohn Institute for Employment Research, November 1968), Mark M. Hauser and Paul Burrows, *The Economics of Unemployment Insurance* (London: George Allen and Unwin, 1969), and International Labour Office, *Unemployment Insurance Schemes*, Studies and Reports, n.s., no. 42 (Geneva, 1955), pp. 101–2.

30. House of Commons *Debates*, April 19, 1971, p. 5054.

31. Ibid., June 10, 1971, p. 6593.

32. House of Commons, Standing Committee on Labour, Manpower and Immigration, *Minutes of Proceedings and Evidence*, p. 19 (hereinafter referred to as SCLMI, *Minutes*). A month later, however, he cautioned that the two mandatory interviews were not intended as policing actions. Ibid., November 3, 1970, p. 15.

33. See C. Michael Lanphier et al., *An Analysis of Attitudes Toward Unemployment Insurance* (Toronto: Institute for Behavioural Research, York University, 1970), for a national survey conducted in spring 1968, indicating widespread though cautious support for increased coverage and benefits.

34. Johnson, "A Minister as an Agent," pp. 620–22. It should be noted that the Department of Finance had supplied the unemployment forecasts which formed the basis for the proposals, and these were low. Moreover, according to Mackasey, key officials in the department and the Treasury Board supported the White Paper. Interview with Bryce Mackasey, Ottawa, February 1982.

35. SCLMI, *Minutes*, September 15, 1970, p. 10.

36. Ibid., p. 29.

37. Ibid., p. 12.

38. D. Allen said before the Standing Committee: "We have not forecast unemployment rates for the nineteen seventies except insofar as we supposed a certain pattern of unemployment would prevail." SCLMI, *Minutes*, September 16, 1970, p. 108. The commission relied on Finance Department forecasts of around 4 percent unemployment for the 1970s. Interview with Bryce Mackasey, Ottawa, February 1982.

39. SCLMI, *Minutes* September 16, 1970, p. 142, *Facts and Figures Unemployment Insurance in the 70's*, table entitled "Forecast of Benefit Costs in 1972 with Proposed Plan at Various Unemployment Rates."

40. On the way in which the 1935 act was intended to divide the working class, see J. L. Cohen, *The Canadian Unemployment Insurance Act—Its Relation to Social Security* (Toronto: Thomas Nelson and Sons, 1935), chaps. 6–7.

41. John Saywell, ed., *Canadian Annual Review of Politics and Public Affairs 1971* (Toronto: University of Toronto Press, 1972), p. 358.

42. John Saywell, ed., *Canadian Annual Review of Politics and Public Affairs 1972* (Toronto: University of Toronto Press, 1974), pp. 353–55.

43. The program also encountered administrative difficulties at the beginning. Since some parts of the 1955 act remained temporarily in force after 1971, the commission had to deal with two pieces of legislation simultaneously. The change-over to computers was made at the same time, adding to the confusion. Thus the cost escalation was probably due to a higher than expected unemployment rate, administrative errors, the entry of newly covered occupations at subsidized contribution rates, and abuse.

44. Unemployment Insurance Commission, *Annual Report 1973* (Ottawa, 1974), p.

7. As the *Annual Report* put it: "The Separation Certificate was replaced by the Record of Employment, making it possible to cross-check by computer the validity of the information provided by the claimant and the employer."

45. Ibid., p. 4. Benefit control costs increased 68 percent in 1973 over 1972, compared to a 15 percent increase in total administration costs for the same period.

46. "The initiatives undertaken in 1975 shifted the emphasis of the system toward preventative measures," Unemployment Insurance Commission, *Annual Report 1975* (Ottawa, 1976), p. 2. The experimental Special Job Finding and Placement Drive alone was successful in disqualifying or disentitling over 80,000 claimants.

47. House of Commons *Debates*, October 27, 1975, p. 8568.

48. On the social security review see A. W. Johnson, "Canada's Social Security Review 1973–1975: The Central Issues," *Canadian Public Policy* 1, no. 4 (1975): 456–72; Christopher Leman, *The Collapse of Welfare Reform* (Cambridge, Mass.: MIT Press, 1980); Rick Van Loon, "Reforming Welfare in Canada," *Public Policy* 27 (1979): 469–504; and chap. 3 above.

49. Interview with senior official, Ottawa, February 1982.

50. Strictly speaking, the program's cost problem should be conceptualized as one of overpayments, rather than simple abuse. Abuse of the system, in the sense of knowingly receiving benefits when ineligible for them or remaining on benefits longer than "necessary," is one *explanation* of overpayments. Though abuse in this sense certainly exists, it is unlikely to be a major explanation for overpayments. Abuse, by definition, is difficult to detect and is even harder to quantify, but two major American studies of the phenomenon (for "working violators"—those who collect benefits while secretly working) suggest that it is not typically more widespread than 0.1 to 2.4 percent of benefits; see Leonard P. Adams, *Public Attitudes toward Unemployment Insurance* (Kalamazoo, Mich.: The W. E. Upjohn Institute for Employment Research, December 1971), chap. 6, and Joseph M. Becker, *The Problem of Abuse in Unemployment Benefits: A Study in Limits* (New York: Columbia University Press, 1953), chap. 11. Recent Canadian evidence suggests that of $290 million in undetected UI overpayments, 20 percent was due to some form of claimant fraud, while the rest was due to employer and commission errors; see Auditor General of Canada, *Annual Report* (Ottawa, 1979).

51. The main contributions to this debate are Frank T. Denton et al., *Unemployment and Labour Force Behaviour of Young People: Evidence from Canada and Ontario* (Toronto: University of Toronto Press for the Ontario Economic Council, 1980); Economic Council of Canada, *People and Jobs* (Ottawa, 1976), pp. 143–70; Christopher Green and Jean-Michel Cousineau, *Unemployment in Canada: The Impact of Unemployment Insurance* (Ottawa: Economic Council of Canada, 1975); Herbert G. Grubel et al., "Real and Insurance-Induced Unemployment in Canada," *Canadian Journal of Economics* 8 (1975): 174–91, Herbert G. Grubel et al., "Real and Insurance-Induced Unemployment in Canada: A Reply." *Canadian Journal of Economics* 8 (1975): 603–5; Herbert G. Grubel and Michael A. Walker, eds., *Unemployment Insurance: Global Evidence of Its Effects on Unemployment* (Vancouver: The Fraser Institute, 1978); Derek P. J. Hum, *Unemployment Insurance and Work Effort: Issues, Evidence, and Policy Directions* (Toronto: Ontario Economic Council, 1981); S. F. Kaliski, "Real and Insurance-Induced Unemployment in Canada," *Canadian Journal of Economics* 8 (1975): 600–603; Fred Lazar, "The Impact of the 1971 Unemployment Insurance Revisions on Unemployment Rates: Another Look,"

Canadian Journal of Economics 11 (1978): 559–70, and Samuel A. Rea, Jr., "Unemployment Insurance and Labour Supply: A Simulation of the 1971 Unemployment Insurance Act," *Canadian Journal of Economics* 10 (1977): 263–78.

52. House of Commons *Debates*, October 27, 1975, p. 8567. Andras confirmed this in committee testimony; see SCLMI, *Minutes*, 13 November 1975, pp. 17–18.

53. SCLMI, *Minutes*, November 13, 1975, p. 18.

54. House of Commons *Debates*, February 1, 1977, p. 2591.

55. Ibid.

56. Ibid., p. 2592.

57. Ibid., November 9, 1978, p. 983. Apart from these legislative changes, the commission's control procedures were further tightened, to the extent that commission officials were allegedly expected to disallow between 40 and 60 percent of all claims; see R. B. Byers and John Saywell, eds., *Canadian Annual Review of Politics and Public Affairs 1978* (Toronto: University of Toronto Press, 1980), p. 9.

58. This is essentially the notion of "less eligibility." See Struthers, "Two Depressions," p. 78, and John A. Garraty, *Unemployment in History* (New York: Harper and Row, 1978) chap. 4, for discussions of the concept.

59. See Department of Manpower and Immigration, *Employment Strategy* (Ottawa, 1976). The developmental use of UI funds was hinted at even in the 1975 changes, so the idea of an active labour management policy had early roots. Interestingly, some department officials resisted the use of UI for job creation—it was an idea that came more from the political than the bureaucratic level. Interview with Bud Cullen, Ottawa, February 1982.

60. Interview with Bud Cullen, Ottawa, February 1982.

61. In 1978, for example, Cullen had wanted to reduce the benefit rate to 50 percent, but eventually settled for 60 percent when he introduced Bill C-14. The variable entrance requirement of ten to fourteen weeks was disliked by the department as well because of the administrative problems it posed, but had to be accepted when the original proposal for a uniform twelve-week requirement was attacked.

62. House of Commons *Debates,* June 23, 1975, pp. 7027–28. The intention to tighten UI was announced in the 1974 Throne Speech, ibid., September 30, 1974, p. 5.

63. Ibid., March 31, 1977, pp. 4533–39. Because of revisions made to the original proposals, especially the substitution of the variable entrance requirement, the estimated annual savings were reduced to $135 million.

64. Interview with Bud Cullen, Ottawa, February 1982.

65. Prime Minister's Office, *Notes for the Prime Minister's Address on National Television* (Ottawa, August 1, 1978).

66. Dingledine, *Chronology of Response*, pp. 83, 112.

67. Interview with Bud Cullen, Ottawa, February 1982. Cullen was even advised by one colleague that the UI Account be renamed the *Employment* Fund.

68. Johnson, "A Minister as an Agent," pp. 618–19, 624.

69. Interview with Bryce Mackasey, Ottawa, February 1982.

70. Interview with senior official, Ottawa, February 1982.

71. House of Commons *Debates*, April 19, 1971, p. 5039.

72. Employment and Immigration Canada, *Unemployment Insurance: Interprovincial Transfers*, Task Force on Unemployment Insurance, Technical Study 9 (Ottawa, 1981) p. 12.

73. Interview with Bryce Mackasey, Ottawa, February 1982.

74. Interview with Bud Cullen, Ottawa, February 1982.

75. SCLMI, *Minutes*, November 30, 1978. Ontario's objections focused less on increases in welfare costs than on lack of consultation.

76. For example, see House of Commons *Debates*, November 9, 1978, p. 984. Cullen estimated that the 1978 changes would increase net provincial welfare costs in 1979–81 by $68.8 million.

77. One partial measure relevant to the dispute is the increase in Canada Assistance Plan (CAP) expenditures. Total provincial CAP expenditures increased by $149.1 million between 1979 and 1981; see Canadian Tax Foundation, *The National Finances 1980–81* (Toronto: The Canadian Tax Foundation, 1981), p. 128. Not all of this increase would have been due to UI cuts, but it does appear that Ottawa underestimated the effects of Bill C-14.

78. For data on UI's redistributive effects, see J. E. Cloutier, *The Distribution of Benefits and Costs of Social Security in Canada 1971–1975*, Discussion Paper No. 108 (Ottawa: Economic Council of Canada, February 1978); Employment and Immigration Canada, *Distributive and Redistributive Effects of the UI Program*, Task Force on Unemployment Insurance, Technical Study 10 (Ottawa, 1981); Employment and Immigration Canada, *Income Redistribution through UI: An Analysis by Individual and Family Income Class in 1977*, Task Force on Unemployment Insurance, Technical Study 11 (Ottawa: 1981); and Alister M. M. Smith et al., *Poverty and Government Income Support in Canada, 1971–1975: Characteristics of the Low Income Population*, Discussion Paper No. 130 (Ottawa: Economic Council of Canada, April 1979).

79. Douglas Brown and Julia Eastman, *The Limits of Consultation* (Ottawa: Minister of Supply and Services, 1981).

80. Interview with senior official, Ottawa, February 1982.

81. W. Irwin Gillespie, "Postwar Canadian Fiscal Policy Revisited, 1945–1975," *Canadian Tax Journal* 27 (1979): 265–77.

82. Alan C. Cairns, "The Governments and Societies of Canadian Federalism," *Canadian Journal of Political Science* 10 (1977): 695–725.

83. Interview with senior official, Ottawa, February 1982.

Chapter Six

Restructuring Family Allowances: "Good Politics at No Cost"?

ANDREW F. JOHNSON

Few contemporary observers of Canadian federalism would dispute J. R. Mallory's claim that "governments find themselves making decisions all the time which can be effective only if taken in concert with other governments."[1] Mallory's remark is especially applicable to decision making in the realm of income security policy. Canada's myriad of income security programs are so closely related that a program change initiated by one level of government will most certainly trigger changes in programs administered by other levels. The task force report prepared for the provincial ministers of social services comments that by the early 1970s "as income security programs . . . increased in scope, complexity, and number it became more apparent that no single program could be considered in isolation from another."[2] And yet, the same report laments the federal government's apparent unwillingness "to maintain serious consultations with provincial governments."[3]

In 1978 the minister of finance, Jean Chrétien, hailed major changes to the federal family allowances program as "one of the most significant policy reforms of the decade."[4] The changes were a milestone in the sense that they represented a shift from a universal to a selective program. Moreover, they served as a basis for subsequent modifications to the program in 1982. Despite the significance of the alterations to the family allowances program since 1978, available evidence clearly demonstrates that the provinces were not involved in the decision-making process. Thus the purpose of this chapter is to explain why the provinces were not involved and, more importantly, to determine how effective the federal government has been in attaining its purported goal of a more redistributive system in the absence of concerted decision making.

Towards a Child Benefits System

Constraining expenditures and helping those most in need were the two objectives that the federal government set for itself as the post-controls period began in 1976.[5] A strategy to fulfil these objectives was also provided; income transfers were to be integrated with the income tax system. Such was the recipe that was used to restructure the family allowances program in 1978 and in 1982 since it has become apparent that the program was costly and not particularly redistributive.

By 1977 family allowance payments amounted to over $1.9 billion, three times as much as they had been prior to the previous program reform which had been approved four years earlier.[6] Costs were expected to continue to climb because benefits were indexed to the cost of living. Allen Lambert, the chairman of the Royal Commission on Financial Management and Accountability, was quick to recognize that if income security programs such as family allowances continued to increase at previous rates, the income tax burden would become intolerable.[7] Significantly, he singled out family allowances as a case in point by recommending a means test for that program as a way to cut spending. A means test would have curbed expenditures by directing payments to those most in need.

The family allowances program held the dubious distinction of being the least redistributive of the federal government's five most expensive income security programs.[8] While net benefit payments were moderately progressive, the costs of the program were borne unequally among family income groups. In other words, the income tax system was perceived as a major obstacle to forging a more redistributive system of family allowances. Thus, the Economic Council of Canada commented that "if the personal income tax exemption for young dependents is considered in conjunction with the program itself, the effect on income redistribution is regressive, with the highest income quintile receiving the largest proportion of net benefits."[9]

The federal government had already identified a strategy to make income security programs more redistributive. Thus it appeared to be more or less consistent with its rather vague intentions of the immediate post-controls period when it used the income tax system to redress regressivity in the family allowances program. In 1977, a $50 child tax credit was provided to families earning incomes of less than $26,000. However, within a year, the minister of finance admitted that the redistributive intent of child tax credits had not been realized;[10] it was of little value to the majority of low income earners who did not pay income taxes. Nevertheless, the existence of a child benefits system had been recognized. Furthermore, it had been recognized that the redistributive thrust of the family allowances program could not be altered without simultaneous modifications to related child benefits included in the income tax system.[11] Moreover, the child benefits system was ripe for reform because its three elements worked at cross purposes.[12] The family allowances program provided substantial benefits for low income families; child tax credits largely benefited middle income families; and the child tax exemption continued to be of greatest value to high income families because it reduced the amount of income which was taxed at the highest rate and in some instances moved the taxpayer into a lower tax bracket with a lower marginal rate.

The 1978 reform of family allowances was fully compatible with the government's objectives for income security programs in the post-controls period and was fully aligned with its strategy for redistribution. First, family allowance payments were reduced by 23 percent, from $312 per annum to $240. Second, the $50 child tax credit was replaced with a $200 refundable child tax credit payable to families earning less than $18,000 per annum; its value was to be reduced by 50 percent of family income in excess of $18,000.[13] However, the most regressive element of the child benefits system, the child tax exemption, was not altered substantially.[14] In other words, savings accrued by the reduction in family allowance payments were to be funnelled into the pockets of lower-income families via the refundable child tax credit. The new package of benefits was to cost an additional $35 million which was, from the minister of finance's perspective, a scheme that would be virtually self-financing.[15] It was thought that a major step towards a more progressive system of child benefits had been accomplished with meagre cost implications.

However, costs continued to rise. By 1982 overall family allowances payments surpassed 1977 levels by about $3 million. Costs were expected to continue to rise due to the indexation of benefits. In addition, revenues lost through the refundable child tax credit had exceeded expectations.[16] More families than initially expected had applied for and received the credit. Forgone revenues were estimated to be approximately $1 billion, slightly less than half of the total disbursements on family allowances. Clearly, the child benefits system was a primary candidate for the program of expenditure restraint announced in the June budget. Thus family allowances was one of the first programs to be cut by the government's "six and five" program. Full indexation of family allowances was to be suspended by January 1983. Benefits would be limited to a 6 percent cost of living adjustment in 1983 and to a 5 percent adjustment in 1984. The refundable child tax credit was to remain fully indexed to the cost of living and a "one shot" $50 increase was to be added for 1983 in order to compensate lower-income families for the capping of their family allowances.[17] Although the minister of health and welfare had long advocated the elimination of the child tax exemption, that element of the child benefits system had been left untouched.

Hence the 1978 formula was resurrected in 1982 with similar results. Costs were cut. Total savings were expected to amount to $70 million; approximately $320 million were expected to be shaved from the family allowances program but $250 million were to be channelled into the refundable child tax credit. In theory, a small measure of redistribution was achieved by using the income tax system to transfer funds to lower-income families. However, in practice, the full value of the tax credit has not been passed on to low-income families who are most in need of financial assistance. It appears that many provinces have quietly prevented their welfare recipients from receiving the tax credit benefit.

The Quiet Subversion of the Provinces

The 1978 and 1982 changes to the child benefits system indirectly affected the financing of provincial income security schemes. Provincial social assistance plans are income tested; that is, all sources of income, including provincial and federal transfers, may be considered in establishing social assistance benefit levels. Thus reductions in child benefits may force the provinces to pour more monies into social assistance payments in order to maintain desired benefit rates. Most provinces claim to maintain a "summing interaction" with family allowances; that is, the amount of social assistance a claimant receives does not take into account the amount of family allowances the claimant may also receive.[18] However, the interaction is difficult to monitor. In 1978, only three provinces had statutory increases in social assistance; currently, only two, Quebec and Nova Scotia, have statutory increases.[19] The remaining provinces increase social assistance levels at ministerial discretion. While some provinces formulate rate increases on the basis of detailed information pertaining to income and other types of assistance available, officials concede that others, especially the smaller provinces, make increases on "a purely *ad hoc* basis."[20] The point is that the procedures used for determining social assistance benefit increases do not guarantee that federal attempts to target child benefits to the lowest-income families will succeed. After all, even statutes can be amended. The provinces can accept federal initiatives. Alternatively, they can openly reject or quietly subvert federal measures.

Initially, the provinces did not choose any of these alternatives. They simply did not react to the proposals. Clearly, this was of considerable concern to the minister of health and welfare, Monique Bégin, because the opposition threatened to filibuster the bill unless provincial acceptance was secured. Hence, Bégin told the House of Commons that she had sent letters to her provincial counterparts in late October of 1978 urging them to pass on the full benefits of the tax credit to social assistance recipients.[21] Further representations were made, including discussions with her provincial counterparts at the meeting of welfare ministers held in late November. Only five provinces had officially indicated that their cabinets were about to accept the new scheme. In view of the delay, Bégin urged pressure groups and MPs to do what the federal government would not—to lobby with the provinces in order to gain their acceptance. Thus, during debate, Bégin presented her position vis-à-vis the provinces: "It is good politics at no cost to the provinces. It is federal tax payers' money which will be transferred to individual Canadian families by a program similar to family allowances. We do not think it should become an additional transfer payment to the provinces...I invite voluntary associations interested in the development of social policies or my colleagues in Parliament to make their views known to their provincial governments."[22]

It has been claimed that subsequently "scarcely a provincial voice was raised in dissent" as the bill was transformed into law.[23] However, once the bill became law, Quebec raised its voice. Quebec refused to transfer the full benefits of the refundable child tax credit to welfare recipients with children by reducing their welfare payments by an almost equal amount. Instead of receiving the statutory increase of 9 percent for social assistance payments in 1979, mothers with children were to receive a 4.5 percent increase. At the same time, Quebec's minister of social affairs, Denis Lazure, tabled legislation to reduce Quebec's family allowance payments by 23 percent. In effect, Quebec's actions erased the benefit of the tax credit for the lowest-income families and transformed it into a transfer to the province.

Lazure used familiar arguments to defend his government's actions: Quebec has an integrated income security system and, therefore, cannot tolerate federal intrusions, however indirect.[24] According to Lazure, twenty years of unilateral federal policy making in the field of income security was tantamount to "guerilla tactics" designed to "frustrate and humiliate" Quebec in exercising its *de jure,* if not *de facto,* jurisdiction over income security policy.[25] However, the specific logic of Lazure and his government's initial rejection of the refundable child tax credit was made clearer in a document prepared for the Quebec minister of state for economic development:

> Les taux de l'aide sociale au Québec sont établis de façon à ce que, combinés aux allocation familiales, il se situent à un niveau inferieur au salaire minimum; ceci afin de ne pas desinciter au travail les bénéficiaires. Lorsque le nouveau programme de crédit d'impôt fédéral a été introduit, il a fallu obligatoirement ne pas indexer au même rythme les barèmes d'aide sociale pour les familles avec enfants, afin de ne conserver l'écart avec le salaire minimum. C'est un exemple supplémentaire pour signaler la nécessité de repenser les deux programmes en même temps.[26]

Lazure also objected to the revisions in principle because the federal government was perceived to have unilaterally breached an agreement reached in 1973 whereby the provinces could vary family allowance payments.[27] The federal government's reduction in payments was seen as an imposition on Quebec to lower its payments or to make up the shortfall with its own revenues. Quebec was apparently hard pressed to raise its family allowance payments because its statutory indexation of social assistance payments for 1979 was expected to cost $67 million, a price that it could ill afford. Finally, Lazure was disturbed by the administrative problems that he foresaw in implementing the refundable child tax credit.

Manitoba followed Quebec's lead by refusing to pass on the full value of the refundable child tax credit to its social assistance recipients. However, by April 1979 Manitoba had joined with the other provincial governments in assuring Ottawa that it would not absorb the value of the tax credit. The governments of Quebec and Manitoba appear to have recognized the common sense in Bégin's claim that it was "good politics." While Manitoba's Conservative government might have had little difficulty in justifying its rejection, the social democratic Parti Québécois government would have been strained to defend its alleged position of "playing politics on the backs of the poor."[28] More to the point, both governments began to realize that continued opposition could backfire. Provincial opposition was based on rather complex arguments and statements of principle, hardly the right stuff to stir voter antipathy to the federal government. Moreover, the family allowances program is a "sacred cow," to borrow one provincial official's choice description.[29] Opposition to the scheme could have been easily construed or misconstrued by the federal government into a clear and simple issue, an affront to motherhood. In short, the federal government had the political advantage, especially since the new scheme had all-party support. Finally, Van Loon claims that the provinces had become sympathetic to tax credits during the federal-provincial negotiations conducted in relation to the social security review. According to Van Loon, "the Review had accustomed people to the idea of income supplementation and refundable tax credits."[30] That may explain the increased use of these devices by both levels of government but it does not entirely explain provincial willingness to accept a federal initiative, especially one that is not fully compatible with provincial income security policies. It seems likely that the provinces were quick to see that cost implications of the federal plan would not significantly affect them. In the long term, the provinces could simply appropriate the tax credit, if necessary.

The provinces did not rush to appropriate the tax credit. Quite the contrary. New Brunswick and Nova Scotia allowed welfare recipients to keep their tax credits and to receive their statutory increases in social assistance. British Columbia, Saskatchewan, and Prince Edward Island raised their social assistance payments per child to match the drop in family allowances. Ontario, on the other hand, raised its social assistance payments by only percent 6, which was well below the rate of inflation in 1979.[31] Although the outcome may not have been intentional, Ontario's decision amounted to a quiet subversion of federal intentions to allocate more funds to a large segment of low-income families. Other provinces could do the same because the timing and size of social assistance increases are not prescribed by law in most of the provinces. Leonard Shifrin put the case another way: "If, for example, a province planning a $30 rate hike decides to appropriate a $20 benefit coming from Ottawa, all it has to do is cut back the intended increase to $10, and no one will be the wiser."[32] Shifrin, writing in 1979, added: "the fate of indirect interception may yet befall the child tax credit in some provinces, but the rumour mill hasn't come up with any evidence thus far." However, the rumour mill of 1983 suggests that most of the provinces have deducted the value of the tax credit by 100 percent in the last four years.[33] In December 1982, Bégin admitted that there is a close relationship between the child benefits system and social assistance benefits but that "none of that has been explored."[34] Officials of Health and Welfare confirm that no study has been undertaken to assess the relationship in this "grey area."

Not a single voice of dissent was raised when the federal government revised the child benefits system again in 1982. The provinces had long since recognized that they could either quietly accept or quietly subvert federal intentions to redistribute income without the political risks that might accompany a public rejection. Quebec, for instance, appears to have caught on quickly. This time Quebec agreed to pass on the full value of the increased tax credit. But Quebec had quietly reduced its social assistance payments for mothers with children in January 1982 and intended to raise payments by only 2 percent in 1983. However, in 1978 and in 1982, there was another factor related to costs that obviated the need for provincial protests: the dollar amounts involved in the restructuring of family allowances were not great. The 1978 changes were to cost the federal government $35 million; the tax revenues lost by the provinces due to the lowering of family allowance payments were negligible. The $70 million to be saved from the second round of changes were hardly going to break the provinces either. In both instances, the poorer provinces stood to gain because funds were to be reallocated to lower-income families. At the same time, the richer provinces had no need to be overly concerned about costs. An official from the Ontario Ministry of Community and Social Services succinctly summarized his government's view of the matter: family allowances tend to be more costly to Ontario residents as a whole than to residents of other provinces because benefits are taxable and because Ontario has higher marginal taxation than other provinces.[35] In any event, the cost of the changes was small by comparison to the other financial matters that the provinces had to worry about.

In 1978 the provincial treasurers and ministers of finance were still trying to assess the impact of the Established Programs Financing arrangements on their treasuries. In April 1977 the federal government had given notice of its intention to reduce spending on transfers for the established programs (medicare, hospital insurance, and post-secondary education). Under the new arrangements, cost-sharing for these programs was replaced by a "block fund," which, unlike the former, is not related to actual program costs. Block-funding was expected to reduce provincial revenues. The restructuring of family allowances coupled with legislation designed to generate massive cutbacks in the unemployment insurance program were announced against this backdrop. The federal government proposed to save an estimated $655 million in 1979–80 by amending the Unemployment Insurance Act and a further $935 million in 1980–81.[36] While most of the savings were to be offset by additional disbursements for job creation, it was estimated that the cutbacks would cost the provinces additional welfare payments of $25.5 million in 1979–80 and $43.4 million in 1980–81. In addition, in September 1978, the prime minister had announced that $370 million would be shaved from the Canada Assistance Plan and related expenditures.[37] The provinces jointly reacted to these cutbacks by denouncing the federal government's "cavalier attitude" which had "denied provincial governments the opportunity to examine the far-reaching implications of these changes on provincial taxpayers."[38] However, their statement was addressed to federal intentions to effect cutbacks of considerable magnitude. The restructuring of family allowances was brushed aside while the provinces attempted to persuade the federal government to delay the implementation of other and more costly measures.

In 1982, once again the provinces were not in a suitable position to harangue the federal government about the cost implications resulting from the revisions to the child benefits system. The provinces were also faced with mounting deficits and declining revenues. Supported by a rising tide of social conservatism, the provinces were enacting legislation to restrain expenditures in general and to trim social security costs in particular. They could not criticize the federal government for doing what they were doing. Indeed, "no cost" added to "good politics" made the revisions palatable to the provinces.

However, both sets of changes also made good political sense and involved insignificant costs for the federal government. Why didn't the federal government therefore use these opportunities to consult with the provinces as a modest gesture of good will and to ensure that its redistributive intentions were fully realized?

First and foremost, federal officials insist that there has been no good reason to do so because family allowances and related programs lie clearly within the federal government's authority to make direct payments to Canadian citizens.[39] In his study of Canadian social security policy, Banting recognizes the federal government's growing predisposition to steadfastly safeguard its authority to legislate in the field of income security.[40] According to Banting, income security programs are "instruments of statecraft" which provide the federal government with handsome opportunities to forge patron-client relationships with millions of Canadians. Income security programs therefore enhance the federal government's political legitimacy in the eyes of Canadians. What better way to reach out to Canadians than through the family allowances program which benefits 3.6 million mothers and through the refundable child tax credit which benefits 2.5 million mothers? What better way to erode political legitimacy than to consult with the provinces over this vital instrument of statecraft?

Second, federal officials claim that the child benefits system has never been a "priority matter." The restructuring of family allowances has been but a small part of the government's overall imperative to reduce expenditures and thereby to curb inflation. The 1978 Speech from the Throne described the introduction of the new child benefits system as one of several measures to reduce inflation.[41] In 1982, Bégin repeatedly stressed that cutbacks in family allowances and in old age security payments had a much broader purpose than simply to trim expenditures and to set an example of fiscal restraint; they were part of a general strategy for economic recovery launched in the June budget.[42] The federal government has been unwilling to brook provincial interference in the development of parts of an overall package to regenerate the economy. Moreover, the Department of Finance has been the conduit of the federal government's imperative of restraint since the mid-1970s. Senior officials of departments within the Social Affairs Envelope take pains to point out that "Finance changed the rules of the game so that departments would be more cost conscious."[43] One new rule has been to prevent departments from initiating proposals without the benefit of very close scrutiny by interdepartmental structures and by central agencies. In the realm of income security this rule has been superseded by another: the Department of Finance has been charged with initiating revisions to programs. The details of the initial restructuring of family allowances were first announced in the August 1978 minibudget and the details of the subsequent revisions were announced in the June 1982 budget. In other words, while the 1973 amendment to the Family Allowances Act was largely an expenditure change, recent revisions have been largely income tax changes. The generic differences of the changes has led to differences in federal-provincial interaction in the policy-making process. Officials from Health and Welfare point out the obvious: the budgetary process is secretive and thus prohibits the inclusion of the provinces in specific policy-making processes.

Finally, there appears to be a consensus among officials of Health and Welfare that there is a reluctance to consult with the provinces because their positions are predictable; the federal government can only expect disagreement. Bud Cullen, a former minister of employment and immigration, adequately expressed this view while referring to amendments to the unemployment insurance program that were tabled in conjunction with the restructuring of family allowances in 1978:

> At the federal level, we initiate changes in federal legislation and discuss it with them [the provinces]. They thought that before we'd done anything or got cabinet approval, we should talk to them. If I can't get it through my caucus and cabinet, then there is no point of going through the headache of going and having the provinces unload on us. Once your cabinet and caucus are prepared to back you, then you can take it to the provinces and then have a discussion. Now whether you call that "consultation," I don't know.[44]

In 1978, it took three weeks for cabinet to agree to the restructuring of family allowances. In 1982, it took three months, punctuated by contradictory statements of cabinet ministers and public opposition by groups of Liberal backbenchers, for cabinet and the Liberal caucus to agree to the changes. Under these circumstances, the federal government could hardly afford the luxury of inviting the provinces to participate in the policy-making process. However, if the federal government continues to deny itself this luxury, over half a million families at the lowest end of the income scale may well be denied the full benefits of the child benefits system.

Reforming the Child Benefits System

The child benefits system is likely to be subjected to changes in the near future. In 1982, Flora MacDonald, then the Progressive Conservative social affairs critic, called for a comprehensive review of the system.[45] The Liberals acknowledged the need for a "rational discussion and careful examination of the issues" related to the system.[46] Furthermore, the major political parties are promoting two common objectives for change: first, costs must be restrained and, second, regressive features must be removed.

The total cost of the child benefits system amounts to $4 billion; $2.2 billion is paid out through the family allowances program; $1 billion is disbursed through the refundable child tax credit program; and forgone revenues from the child tax exemption amount to approximately $800 million. The Conservatives endorsed the objective of restraining costs in a rather oblique but, nevertheless, heavy-handed manner while enjoying their brief tenure of office. The Clark government proposed to terminate family allowances, the most expensive element of the system, by 1981. The record of Liberal governments also demonstrates sensitivity to costs. Thus Bégin commented in October 1982 that in the next few years it was highly unlikely that additional funds would be directed to the system, for the "hundreds of millions of dollars" that had been available "no longer exist."[47] She added that redistribution should be the basis for any future changes to the system but that redistribution would have to be generated from funds already within the system. Bégin and her Conservative counterpart designated the most regressive feature of the system, the child tax exemption, as the likely source of funds for redistribution. However, Bégin cautiously noted that her views did not necessarily correspond to government policy because tax measures were under the jurisdiction of the minister of finance, not the minister of health and welfare.

Advisory groups, community groups, and policy analysts appear to support the contention that the child tax exemption should be abolished. However, there are two competing proposals to make the system more progressively redistributive with savings derived from the child tax exemption. One recommends that the savings be directed into the refundable child tax credit program while another holds that family allowances be the vehicle for redistribution.

The National Council of Welfare favours abolishing the child tax exemption and applying the proceeds to the child tax credit program.[48] Its scheme for restructuring the system would include lowering the eligibility threshold from its current level of $26,330 to $21,000 so that the child tax credit could be raised by 68 percent,that is, from $343 to $575. The family allowance program would not be altered; payments decrease as income increases because benefits are taxable. The council claims that its proposal would not add one cent to government spending and would provide a boost for low and modest income earners. For instance, a family with two children, earning less than $21,000, would have received $1,150 in 1983 as opposed to $686 under the existing program.

Economist Jonathan Kesselman, on the other hand, advocates abolishing the child tax exemption and the refundable child tax credit.[49] The savings would be used to increase family allowances by 145 percent. Thus in 1982 payments would have amounted to $65.93 a month or $791 per annum, per child, Kesselman proposes a special tax recovery device to recover increasing portions of family allowance payments at higher family income levels. The plan is unquestionably redistributive and, according to Kesselman, the government would have saved about half a billion dollars had his plan been implemented in 1982.

The proposal for a 145 percent increase in family allowance payments is not as outrageous as it may seem at first glance. After all, the Canadian Council of Social Development assesses the total value of family allowance payments to be about the same level as it was in 1976 and about half of what it was in constant dollars.[50] Moreover, the combined value of the child tax exemption and the refundable child tax credit is roughly equal to 100 percent of the value of total family allowance payments. In addition, a long list of administrative and social arguments have been advanced to support enriched family allowances over increased child tax credits.[51]

Several of the frequently cited arguments run as follows: universal family allowances are administratively simple and inexpensive. A parent merely files one application and a child receives benefits until the age of eighteen. However, a parent must file an income tax return annually in order to apply for the child tax credit. In 1978, it was estimated that the Department of National Revenue required an additional 350 person-years to process approximately 1.5 million income tax returns which would not have been filed otherwise.[52] Family allowances do not pose budgeting problems for families in need because payments are made monthly rather than in a yearly lump-sum as are child tax credits. Furthermore, child tax credits are slow to respond to changes in family income because an income test is applied before benefits are disbursed, not after. The National Council of Welfare's proposal to divide the credit into three instalments would only provide a partial remedy to these problems. In the final analysis, the family allowance demogrant is stigma-free whereas the selective system of child tax credits smacks of residual welfare; children are entitled to family allowances by right, not by social beneficence. There is still another advantage which is crucial in the absence of concerted federal-provincial decision making: enriched family allowances are likely to be more acceptable to the provinces.

The federal government has the right to pay child tax credits. However, Michael Mendelson perceptively notes that "matters become less clear as credits become further removed from the tax system" because "the right of the federal government to run a general income supplement or assistance program becomes unclear."[53] It is conceivable that child tax credits could be construed as charities under provincial jurisdiction. On the other hand, enriched family allowances are likely to be welcomed by provinces such as Manitoba, Saskatchewan, and Quebec. Increased payments would provide a much needed increment to their income supplementation programs which are designed to complement family allowances.[54]

In addition, a reliance on child tax credits is accompanied by the risk that the provinces will appropriate the benefits to those at the lowest rungs of the income ladder. This is not to exaggerate the problem. Indeed, about five times as many low and modest income families receive the full benefit as those who do not. However, it is still a major problem insofar as the raison d'être of the child benefits system remains to help those in need. The enriched family allowances proposal would largely avoid this problem for two reasons: first, the magnitude of the increases would present political difficulties for provinces intent on quietly subverting the redistributive thrust. Second, the provinces would have less incentive to do so. By Kesselman's accounting, the provinces would gain about $180 million from the joint abolition of the child tax exemption and family allowance taxability, if his scheme were adopted.

Despite the advantages, the federal government is unlikely to follow a course that vaguely resembles Kesselman's proposal. Conservatives and Liberals alike do not appear to favour a universal system of increased family allowances. Moreover, while the child tax credit option is good politics at no cost, the family allowances option is bad politics at no cost. The restructuring of family allowances plays a major part in the politics of restraint. However, the child tax credit option, unlike the family allowances option, provides what governing parties require in order to be successful at the politics of restraint, namely a fiscal illusion. A tax expenditure such as the refundable child tax credit provides redistribution without the political liability of increases in public spending. Thus the challenge of the 1980s will likely be to ensure that the continued erosion of family allowances, combined with the enrichment of child tax credits, benefits those most in need. That challenge will require concerted federal-provincial decision making in the restructuring of family allowances.

NOTES

1. J. R. Mallory, *The Structure of Canadian Government* (Toronto: Macmillan, 1971), p. 37.

2. Interprovincial Conference of Ministers Responsible for Social Services, *The Income Security System in Canada* (Ottawa: Canadian Intergovernmental Conference Secretariat, 1980), p. 27.

3. Ibid, p. 28.

4. House of Commons *Debates*, October 31, 1978, p. 652.

5. Canada, *The Way Ahead: A Framework for Discussion* (Ottawa: Minister of Supply and Services, October 1976), p. 26.

6. In 1973 the Family Allowances Act was amended. Under the new act benefits were increased substantially and indexed to increase annually with the Consumer Price Index. Benefits were also made taxable. For a detailed discussion of these and other changes that were proposed in the early 1970s see Simon McInnes, "Federal-Provincial Negotiation: Family Allowances 1970–1976" (Ph.D. thesis, Carleton University, 1978).

7. *Toronto Star*, December 17, 1977.

8. J. E. Cloutier, *The Distribution of Benefits and Costs of Social Security in Canada, 1971–1975* (Ottawa: Economic Council of Canada, Discussion Paper No. 108, February 1978). See pp. 24–31 for a detailed analysis of the redistributive impact of family and youth allowances.

9. Economic Council of Canada, *A Time for Reason (Fifteenth Annual Review)* (Ottawa: Minister of Supply and Services, 1978), p. 110.

10. House of Commons *Debates*, October 31, 1978, p. 652.

11. Canada, *Integration of Social Program Payments into the Income Tax System: A Discussion Paper* (Ottawa: Department of Finance, November 1978), p. 33.

12. National Council of Welfare, *Bearing the Burden, Sharing the Benefits*, Ottawa, March 1978.

13. Brigitte Kitchen, "A Canadian Compromise: The Refundable Child Tax Credit," *Canadian Taxation* 1, no. 3 (Fall 1979): 44–51, provides a detailed analysis of the 1978 changes.

14. The differential exemption rate for children under sixteen and children over sixteen was abolished.

15. House of Commons *Debates*, October 31, 1978, p. 653.

16. Interviews. Interviews were conducted with officials from the Department of Health and Welfare and from provincial ministries of social services during September and October 1983.

17. The income threshold for eligibility was raised to $26,330 in 1982.

18. Interprovincial Conference, *Income Security System*, p. 104.

19. New Brunswick recently abolished statutory increases.

20. Interviews.

21. House of Commons *Debates*, November 29, 1978, p. 1625.

22. Ibid.

23. Rick Van Loon, "Reforming Welfare in Canada," *Public Policy* 27, no. 4 (Fall 1979): 499.

24. See the remarks of Mr. Gauthier, MP (Roberval) in House of Commons *Debates*, February 7, 1979, p. 2994.

25. Denis Lazure, *Les contentieux Québec-Ottawa dans le champ des affaires sociales* (Montreal: Notes pour un discours de Monsieur Denis Lazure [Ministre des Affaires Sociales] prononcé devant la Société Saint-Jean-Baptiste, 16 janvier 1978), pp. 30–31.

26. Québec, *L'impact des transferts sur la répartition des revenus du Québec 1967–1975* (Québec: Office de planification et de développement du Québec, 1979), p. 76.

27. In 1973 an agreement was reached whereby a provincial government may request the federal government to vary the rates payable under the Family Allowances Act in that province on the basis of the age of the child or the number of children in the family, or both, provided the smallest monthly payment in that province is at least 60 percent of the federal rate and the average monthly amount paid for all children in that province is equal to the monthly federal rate. The provinces of Alberta and Quebec took this option. In addition, Quebec has its own family allowances program.

28. *Montreal Star*, February 10, 1979.

29. Interviews.

30. Van Loon, "Reforming Welfare," p. 499.

31. Leonard Shifrin, "Federal Tax Credit Means Nothing in Quebec," *Montreal Star*, February 16, 1979.

32. Ibid.

33. Interviews.

34. House of Commons, Standing Committee on Health, Welfare and Social Affairs, *Proceedings*, December 9, 1982, p. 54.

35. Interviews.

36. Canada, *Detailed Impact of the 1978 Changes to the Unemployment Insurance Act* (Ottawa: Employment and Immigration Commission, November 1978), p. A-2.

37. *Montreal Gazette*, September 9, 1978.

38. *Canadian News Facts*, September 10, 1978, p. 2010.

39. Interviews.

40. Keith A. Banting, *The Welfare State and Canadian Federalism* (Kingston and Montreal: McGill-Queen's University Press and the Institute of Intergovernmental Relations, Queen's University, 1982), p. 177.

41. House of Commons *Debates*, October 11, 1978, p. 2.

42. Ibid, October 28, 1982, p. 21194.

43. Interview, July 1981.

44. Interview with Bud Cullen, November 1980.

45. House of Commons *Debates*, October 28, 1982, p. 21180.

46. Ibid, November 3, 1982, p. 20341. The remarks were made by the minister of finance, Marc Lalonde.

47. Ibid, October 218, 1982, p. 21178.

48. National Council of Welfare, *Family Allowances for All?* (Ottawa, March 1983). Also see National Council of Welfare, *The June 1982 Budget and Social Policy* (Ottawa, July 1982).

49. Jonathan R. Kesselman, "Family Allowances: How to Save and Pay to All," *Financial Post*, December 11, 1982.

50. House of Commons Standing Committee on Health, Welfare and Social Affairs, *Proceedings*, December 13, 1982, pp. 9–13 provides a statement by the CSSD.

51. Jonathan R. Kesselman, "Credits, Exemptions and Demogrants in Canadian Tax-Transfer Policy," *Canadian Tax Journal* 27, no. 6 (November-December 1979): 676–82, and Dennis Guest, "Canada's Universal Family Allowance System—the Keystone of a Guaranteed Annual Income," a paper delivered at the annual meeting of the Society for the Study of Social Problems, Detroit, August 1983.

52. Kesselman, "Credits, Exemptions," pp. 679–80.

53. Michael Mendelson, *Universal or Selective? The Debate on Reforming Income Security in Canada* (Toronto: Ontario Economic Council, 1981), p. 58.

54. See chap. 7.

Chapter Seven

The Working Poor, the Canada Assistance Plan, and Provincial Responses in Income Supplementation

DEREK P. J. HUM

In 1979 over two and one-half million Canadians lived in poverty.[1] Of greater significance is the fact that approximately 55 percent of poor families were headed by individuals in the labour force. This group is often referred to as the "working poor."[2] The working poor typically receive no aid because the Canadian social assistance system assumes a clear-cut dichotomy between those who cannot or should not work (the aged, the blind, the disabled, women with small children, and so on) and those deemed able-bodied and, therefore, employable. Those capable of working are expected to meet their needs through employment; consequently only the unemployables are considered worthy of public support. Although a variety of policies directed towards working Canadians with low incomes have evolved, these are generally independent of social assistance programs cost-shared under the Canada Assistance Plan.

By the early fifties, the employable-unemployable dichotomy had become entrenched in Canadian policy thinking. The employables were to be protected by minimum wage legislation to ensure income adequacy. Fiscal and monetary policies would maintain full employment, and unemployment insurance would give protection against the risk of unemployment. On the other hand, the unemployables—the aged, the blind, and the disabled—would receive support through federally cost-shared provincial programs. Aid for the residual "unemployed but employable" group, which did not qualify for unemployment insurance, continued as a joint responsibility of municipalities and provinces. The federal government extended cost-sharing to provincial programs providing assistance to this group through the Unemployment Assistance Act in 1956. But despite this patchwork of programs, many workers still faced inadequate income—even those working full-time year round.

The working poor attracted attention during federal-provincial meetings leading up to the Canada Assistance Plan. Initially, discussion centred on ways to deal with those technically employable but chronically unemployed. The scope of the discussion eventually expanded and three new ideas were considered for inclusion in CAP: rehabilitation of those on welfare to make them self-supporting, community development, and community work programs. Although the second draft of the CAP legislation included provisions for work training programs, the community work program proposal was modified under pressure from the Department of Labour and the more restrictive work activity provisions of the current legislation emerged.[3] In any case, the consolidation and extension of federal cost-sharing and the introduction of a "needs test" under the Canada Assistance Plan were potentially more significant for the working poor. The lone requirement under CAP was that a person be "in need"; therefore, provincial assistance to those working part or full-time but who were also "in need" became cost-sharable for the first time.

This chapter examines income maintenance for the working poor within the context of the Canada Assistance Plan provisions. Some necessary background and descriptive statistics on several initiatives and programs in Canada that affect the working poor are followed by a formal discussion of the policy issues involved in delivering income assistance to the working poor, in particular, the related issues of costliness of payments, the adequacy of such payments, and the advantages of limiting them to identifiable groups like the working poor. The important issue of work disincentives is mentioned since the fear that income transfers to those able to work will create large-scale voluntary unemployment is a major political concern. Finally, some provincial responses in income supplementation are considered.

Canadian Policy and the Working Poor

Concern over the adequacy of wages led Manitoba to introduce minimum wage laws as early as 1918. Eventually, other provinces followed but minimum wage laws alone were insufficient to help the working poor. Unemployment became the major policy concern. The federal government enacted the Federal Unemployment and Social Insurance Act in 1935 to deal with widespread unemployment but this act was declared ultra vires. The federal and provincial governments agreed to a constitutional amendment enabling federal action, and the Unemployment Insurance Act received royal assent on August 7, 1940, thereby providing a national unemployment insurance scheme for all Canadians.

Because the unemployment insurance program was initially designed according to insurance principles, many Canadians in seasonal or high risk jobs were excluded. As a consequence, the act had only a limited impact on the working poor. Major changes were introduced in 1955 to expand coverage but it was not until 1971 that the unemployment insurance program moved

TABLE 1

PERCENTAGE DISTRIBUTION OF LOW-INCOME FAMILIES, AND UNATTACHED INDIVIDUALS BY SELECTED CHARACTERISTICS, 1979

	Families		Unattached Individuals	
	Low Income	Other	Low Income	Other
Totals	100.0	100.0	100.0	100.0
Estimated numbers ('000)	628	5387	809	2508
By employment status of head				
In labour force	50.5	83.6	26.7	76.4
Employee	36.9	74.9	24.2	72.6
Employer	13.6	8.8	2.4	3.8
Not in labour force	49.5	16.4	73.3	23.6
By weeks worked by head				
None	48.4	12.8	66.4	19.3
1–19 weeks	11.1	2.3	11.7	3.5
20–29 weeks	6.1	3.1	5.7	4.5
30–39 weeks	4.9	3.7	3.2	5.0
40–49 weeks	4.8	5.0	2.9	6.5
50–52 weeks	24.7	73.2	10.1	61.2
By full/part-time status of head[1]				
Full-time worker	22.4	71.2	7.3	57.9
Part-time worker	29.2	16.0	26.3	22.8
Did not work	48.4	12.8	66.4	19.3
By major source of income				
No income	1.6	0.0	6.3	0.0
Earned income	38.1	88.5	25.8	76.9
Wages and salaries	29.0	82.9	23.6	74.5
Self-employment	9.1	5.6	2.2	2.4
Transfer payments	53.8	6.9	61.4	11.1
Investment income	3.4	2.8	3.2	7.1
Miscellaneous	3.1	1.9	3.3	4.9

SOURCE: Statistics Canada, *Income Distributions by Size in Canada*, 1979, table 87, pp. 170–73.

1 A full-time worker is a person who worked, mostly full-time, 50–52 weeks in 1979. A person who worked 50–52 weeks but mostly part-time or worked less than 50 weeks in 1979 is treated as a part-time worker.

significantly towards encompassing income maintenance. Although a new act in 1971 provided virtually universal coverage, it did not address the fundamental problem of the working poor, namely, inadequate income.

Interest in the plight of the working poor intensified in the late sixties. Both the Special Senate Committee on Poverty (the Croll Committee)[4] and the Castonguay-Nepveu Commission[5] directly addressed the issue. Both recommended the introduction of a guaranteed annual income (GAI), differing only in mechanics. The Croll Committee recommended a federally administered, federally financed negative income tax (NIT) uniformly applied across Canada. In contrast, the Castonguay-Nepveu Commission recommended a provincially operated two-tier program.

In 1970 a federal White Paper, *Income Security for Canadians*, proposed a Family Income Security Plan (FISP) to replace universal family allowances.[6] Under the FISP proposal, low-income Canadians, working or not, would be eligible for financial assistance. The assistance would be greater than family allowance, but would decline with income. The proposal was brought before the House of Commons in 1972, but allowed to die amid protests from federal opposition parties and private citizens.

In 1973 the federal and provincial governments again embarked on an attempt to reform the Canadian income security system. The federal government's *Working Paper on Social Security in Canada* declared that "the incomes of those that are working but whose incomes are inadequate by reason of family size . . . or by reason of their employment (low paying self employment or intermittent or partial employment) [should be] sufficient to meet their needs."[7] After two years of negotiations, a proposal emerged to replace the Canada Assistance Plan with an income support and supplementation scheme. However, several provinces rejected the proposal. Consequently, the failure of the review not only left the working poor without an income supplementation program; there were also wider implications since it placed in jeopardy programs developed by some provinces in anticipation of new cost-sharing arrangements.

An alternative method of providing income supplementation is through the personal income tax system; for example, refundable tax credits. A variety of tax credit schemes are now in place, but these have primarily developed around specific issues or recipient groups which enjoy considerable public support (e.g., the financial difficulties of renters and the elderly). Because provincial tax credit programs are financed solely from provincial revenues, most provinces have not adopted this approach. The major tax credit program is the federal government's refundable child tax credit, introduced in January 1979. Although this program provides some income to the working poor, it was not designed expressly for this group.

The many programs that now exist have not solved the problems of the working poor. There are a variety of reasons for this. First, minimum wage

TABLE 2

NET MINIMUM WAGE INCOME AS A PERCENTAGE OF SOCIAL ASSISTANCE INCOME BY PROVINCE AND FAMILY SIZE, 1980*

	Nfld.	P.E.I.	N.S.	N.B.	Que.	Ont.	Man.	Sask.	Alta.	B.C.
One adult	143	125	120	152	177	174	153	164	155	145
Two adults	93	98	91	101	128	109	112	119	102	101
One parent, one child	88	91	88	95	132	102	105	104	103	89
One parent, two children	83	79	74	91	121	90	89	87	86	76
One parent, three children	80	72	67	88	116	81	79	83	78	68
Couple, one child	89	85	77	95	120	97	94	98	87	85
Couple, two children	85	78	70	92	114	88	84	92	79	76
Couple, three children	83	71	64	89	111	81	76	87	74	71

SOURCE: National Welfare Council, *The Working Poor: People and Programs*, p. 101.

*Minimum wages are net employment-related expenses, and for single parent families, child care costs, to allow a more realistic comparison than if gross minimum wage incomes were used.

rates remain low—and become less and less likely to ensure an adequate income level as family size increases.[8] This is apparent from inspecting table 2, which compares the income available from working at the minimum wage with the amount of social assistance. While there is substantial variation across provinces, only for Quebec does the minimum wage income exceed the social assistance level. Additionally, for all provinces the ratio of minimum wage income to social assistance payments declines for both one and two-parent families as the number of children increases. This is due to two factors. First, minimum wage rates do not take account of the family responsibilities of the worker. On the other hand, social assistance levels are invariably adjusted to family size. In sum, families in all provinces except Quebec generally receive more money from social assistance than they would from working at the minimum wage. Furthermore, the income advantage from social assistance grows larger as the number of children increases.

Even when various provincial income supplementation programs are taken into account, the income of low- (and minimum) wage workers remain below

TABLE 3

A COMPARISON OF MINIMUM WAGE, SUPPLEMENTED INCOMES, AND SOCIAL ASSISTANCE EXPRESSED AS A PERCENTAGE OF THE STATISTICS CANADA POVERTY LINES, 1979–80, FOR A FAMILY OF FOUR[1]

	Annual Minimum Wage Income	Supplemented Annual Income[2]	Social Assistance
Newfoundland	53.2[3]	59.7	66.1
	(59.2)[4]	(66.3)	(74.1)
Prince Edward Island	(58.6)[4]	(65.3)	(70.5)
Nova Scotia	52.4[3]	58.8	58.8
	(58.2)	(65.3)	(65.3)
New Brunswick	53.2[3]	59.7	61.5
	(59.2)	(66.3)	(68.4)
Quebec	61.9[5]	77.4	61.9
	(73.5)	(91.8)	(73.5)
Ontario	53.3[5]	61.9	59.3
	(63.3)	(73.5)	(70.5)
Manitoba	54.2[5]	64.5	68.8
	(64.3)	(76.5)	(81.6)
Saskatchewan	67.1[3]	80.8	61.5
	(74.5)	(89.8)	(68.4)
Alberta	53.3[5]	60.2	90.3
	(63.3)	(71.4)	(107.1)
British Columbia	53.3[5]	60.2	78.3
	(63.3)	(71.4)	(92.9)

SOURCES: Annual minimum wage income, supplemented incomes, and social assistance are from David Ross, *The Working Poor: Wage Earners and the Failure of Income Security Policies*, p. 58. Poverty lines are from Statistics Canada, *Income Distributions by Size*, 1979, p. 20.

1 Adapted from Ross, *The Working Poor*, p. 58.
2 Supplemented annual income is the net cash supplement available from all sources in 1979 at the particular annual minimum wage. Income (benefits minus taxes and premiums).
3 Poverty line adjusted for size of largest provincial urban centre—population 100,000–499,000.
4 Poverty line for centres with population less than 30,000.
5 Poverty line adjusted for size of largest provincial urban centre—population over 50,000.

the poverty line (see table 3). Furthermore, not all provinces have supplementation programs. Low-wage workers in any of the Atlantic provinces, for example, do not receive provincial supplementation. And as noted, substantial work disincentives exist in provincial programs in all but four provinces (Quebec, Ontario, Nova Scotia, and Saskatchewan) since minimum wage earners (heads of a family of four) would be better off drawing social assistance (see table 3, columns 2 and 3).

INCOME TRANSFERS TO THE WORKING POOR

What are the major issues surrounding income transfers to the working poor? These may be examined by focusing on the relationship between program design (tax rate schedule, "tagging," and the like) and policy trade-offs (costs of program, adequacy of benefits, and so on) within the generic framework of the NIT mechanism.[9]

Every income transfer program embodies some basic support level to which families are entitled if they have no other income, and some "tax" rate by which this amount is reduced for each dollar of earnings. Consequently, a welfare program may be characterized succinctly in terms of the parameters of a negative income tax plan; namely, the basic support or "guarantee," S, and the benefit reduction (or offset) rate, B. A break-even point is given by S/B,; it is that income level at which cash transfers or "negative taxes" are no longer paid.

The higher the support level chosen (S) and/or the lower the offset tax rate (B), the higher will be the break-even point. Consequently, the proportion of the population receiving cash transfers will be larger, and the total program costs will be larger, or equivalently, the average tax rate necessary to finance the program will be higher. The cost of an income assistance program is therefore greater with higher basic support levels and lower offset rates. High support levels are often advocated on grounds of "income adequacy," either because the basic support level S is judged to be unacceptably short of some absolute poverty line or because the basic support level is considered too small a fraction of the average income standard in Canada. But high support levels may foster undesirable incentives. For example, they may cause families to break up;[10] or again, high support levels and low tax rates may combine to diminish work effort. In fact, the work disincentive effect of a guaranteed income was the principal policy issue which led to several American experimental studies of the negative income tax, and it remains the centre of controversy still.[11]

The fundamental policy conflict between program costs, adequacy of benefits, and incentive structures may be set out more formally. Consider a negative income tax program defined by

$$T = -au + tY \tag{1}$$

where T is "negative" tax payments, a is the fraction of average per capita income (u) received by a person with zero income, so that au is the basic support level. The marginal rate of taxation on earnings (Y) is represented by t. Slight rearrangement of (1) yields the more familiar payment formula usually identified with a NIT design:[12]

$$\begin{aligned} P = -T &= au - tY \\ &= G - tY \end{aligned} \tag{2}$$

Summing (1) over all individuals in society, and dividing by total income yields

$$\sum T_i = \sum (-au) + \sum tY_i$$
$$= -anu + t\sum Y_i$$

Hence

$$\sum T_i \Big/ \sum Y_i = g = -a + t,$$

or

(3) $$g = -a + t$$

Equation (3) establishes the fundamental trade off.[13] The magnitude g is the ratio of net taxes collected to total income and can be taken as a measure of program cost. Higher levels of support (an increase in a) can only be achieved by higher costs (an increase in g) or at the expense of higher marginal tax rates. Since high marginal tax rates are associated in economic theory with labour supply reductions, the effect of higher marginal tax rates on individual behaviour is usually phrased in terms of work disincentives. However, the direct cash transfer itself (au) may also engender effects such as family splitting and marital dissolution.

The policy conflict between generosity (a), incentives (t), and costs (g) implied by Equation (3) is also helpful in identifying the major concerns of the different professional groups. The focus of academic economists on labour supply and the tax structure (t) reflect their concern with work incentives, productivity, and labour markets. The quest by the social work profession for an "adequate income" for the poor is typically expressed in attempts to define the "poverty line" and to argue for increased assistance levels (a). Finally, the overall financial costs to government (g) is often the chief concern of public officials, particularly those in Finance and Treasury departments. The point remains that a fundamental conflict exists among costs, incentives, and benefits. Whatever the special pleading of any particular group, no program can be so designed that simultaneously "does not cost too much," "provides adequate benefits," and "has no work disincentives." The virtue of the negative income tax lies in its income-testing feature whereby benefits are scaled inversely to income; it is this basic principle that allows some scope for compromise.

In contrast to the tidiness, elegance, and advantages of a NIT design, current social assistance programs are often fragmented, duplicated, complicated, and distorted.[14] Particularly the object of criticism is the use of what Akerlof calls "tagging," by which is meant the use of various characteristics to identify particular groups for special treatment.[15] Income transfer programs become "categorical" as a result of such tagging. Some categorical programs employ demographic characteristics such as age or family status, and these are called demogrants; for example, Old Age Security and family allowances. Other categorical programs are based upon "subjective" tests such as "availability for work" (for example, unemployment insurance) or "likelihood of need" (Canada Assistance Plan). Income transfers are given to specific categories of people on the basis of assumed need in these cases. Therefore, the relationship between categorical transfer programs (that is, tagging) and the extent to which poverty is reduced depends upon whether the group singled out for special treatment and the low-income population are one and the same. Tagging is one means of improving the policy trade-off implied by Equation (3).

Suppose the poor comprise a fraction p of the population, and that they can be unambiguously "tagged." The poor are given a basic support level of, say, $S = au$; the non-poor are not given any support level. Everyone is subject to a common marginal tax rate t. The set of programs then comprise

$$T_i = -au + tY_i \qquad \text{for } p$$

$$T_i = 0 + tY_i \qquad \text{for } 1 - p$$

It is easy to show that tagging results in Equation (3) being amended to:[16]

$$g = -pa + t \tag{4}$$

Equation (4) reveals that the ability to tag the poor improves the trade off between g, t, and a. In particular, tagging allows for higher support levels for the poor with less distortion to the tax structure. But tagging may be costly to administer, and may even induce individuals to alter their characteristics in order to qualify for special treatment. The commonly cited example in Canada is unemployment insurance where it is alleged that significant numbers feign job search in order to be tagged as "available for work" and hence qualify for benefits.[17]

The justification for tagging in terms of an anti-poverty objective must therefore lie in the view that tagging is relatively cheap to administer, tagging will not create opportunities for individuals to alter their condition so as to receive benefits, and that the tagged group and the poor are one and the same. The first two of these conditions perhaps explain the popularity of demogrants; the last condition is an empirical one and is not generally satisfied by many of the tags frequently used in Canada (for example, unemployment insurance).[18]

The foregoing discussion suggests the following important policy questions. Should income transfers be delivered on a categorical or tagging basis? Or should the transfer system focus upon the income-testing principle? Should the working poor constitute a separate group for treatment? And can an appropriate tag be devised to identify this group? Finally, what special features, if any, would be necessary for a program designed especially to aid the working poor?

Despite the heated debate over categorical versus income-tested programs, the general superiority of one transfer method over another cannot be established. Income-tested transfers can reduce poverty to a greater extent than categorical programs if the tagged groups do not correspond closely to the low income population. On the other hand, tagging may create less distortion to the incentive structure; it may also select those in special need (for example, manpower programs, social services) very efficiently.[19] In short, the policy gains of any redistribution must be weighted against the losses due to adverse incentive effects.

The more narrow policy issues concern whether or not the working poor group should be tagged, whether or not a sufficiently discriminating tag can be found, and whether or not special programs for the working poor are necessary. Because every tag implies a social (or political) judgement concerning the "worthiness" of the recipient group, the question whether the working poor should receive special attention is highly controversial; the focus of the controversy being the alleged work disincentive effects.

The Working Poor and Work Incentives

Policy interest surrounding this controversy is easy to understand. The greater the reduction in work effort, the larger the cost to society of income maintenance for the working poor. Further, because society expects the able-bodied to work, any work disincentive effect attributed to income transfers will erode public support for assistance programs.

Worry over the possible work disincentive of income transfers has led policy-makers to retain the basic distinction between the working poor and all others who are poor. For example, discussion of possible guaranteed income designs retain the notion of a separate guarantee support level for the working poor (for example, the Castonguay-Nepveu proposal) who are to be distinguished (tagged) from the general population on the basis of various "employment-availability" or "work-eligible" tests.[20] In sum, the work disincentive issue provides a prima facie basis for retaining a very important categorical distinction in income maintenance.

However, the magnitude of any labour supply reduction due to income transfers is an empirical matter. The importance of reliable estimates of labour supply withdrawal has occasioned five large-scale social experiments in negative income taxation–four in the United States and one in Canada. The results from the American experiments are the best prime source of information about the probable work disincentive effect of income transfers to the working poor. Although the estimated withdrawals differ in each experiment, and significantly by demographic group, the disincentive effect may be as low as 2.5 percent or as high as 20 percent.[21] That is, individuals receiving a guaranteed income tend to work less than a demographically similar group by about 2.5 percent, though some worked 20 percent less than their counterparts who did not receive the guaranteed income. Whether these magnitudes are too high to justify a universal guaranteed income for all is a matter of political judgement. However, the experiments also reported favourable (and unfavourable) response effects unrelated to work effort so that any conclusion drawn about the economy-wide or social effects of a universal income maintenance program should be based on broader considerations than purely those of work reduction.

The question remains whether or not the working poor should be categorized as a distinct group for income maintenance and if so, how this should be done. Since society will wish to provide income transfers to the population in need but at the same time demand the reciprocal obligation of its members to contribute to their support according to their capacity, the issue of work disincentive is likely to recommend continued categorization. But categorization may be less objectionable and administratively cumbersome if "self-categorization" is adopted. Rather than rely upon various subjective assessments of eligibility, an income maintenance strategy designed to include the working poor might profitably consider wage subsidy or earning supplementation mechanisms. The exact details and administrative advantages of such schemes are not of concern here;[22] the important point is that such designs minimize work disincentives for the working poor and confine transfers to those who work a positive number of hours.

The major limitation of the current CAP arrangements remains the fact that despite its avowed attempt to abandon the traditional categorical approach, a categorical approach with respect to the working poor persists. The tag "eligible for employment" in practice meant "ineligible for assistance." But the criticism of CAP with respect to the working poor is concerned less with the principle of categorization per se than with the inequity of a system in which assignment to one category rather than another results in vastly different rewards for those in "need or likelihood of need." As Kesselman writes: "If all categories were to be rewarded, but on different conditions, then the incentives for individuals to falsify their true traits would be reduced. Further, the magnitudes of inequity . . . would be lessened."[23] Some categorization scheme to segregate the working poor from those who cannot or should not work is therefore probably necessary. What is unsatisfactory is to ignore the working poor altogether. And despite the attempt by CAP to move away from the categorical approach, the working poor are generally still excluded from provincial income maintenance programs.

PROVINCIAL RESPONSES IN INCOME SUPPLEMENTATION

Only three provinces—Saskatchewan, Quebec, and Manitoba—have implemented general income maintenance programs which apply to the working poor population. (See Appendix.) The Saskatchewan Family Income Plan (FIP) was the first such program. The FIP program provides monthly payments to families with dependent children and was introduced as a transitional program to be merged eventually with whatever income supplementation scheme resulted from the social security review.[24] When no such scheme emerged, Saskatchewan was forced to seek funding for the program under CAP, but since cost-sharing eligibility under CAP was restricted to needs-tested recipients, not all of the expenditures under FIP were shareable. As a consequence, eligibility conditions have been tightened,[25] benefit levels have been allowed to decline under FIP, and political support for the program has lessened.[26] Nonetheless, the Family Income Plan was an important development. As an income-tested program FIP incorporated a tax back rate of less than 100 percent; thus, in contrast to other social assistance programs FIP provides substantial work incentives.[27] Significantly, the Saskatchewan program also established provincial jurisdiction over this type of supplementation program, thereby assuring some measure of integration with provincial social assistance schemes. The Family Income Plan therefore established a precedent. The needs test requirement of the Canada Assistance Plan proved to be a major stumbling block, however. Whereas income-tested programs allow income supplementation to be paid to those leaving social assistance in order to smooth the transition to work, a needs-tested program does not.

Under pressure to deal with the problems of the working poor and to overcome the lack of work incentives in the existing social assistance system, other governments began to consider supplementation programs of their own. The only other provinces to follow Saskatchewan's lead and establish fairly general income-tested programs providing direct cash payments to poor families are Quebec and Manitoba. Quebec introduced its Work Income Supplementation Program in 1979 designed specifically to aid the working poor.[28] The Quebec plan operates as a supplement to earned income and is self-categorizing. Only those who work, and have low earnings relative to their overall family needs, receive income supplements. The income supplements decline as income increases and are designed so as to integrate with the province's other income security programs. The Quebec program represents a significant advance in income maintenance for the working poor. Not only is the program self-categorizing, it is also harmonized with other programs such as family allowance and minimum wage laws. It may be seen as the culmination of efforts in this direction over a lengthy period and a reflection of Quebec's traditional stance of "going it alone" in matters of social policy if need be, even to the extent of eschewing cost-sharing under CAP.

The Manitoba program is called the Child Related Income Support Program (CRISP) and was introduced in 1981.[29] The proposals were announced in 1980 as a White Paper appended to the budget speech. As its name suggests, the program is child-related in terms of determining eligibility. It delivers cash supplements based upon income rather than earnings, and consequently is not specific to the working poor although it may include those working poor with children. The CRISP program was introduced by the Conservative government but in its initial year of operation the New Democratic Party assumed office and formed a task force to review social assistance. Although the task force has issued its report (the Ryant report), no action has been taken. Consequently, the fate of CRISP and the future direction of income maintenance policy in Manitoba are uncertain.

It is important to note the very special circumstances which led the three provinces which have income supplementation programs to introduce them. Saskatchewan introduced its plan to establish a claim over jurisdiction and in anticipation of new cost-sharing arrangements. It also wanted to integrate its program with the Saskatchewan Assistance Plan. Quebec has long had a history of harmonizing its social programs and its introduction of a program for the working poor reflects its ongoing resolve to develop an independent and comprehensive social security system specific to its provincial needs. Manitoba, arguably, introduced the CRISP reforms only when the Conservative government faced an approaching election and was fearful that its earlier and severe restraint policies would be too well remembered. If the initiatives of Saskatchewan, Quebec, and Manitoba can be ascribed to particular circumstances, then the more important question remains why there are so few provincial responses to the working poor.

Part of the explanation is due to the cost-sharing arrangement of CAP, in particular the requirement of a needs test. The needs test forced Saskatchewan to make a number of design concessions in order to obtain limited funding. Quebec's refusal to institute a nominal needs test and Manitoba's silence on whether it will do so means that income supplementation programs aimed at the working poor can be costly to the provinces. The "need or likelihood of need" phrasing of the Canada Assistance Plan Act is therefore a considerable obstacle to the future development of provincial income maintenance policy for the working poor. Yet in another sense, the CAP Act is merely a symbol. The deeper issues involve program design, social philosophy, and jurisdiction.

The CAP was an attempt to decategorize income maintenance. However, the greatest strides, both by provinces and the federal government, have been in programs targeted towards the elderly. In short, categorical programs continue to be the favoured delivery design, not only to limit costs, but also as a means of extending programs solely to those groups commanding wide sympathy. There is also the tendency for both governments to become involved with groups favoured by the public, such as the aged or children. The converse proposition is that neither government wants to embark on income maintenance for the working poor since these programs would be costly and not particularly popular. In other words, the working poor have yet to conjure up as sympathetic an image of the needy Canadian as say, the pensioner, in the mind of the public. Until that happens, low-income wage earners will continue to attract mere lip service from governments at both levels. Consequently, despite all the attention given to constitutional matters in Canada, jurisdiction for the working poor remains an unsettled question.

Conclusion

The condition of the working poor may grow worse in the future. Since 1975, increases in the minimum wage have not kept pace with inflation.[30] Furthermore, unemployment remains high and the unemployment insurance program has been revised by tightening eligibility. Introduction of federal and provincial income supplementation and tax credit schemes has intensified problems of coordination. As provinces initiate programs in response to local pressures and demands, program stacking may occur, affecting tax rates and making integration of different programs difficult. Provinces have also become increasingly vulnerable to unilateral federal initiatives; reductions in federal program outlays (as with unemployment insurance) may increase provincial assistance expenditures. Cooperation between levels of government has been affected and is perhaps now at an all-time low. The need for a coordinated income supplementation scheme is probably more important today than ever. Yet difficulties associated with the issues of income adequacy, program cost, work incentives, and jurisdictional responsibility remain.

The Canada Assistance Plan sought to shift the focus of transfers from groups of "deserving poor" to all "in need or likelihood of need." But the issue of the "working poor" was never satisfactorily addressed. This was partly the result of the divided and unsettled jurisdiction for the working poor, partly because of concern to preserve work incentives among this group, but also because the wording of CAP inhibited extending cost-sharing for programs to the working poor. At a minimum, the CAP legislation should be revised to facilitate the use of income-testing in place of the "need or likelihood of need" condition.

APPENDIX

SUMMARY OF INCOME-TESTED SUPPLEMENTATION PROGRAMS

Programs	Date of Implementation	Jurisdiction	Cost-sharing	Details
Income-Tested Direct Transfer Programs				
Saskatchewan Family Income Plan	1974	Provincial	Limited cost-sharing under CAP	Maximum benefit of $50 per month per child for first three children; $40 a month for each additional child. If after tax income <6,200 the maximum benefit is payable. Payments reduced by $0.50 for every dollar of income above the limit for maximum benefits.
Quebec Work Income Supplement Plan	1979	Provincial	None	Applicants complete a special form with their provincial income tax returns and submit it to the Quebec Department of Revenue which determines eligibility and amount of benefits. The program assures that families and individuals are financially better off working than on welfare. Those earning less than or equal to what they would receive under social assistance can apply for an income supplement equal to 25% of the earnings. Maximum benefits go to those earning incomes equal to the social assistance level. Benefits are reduced by one dollar for every three dollars of earnings above the social assistance level.
Manitoba Child-Related Income Support Program	1981	Provincial	None	Maximum benefits of $30 a month per child. If total family income (including federal family allowances and child tax credits) adjusted by $500 per child <$7,500 the maximum benefit is payable. Benefits reduced by $0.25 for every dollar of income above the maximum.

Tax Credit Programs				
Ontario Tax Credits	1972	Provincial	None	Property tax credit = $180 or occupancy cost (whichever is less), plus 10% of occupancy cost. Occupancy cost defined as 20% of rent or property taxes paid. Sales tax credit = 1% of total personal income tax exemptions. If taxable income is greater than $1,820 the combined property and sales tax credit is reduced by 2% of taxable income.
Alberta Renter Assistance Tax Credit	1973	Provincial	None	$80 plus 5% of annual rent less 1% of taxable income; the minimum annual credit is $50 and the maximum is $250.
B.C. Rent Aid Renters' Tax Credit	1975	Provincial	None	10% of annual rent or $150 minus 1.5% of taxable income (whichever is less) to a maximum of $150.
Manitoba Tax Credits	1974	Provincial	None	Cost of living tax credit = 3% of total personal income tax exemptions less 1% of net family income. Property tax credit = 20% of annual rent or property tax or $475 minus 1% of net family income (whichever is less). Minimum credit is $325, maximum is $475.
Saskatchewan Renters' Tax Rebate	?	Provincial	None	5% of annual rent up to a maximum of $115.
Quebec Real Estate Tax Refund	?	Provincial	None	(For owners and renters) = 40% of real estate tax paid (to a maximum of $1,000) less 2% of 'basic income' (total income minus a personal exemption of $4,150 for singles and $7,190).
Canada Refundable Child Tax Credit	1978	Federal	N/A	$200 per dependent child under the age of 18. Benefits are reduced by $0.05 for every dollar family income exceeds $18,000. The credit is indexed.

SOURCE: National Welfare Council, *The Working Poor: People and Programs*, p. 105–20.

NOTES

This research was supported in part by the Ontario Economic Council and the Social Sciences and Humanities Research Council of Canada under Grant No. 451-81-3739. I am indebted to Frank Strain for invaluable research assistance.

1. Estimate is based upon the Statistics Canada revised low-income cut-offs. The cut-offs take into account family size and size of area of residence and are designed on the basis of 1969 Family Expenditure Survey data. Cut-offs refer to income levels at which family units spend 63 percent or more of their income on food, shelter, and clothing.

2. Data adapted from Statistics Canada, 1979, *Income Distribution by Size*, Cat. No. 13-207, table 87, pp. 170–73. A detailed profile of low-income Canadians by demographic characteristics is attached as table 3.

3. Leslie Bella, "The Provincial Role in the Canadian Welfare State: The Influence of Provincial Social Policy Initiatives on the Design of the Canada Assistance Plan," *Canadian Public Administration* 22 (1979):439–52.

4. *Poverty in Canada: Report of the Special Senate Committee* (Ottawa: Information Canada, 1971).

5. *Income Security: Report of the Commission of Inquiry on Health and Social Welfare* (Quebec City: Quebec, 1971).

6. Canada, Department of National Health and Welfare, *Income Security for Canadians* (Ottawa: Queen's Printer, 1970).

7. Canada, Department of National Health and Welfare, *Working Paper on Social Security in Canada* (Ottawa, 1973), p.30 (commonly referred to as the Orange Paper).

8. This is not to suggest that the minimum wage is an appropriate policy instrument for eliminating poverty among the working poor. Most low-income workers actually earn more than the minimum wage. Very large increases in minimum wage rates would be required to move most families out of poverty. Moreover, minimum wage rate increases may even exacerbate unemployment problems. See Edwin G. West and Michael McKee, *Minimum Wages: The New Issues in Theory, Evidence, Policy and Politics* (Ottawa: Supply and Services Canada, 1980). Also, the correlation between low wages and low family income may not be as strong as generally presumed. See Wayne Simpson, *The Relation between Wages and Family Income in Canada* (Ottawa: Labour Canada Discussion Paper, 1981).

9. For a discussion of the actual administration of a negative income tax in Canada, see Derek P. J. Hum, "Canada's Administrative Experience with Negative Income Taxation," *Canadian Taxation* 3 (1981): 2–16.

10. J. Bishop, "Jobs, Cash Transfers, and Marital Instability: A Review of the Evidence" (Madison: Institute for Research on Poverty, University of Wisconsin, 1977).

11. See Derek P. J. Hum, "Poverty, Policy and Social Experimentation in Canada: Background and Chronology," and "Negative Income Tax Experiments: A Descriptive Survey With Special Reference to Work Incentives," in *Reflections on Canadian Incomes* (Ottawa: Economic Council of Canada, 1980).

12. Hum, "Canada's Administrative Experience," 1981.

13. George Akerlof, "The Economics of 'Tagging' as Applied to the Optimal Income Tax, Welfare Programs, and Manpower Planning," *American Economic Review* 68 (1978): 8–19.

14. *The Income Security System in Canada: A Report prepared by the Interprovincial Task Force on Social Security for the Interprovincial Conference of Ministers Responsible for Social Services* (Ottawa: Canadian Intergovernmental Secretariat, 1980).

15. Akerlof, "Economics of 'Tagging'," 1978.

16. A proof is given in Akerlof, "Economics of 'Tagging'." An easier alternative useful in manipulating other program designs is as follows:

Since

$$T_i = -au + tY_i \qquad \text{for } p$$
$$T_i = 0 + tY_i \qquad \text{for } (1-p)$$

Hence

$$pT_i = -apu + \quad ptY_i$$
$$(1-p)T_i = \quad + \ (1-p)tY_i$$

Therefore

$$\sum T_i \Big/ \sum Y_i = -pa \sum u \Big/ \sum Y_i + t \sum Y_i \Big/ \sum Y_i$$
$$g = -pa \qquad + t,$$

which is Equation (4).

17. For a review of the evidence, see Derek P. J. Hum, *Unemployment Insurance and Work Effort: Issues, Evidence and Policy Directions* (Toronto: Ontario Economic Council Discussion Paper, 1981).

18. Other policy designs, including the two-tier proposals of the social security review, are indicated in Derek P. J. Hum, *Federalism and the Poor: A Review of the Canada Assistance Plan* (Toronto: Ontario Economic Council, 1983), chap. 5.

19. Manpower programs and social services illustrate the added dimension of in-kind transfers rather than income transfers. In many instances services may be tied to income. CAP permits the use of "tags" to identify special needs in order to calculate income transfers.

20. This proposal was discussed during the social security review; see communiqué, June 1–2, 1976.

21. The experimental results vary widely and have not been subject to much professional scrutiny. A. Basilevsky and Derek P. J. Hum provide a critical evaluation in *Experimental Social Programs and Analytic Methods: An Evaluation of the U.S. Income Maintenance Projects* (New York: Academic Press, 1984).

22. For a discussion see Jonathan R. Kesselman, "Labor Supply Effects of Income, Income-Work, and Wage Subsidies," *Journal of Human Resources* 4 (1969): 275–92, and Jonathan R. Kesselman, "A Comprehensive Approach to Income Maintenance: SWIFT," *Journal of Public Economics* 2 (1973): 59–88.

23. Kesselman, "A Comprehensive Approach," p. 67.

24. David Ross, *The Working Poor: Wage Earners and the Failure of Income Security Policies* (Toronto: Canadian Institute for Economic Policy, 1981), p. 51.

25. See press release, November 8, 1976, "Criticism of FIP Misleading," issued by Saskatchewan Information Services.

26. Graham Riches, "FIP Flops," *Perception* 1 (1978): 42.

27. Although earnings from work do not decrease assistance payments dollar for dollar (100 percent tax back), financial work incentives are quite limited. In most provinces earnings are either sheltered up to some fixed level (with earnings above this amount taxed at a high, usually 100 percent, rate), or a fixed percentage of earned income (gross or net) is exempted. FIP offers greater work incentives because payments are reduced by 50 cents for each dollar earned above a specified level. For a description of FIP see Saskatchewan, Department of Services, *Income Support and Supplementation: The Saskatchewan Experience with FIP and SAP* (1976).

28. For a description of the Quebec program see Edward Tamagno, "The Quebec Income Supplementation Plan," *Canadian Taxation* 1 (1979): 63–66.

29. For an analysis of the CRISP proposals see Derek P. J. Hum and Harvey Stevens, "The Manitoba White Paper on Tax Credit Reform: A Critique," *Canadian Taxation* 2 (1980): 129–34.

30. National Council of Welfare, *The Working Poor: People and Programs* (Ottawa, 1981), p. 104.

Chapter Eight

Trends in Provincial Social Service Department Expenditures 1963–1982

H. PHILIP HEPWORTH

Although there has been recurrent interest in the nature of federal support for provincial social assistance and social service programs,[1] there has been little systematic or comparative analysis of the activities of provincial social service departments in Canada. Utilizing provincial public accounts and annual reports, federally collected statistics, and other historical materials, this chapter provides a detailed comparison of developments in provincial social service departments over the period 1963–64 to 1981–82.

The limitations of such data were identified by the Federal-Provincial Working Group on Costs of Welfare Programs, established in 1969, which cautioned against "drawing any conclusions concerning the relationships of welfare expenditures with those of any other government activity, or with the needs of welfare recipients" due to "inadequacies and inconsistencies in the data, and . . . lack of a uniform approach to data collection by provinces."[2] Nevertheless, the study of provincial social service department expenditures during the last two decades permits an examination of the initial impact of the 1966 Canada Assistance Plan (CAP) and a comparison of provincial trends since then.

The Historical Context

Growth in provincial programs reflects and to a large extent depends on a variety of factors, among which are population growth, changes in age structure, and economic development. The previous history of social programs within a province and other constraints or events also have a bearing on how particular services develop in a given period of time. We should recognize at the outset, therefore, that the introduction of the Canada Assistance Plan found provincial social programs at different stages of development. Moreover, these different starting points—what might be called the inheritance of social programs and facilities—may well account in large part for the persistence of differences between provinces despite the possible equalizing effects of various federal programs. One obvious area where differences may persist is with respect to residential institutions which may have been widely used in some provinces and not in others.

At the same time, there are some influences which affect all provinces. Chief among these is the spread of ideas about social programs. Modern social assistance programs, for example, trace their origins to the introduction of mothers' allowance programs first in Manitoba, then in most other provinces, in the period 1916–39. Similarly child welfare services were introduced first in Ontario, and then in most other provinces in the period 1893–1910. The introduction of old age pensions cost-shared by the federal and provincial governments after 1927 served also to stimulate the creation of social service delivery systems at the provincial level. Economic and social factors played their part in enlarging the provincial role in social services delivery. Whereas from 1867 on, the administration of relief and operation of residential institutions had tended to occur at the municipal or parish level, the provincial governments became increasingly involved during the depression years.

Provincial social service departments, as we know them today, date from the depression years and World War II. Responsibility for administering assistance programs, child welfare services, and institutional care was gradually consolidated and placed in one department in most provinces. The departments grew as the population grew in the 1945–65 period, and gradually professionally trained social workers and administrators were recruited. The introduction of the various cost-shared, categorical assistance programs—the 1952 Old Age Assistance Act, and the 1956 Unemployment Assistance Plan, added materially to the development of the provincial social service departments.

In addition to this steady development of the provincial departments, there were several reasons why further expansion of social programs in the early 1960s was needed. The development of the then existing provincial financial assistance programs, as well as of their categorical federal counterparts, had been piecemeal, so consequently they were not well coordinated or comprehensive and were ill-equipped to tackle the persistent problem of poverty. Unprecedented demands on the child welfare services, due to the rapid and continuing growth of the child population, as well as insecure funding arrangements for these services in several provinces, had created a crisis situation. People sixty-five years and older were growing in numbers and in many cases were impoverished. Rehabilitation and support services for the disabled were fragmentary. Existing community support services were largely located in urban areas, and even so served only a small part of their relevant target populations. Canada's population was still growing rapidly, and new Canadians in particular needed help in establishing themselves. This then was the situation which the Canada Assistance Plan was intended to address, and this is the starting-point for the present discussion of provincial social service department spending trends in the last two decades.

Impact of the Canada Assistance Plan

Because the Canada Assistance Plan grew out of existing cost-shared programs, expanded 50:50 cost-sharing did not represent an immediate doubling of the resources available to the provincial governments for social assistance and welfare services. It is true that mothers' allowance programs were fully cost-shared for the first time. But in the case of welfare services, existing expenditures in the base year, 1964–65, were not cost-shareable; it was only the additional expenditures which were shareable. Nonetheless, the subsequent growth in expenditures was rapid.

Growth in Real Terms

Table 1 reflects total provincial social service department expenditures over the period 1963–64 to 1981–82. Expenditures in real terms expanded by 50 percent between 1963–64 and 1966–67. In Prince Edward Island, British Columbia, and the Northwest Territories, expenditures actually doubled. Only in Nova Scotia and Saskatchewan was the situation virtually static. This initial growth reflects to some extent provincial readiness to make use of the new cost-sharing arrangements.

The full impact of the new legislation came in the period 1966–67 to 1969–70, when growth in real terms exceeded 60 percent. Growth was particularly dramatic in Ontario where spending more than doubled. Saskatchewan again remained static, and growth in Nova Scotia was modest. The western provinces, excluding Saskatchewan, grew by about a third. Table 2 identifies the percentage growth rate in total expenditures by provincial social service departments in three-year periods between 1963–64 and 1981–82.

As table 2 demonstrates, the rate of expansion was sustained in subsequent years. There was a further 50 percent increase between 1969–70 and 1972–73, and 46 percent growth between 1972–73 and 1975–76. Provinces such as Nova Scotia and Saskatchewan, which had been static earlier, suddenly exceeded all other provinces in their real growth rates, Nova Scotia by 187 percent between 1969–70 and 1972–73, and Saskatchewan by 130 percent between 1972–73 and 1975–76. This rate of growth, it must be remembered, was in real or constant dollar terms, so that the sudden burst in current dollar spending would appear particularly dramatic in these provinces and politically might be judged profligate. Nonetheless, this rapid growth represented a catching up with other provinces, or at least with their rate of expansion.

TABLE 1

TOTAL EXPENDITURES (CONSTANT 1971 DOLLARS) BY PROVINCIAL SOCIAL SERVICE DEPARTMENTS, 1963–64 to 1981–82 ($,000's)

	1963–64	1966–67	1969–70	1972–73	1975–76	1978–79	1981–82
Nfld.	27,208.0	33,569.3	44,775.7	51,989.7	62,162.5	63,275.0	61,018.9
P.E.I.	3,645.9	7,726.2	7,655.1	9,342.5	13,685.9	13,844.4	15,296.0
N.S.	12,051.9	12,821.6	14,446.4	41,496.6	58,210.3	69,718.0	75,937.0
N.B.	15,232.6	16,214.2	27,194.7	47,195.5	76,516.8	81,532.3	72,984.6
Que.	177,719.9	287,642.5	479,076.0	683,824.9	904,198.0	1,097,801.2	1,223,983.2
Ont.	78,614.0	120,362.6	269,831.9	394,978.7	617,278.5	683,628.5	723,707.3
Man.	24,414.0	35,604.0	48,897.4	85,127.9	77,164.1	89,685.3	99,515.2
Sask.	23,445.2	23,643.9	23,714.8	42,126.1	96,968.8	108,674.5	121,829.6
Alta.	46,963.1	59,973.1	77,850.5	134,692.5	175,975.3	195,731.5	321,783.5
B.C.	43,297.0	86,067.0	109,490.2	161,354.1	332,967.2	311,496.0	341,532.5
Yukon	511.0	641.4	1,546.4	1,570.2	2,591.4	2,402.9	2,832.8
N.W.T.	577.1	1,156.3	3,322.2	7,003.4	8,609.4	9,745.9	9,706.7
Canada	453,679.8	685,422.2	1,107,801.2	1,660,702.0	2,426,328.1	2,727,535.6	3,070,127.2

TABLE 2

PERCENTAGE GROWTH RATE IN TOTAL EXPENDITURES BY PROVINCIAL SOCIAL SERVICE DEPARTMENTS IN THREE-YEAR PERIODS BETWEEN 1963–64 AND 1981–82 (CONSTANT 1971 DOLLARS)

	1963-64–1966-67	1966-67–1969-70	1969-70–1972-73	1972-73–1975-76	1975-76–1978-79	1978-79–1981-82
Nfld.	23.4	33.4	16.1	19.6	1.8	−3.6
P.E.I.	111.9	−0.9	22.0	46.5	1.2	10.5
N.S.	6.4	12.7	187.2	40.3	19.8	8.9
N.B.	15.3	67.7	73.5	62.1	6.6	−10.4
Que.	61.9	66.6	42.7	32.2	21.4	11.5
Ont.	53.1	124.2	46.4	56.3	10.7	5.9
Man.	45.8	37.3	74.1	−9.4	16.2	11.0
Sask.	0.8	0.3	77.6	130.2	12.1	12.1
Alta.	27.7	29.8	73.0	30.6	11.2	64.4
B.C.	98.8	27.2	47.4	106.4	−6.4	9.6
Yukon	25.5	141.1	1.5	65.0	7.3	17.9
N.W.T.	100.4	187.3	110.8	22.9	13.2	−0.4
Canada	51.1	61.6	49.9	46.1	12.4	12.6

TABLE 3

RANKING OF PROVINCES BY PER CAPITA SOCIAL SERVICE DEPARTMENT EXPENDITURES
1963–64 TO 1981–82 (CONSTANT 1971 DOLLARS)

1963–64 Range $12.13–$57.16	Nfld.	P.E.I.	Alta.	Que.	Man.	B.C.	Sask.	N.B.	N.S.	Ont.
Mean $23.96	57.16	33.76	33.47	32.42	25.73	25.48	25.13	25.01	16.04	12.13
1966–67 Range $16.96–$70.88	P.E.I.	Nfld.	Que.	B.C.	Alta.	Man.	N.B.	Sask.	Ont.	N.S.
Mean $34.00	70.88	67.68	49.53	45.18	40.80	37.13	26.28	24.71	17.13	16.96
1969–70 Range $18.57–$86.77	Nfld.	Que.	P.E.I.	B.C.	Man.	Alta.	N.B.	Ont.	Sask.	N.S.
Mean $52.36	86.77	79.83	68.96	52.59	49.95	49.55	43.30	36.26	24.83	18.57
1972–73 Range $46.31–$112.86	Que.	Nfld.	Man.	P.E.I.	Alta.	N.B.	B.C.	N.S.	Ont.	Sask.
Mean $75.70	112.86	97.60	85.88	82.53	80.63	73.48	71.35	52.01	50.34	46.31
1975–76 Range $70.64–$145.87	Que.	B.C.	P.E.I.	N.B.	Nfld.	Sask.	Alta.	Man.	Ont.	N.S.
Mean $106.15	145.87	136.02	116.28	114.07	112.45	106.15	97.82	75.95	75.17	70.64
1978–79 Range $80.74–$175.06	Que.	B.C.	N.B.	Sask.	P.E.I.	Nfld.	Alta.	Man.	N.S.	Ont.
Mean $115.65	175.06	122.38	116.93	114.18	113.11	110.85	99.05	86.90	82.57	80.74
1980–81 Range $81.95–$187.64	Que.	B.C.	Alta.	P.E.I.	Sask.	Nfld.	N.B.	Man.	N.S.	Ont.
Mean $122.85	187.64	130.30	128.82	122.56	113.17	106.36	104.34	92.37	85.62	81.95
1981–82 Range $83.91–$190.11	Que.	Alta.	Sask.	P.E.I.	B.C.	Nfld.	N.B.	Man.	N.S.	Ont.
Mean $126.12	190.11	143.00	125.82	124.87	124.44	107.48	104.80	96.97	89.61	83.91

THE DEFINITION OF NEED

So far we have left out of consideration the incidence of needs in different parts of Canada. We do not know the extent to which an explicit or implicit demand for services elicits a corresponding supply. We know that regional economic differences exist, and that the proportion of poor people is likely to be higher in some provinces than in others. But obviously a poor province is more constrained in responding to poverty than a wealthy one. Nonetheless, a poor province may decide to provide the needed services, whereas a wealthy one may ignore the problem.

Similar problems exist in the provision of personal social services. Some provinces may attach a higher priority to certain types of perceived needs than to others, and then provide the requisite services; other provinces may act quite differently.

But while there are factors making for diversity in service provision, there are influences likely to elicit similar, if not uniform, responses. Demographic trends are similar across Canada. Social and economic trends often manifest themselves in similar ways in different regions. The federal government uses a variety of fiscal instruments to promote equalization of resources across the country. Similar ideas about social issues tend to be diffused to all parts of the country. The recruitment of trained professional personnel by all provinces also promotes a greater measure of uniform thinking than might have been the case in the past.

GROWTH IN PER CAPITA SPENDING

One measure of response to need might be per capita spending in each province. Table 3 ranks provinces by per capita social service department expenditures over the period 1963–64 to 1981–82. By this token, Newfoundland and Prince Edwad Island spent much higher per capita amounts in 1966–67 than did other provinces, and this level has remained high in these provinces in subsequent years. However, in 1972–73, Quebec overtook these two provinces in per capita spending and has ranked highest among the provinces since that time.[3]

The earlier noted static level of spending in Saskatchewan until the early 1970s is again reflected in the per capita figures, and in ranking levels. Since 1972–73, however, Saskatchewan has maintained per capita spending around the average for the whole country.

Ontario, Nova Scotia, and Manitoba are provinces with consistently low per capita spending levels as compared with other provinces. One possible explanation is the role played by municipalities in providing social assistance and personal social services in these provinces. But municipal spending is taken into account in federal-provincial cost-sharing and in provincial accounts. As at the provincial level, so at the municipal level, some services are not eligible for cost-sharing, but might still be reflected in consolidated provincial accounts. The relative state of development of voluntary services could also account for some low spending in the public sector. Service delivery arrangements are another factor, since these three provinces have, along with municipal agencies, child and family agencies, or children's aid societies operating at the local level. At least one possible hypothesis is therefore that decentralized delivery systems are cheaper to operate than centralized provincial departments.[4]

Since 1966, the municipal role in delivering social services has been substantially modified if not eliminated in several provinces. In New Brunswick the local role of municipalities and children's aid societies was terminated on January 1, 1967. In Alberta, both Edmonton and Calgary have given up their remaining responsibilities for short-term social assistance payments, but along with other municipalities in the province retain a role in the preventive social services area. In British Columbia, the City of Vancouver Social Services Department ceased operation in 1974, along with several children's and family agencies responsible for child welfare. In Winnipeg, the city social services department remains responsible for the delivery of a wide range of social assistance and social services within the metropolitan area.

Spending since the Mid-1970s

After the rapid growth in spending in the period up to 1975–76, it is not altogether surprising that the rate of increase has declined. As we have already seen, some provinces remained static in spending levels even as others advanced dramatically. In fact, even in the 1960s, some provincial reports spoke of the need for restraint. But the period after the 1973 Arab-Israeli war and the resulting oil crisis brought many more signs of deliberate restraint as world economic conditions worsened. At the same time, the raison d'être for social assistance programs would justify more being spent on the victims of recession and poverty. After 1970, the demographic pressures on child welfare services eased, but activity in the enlarged services remained high. Newer services such as child day care and homemaker programs were also coming on stream.

In fact, in real terms there has been continued growth in provincial social service spending since 1975–76. The rate of increase in each of the two three-year periods between 1975–76 and 1981–82 was over 12 percent, but much lower than in the earlier time periods under review. The national averages also conceal cutbacks in real terms in Newfoundland and New Brunswick, and sharp growth in Alberta. The continuing effects of recession are now being seen in other provinces.

Social Assistance and Unemployment

At the beginning of the period under review (1963–64), social assistance payments accounted for between 68 and 97 percent of provincial social service department expenditures, with a national average of 83 percent. In 1980–81, the picture was dramatically different with between 45 percent and 66 percent of expenditures being clearly designated as social assistance payments. Despite the obvious swing towards personal social service spending, a large part of spending on residential care and child welfare services (discussed later in the chapter) is still attributable to maintenance of the people being cared for—for example, foster care payments—so that the predominantly income support character of provincial social services has been retained.

In 1963–64, the highest per capita spending levels—in Newfoundland and Prince Edward Island—coincided with the lowest levels of per capita "provincial gross domestic product" and the highest levels of unemployment. Conversely, Ontario with the highest per capita "product" had the lowest per capita social service spending. But other low "product" provinces like Nova Scotia and New Brunswick had low per capita expenditures, whereas a "prosperous" province like Alberta had high social service expenditures. With minor variations, this somewhat mixed if not contradictory picture remained the same in 1966–67.

By 1980–81, Quebec, with below average levels of prosperity, was the highest per capita social service spender; whereas the two most "prosperous" provinces, Alberta and British Columbia, were the other high spenders. Despite continuing low levels of relative prosperity, Newfoundland and Prince Edward Island had maintained per capita social service spending, whereas the other two Atlantic provinces, Nova Scotia and New Brunswick with somewhat higher levels of prosperity were still low in social service spending. Ontario, no longer a leader in national prosperity, but still above average, retained its low per capita social service spending.

Since 1963–64, the labour force has grown, and along with it (despite a slight fall in 1966–67) the number of unemployed; by 1980–81, three times as many as in 1963–64. Offsetting this increase in the number of unemployed, so far as demands on social assistance are concerned, is unemployment insurance, which was given an expanded role in 1971. But for people who are unemployable, or who run out of unemployment insurance benefits, and are or remain unemployed, recourse to social assistance is almost inevitable.

With population growth of 19 percent between 1966 and 1980, the persistence of poverty among the unemployable and the long-term unemployed, and problems of low income for some sections of the working population, the conditions were present for sustained and even growing demands for social assistance in the last two decades. The present prolonged recession and the associated increase in unemployment are simply added factors maintaining the demands for help. Whereas provincial social service department expenditures rose on a per capita basis by 277 percent in constant 1971 dollars between 1966 and 1980, unemployment rose by 289 percent.

Few provinces, in fact, matched the rate of increase in the number of unemployed in their social service expenditures. Nova Scotia and New Brunswick did so, but then their average per capita expenditures have remained low. Elsewhere, Saskatchewan and British Columbia increased their spending at a rate exceeding that of the increase in the number of the unemployed.

A picture thus begins to emerge of the persistence of poor economic conditions in some provinces or regions, and of particular spending patterns, which may be rooted either in the nature of particular provincial social service delivery systems or in the dominant political values in particular provinces.

Federal Transfers to the Provinces

The nature of federal transfers to the provinces in respect of social assistance and social services has changed over time as programs have changed and modifications have been made to accommodate local circumstances. Because in some ways the Canada Assistance Plan was a successor to the Unemployment Assistance Act, there was little or no break in continuity for some of the relevant services; but the consolidation of categorical federal cost-shared programs and the sharing of mothers' allowance programs did lead to expansion of expenditures. For services newly included, like child welfare services, there was a period of years before implementation was complete and the resulting expansion in services was fully cost shared. There was also a process of continuous modification as some institutions formerly under mental health and correctional auspices were made eligible for cost-sharing. This process led to some provinces forgoing federal sharing for some services which remained under departments other than the social service departments. In order to remedy this perceived inequity between provinces, beginning in 1974 the federal government made agreements relating to nursing homes and young offender services, and these agreements have by and large remained in force until the present time.

Consideration of provincial social service department expenditures in complete isolation from relevant expenditures by other provincial departments is therefore unwise. At the same time, the identification and disaggregation of expenditures outside social service department auspices is also fraught with difficulties, though not impossible. By and large social service department expenditures still provide the firmest ground for the purpose of interprovincial comparison, especially where federal transfers are involved.

Table 4 provides a ranking of provinces by per capita federal contributions to provincial social service departments for the period 1969–70 to 1981–82. The

TABLE 4

RANKING OF PROVINCES BY PER CAPITA FEDERAL CONTRIBUTIONS TO PROVINCIAL SOCIAL SERVICE DEPARTMENTS, 1969–70 TO 1981–82 (CONSTANT 1971 DOLLARS)

	1	2	3	4	5	6	7	8	9	10
1969–70 Range $19.01–$41.43	Nfld.	P.E.I.	Que.	B.C.	Man.	Alta.	N.S.	N.B.	Sask.	Ont.
Mean $23.27	41.43	31.36	28.42	21.88	21.87	21.25	20.89	20.02	19.72	19.01
1972–73 Range $25.74–$46.02	Nfld.	Que.	P.E.I.	Man.	N.B.	Sask.	Alta.	B.C.	N.S.	Ont.
Mean $33.77	46.02	45.55	36.67	34.95	33.88	30.88	30.35	29.22	26.47	25.74
1975–76 Range $33.59–$80.98	P.E.I.	Que.	B.C.	N.B.	Nfld.	Man.	Alta.	Ont.	N.S.	Sask.
Mean $45.68	58.82	55.72	53.32	53.01	46.84	42.79	39.08	37.79	34.99	33.59
1978–79 Range $42.01–$71.45	Que.	P.E.I.	N.B.	B.C.	Nfld.	Sask.	Alta.	Man.	N.S.	Ont.
Mean $53.41	71.45	64.83	62.34	57.30	51.56	47.61	47.22	45.11	43.28	42.01
1980–81 Range $42.53–$77.09	Que.	B.C.	P.E.I.	N.B.	Nfld.	Sask.	Alta.	N.S.	Man.	Ont.
Mean $56.20	77.09	66.57	65.29	64.56	54.33	48.01	47.02	44.94	44.75	42.53
1981–82 Range $42.89–$75.48	Que.	P.E.I.	N.B.	B.C.	Alta.	Nfld.	Sask.	Man.	N.S.	Ont.
Mean $57.08	75.48	74.14	67.05	64.35	56.95	55.50	50.16	47.28	46.32	42.89

per capita federal payments under the Established Programs Financing Act by definition have not been directly related to provincial spending levels since 1977, but a comparison of tables 3 and 4 suggests that a fair measure of congruence remains in the rank ordering of provinces, whether it is based upon per capita spending by provinces or per capita federal contributions. The higher-spending provinces tend to rank highly in terms of the federal contribution and vice versa for the low-spending provinces. Generally, this finding tends to support the accuracy of the data collection process using provincial accounts.

Generally, Newfoundland has slipped from a rank order of 1 or 2 in 1969–70 and 1972–73, to a rank order of 5 or 6 in subsequent years. Saskatchewan's rank order has risen between the earlier and the later years, whereas Manitoba's has fallen. There is otherwise very consistent ranking for most other provinces. Prince Edward Island, Quebec, and with an exception in one year, British Columbia have ranked highly, whereas Nova Scotia and Ontario have ranked lowly both for departmental spending and for federal contributions.

The per capita federal contribution (in constant 1971 dollars) ranged from $19 in Ontario to $41 in Newfoundland, at the beginning of the period under review, to $43 in Ontario and $57 in Newfoundland in 1981–82. The mean per capita contributions have increased from $23 in 1969–70 to $57 in 1981–82 (of which, in recent years, the per capita contribution under the Established Programs Financing Act was about $12.50 in constant dollars).

As a proportion of provincial social service department expenditures, federal transfers have fluctuated between 40 and 46 percent over the years, a small variation when all relevant factors are taken into account. The nature of cost-sharing instruments is such that retrospective adjustments are made in subsequent years to allow for under- or over-payments, and some provincial expenditures are not cost-shareable, so that the federal contribution will tend to be below the 50 percent mark under existing transfer arrangements.

The purpose of such comparisons as these is not particularly to see which province is doing well out of cost-sharing or federal transfers generally; nor does comparison between provinces using expenditure data tell us a great deal about how good the services are in one province compared with another. Rather, the figures and comparisons are best understood in relation to the history and circumstances of particular provinces and the country as a whole during the past fifteen to twenty years. It is obvious that some provinces like Newfoundland had relatively high expenditure levels in the early 1960s because local unemployment levels were high, and some provinces like British Columbia had relatively highly developed child welfare services, and so their expenditures were also high. Generally, therefore, comparisons have to be made with a great deal of caution.

The configuration of legislation, policies, programs, services, organizations, and agencies is obviously different from one province to the next; and even where some indicators appear to be comparable, striking differences between similar or neighbouring provinces illustrate that historically the types of provision made have been different. Moreover, provincial spending priorities may also be different and allow for quite wide variations in expenditure levels.

Even in a so-called centralized country such as Britain, where common legislation and regulations exist, local variation in level and types of services can be very great. A number of attempts have been made to develop sophisticated territorial need indicators, and to some extent these have been useful in pointing out striking differences in levels of basic services, such as meals-on-wheels, homemakers, child welfare, and so on. It becomes apparent that some distinctions can be made between relatively concrete services involving clearly definable units of services and those services which are either discretionary or which require the exercise of professional judgement. Again, comparisons between local governments can be useful since we are then forced to ask why differences occur, how they have occurred, and what they consist of.[5]

The personal social service data most suitable for making consistent comparisons over time in Canada are the statistics on homes for special care collected by the federal government since the late 1950s and child welfare statistics. Since social assistance payments are not readily available for analysis in disaggregated form, we shall look at the statistics on homes for special care and child welfare.

Adult Homes for Special Care

A major area of operations for provincial social service departments is residential or institutional care known under the Canada Assistance Plan as "homes for special care." Adult care institutions were listed for cost-sharing prior to the 1966 Canada Assistance Plan under the 1956 Unemployment Assistance Act. Child care institutions were included along with child welfare services when cost-sharing became available through CAP and are discussed in the next section.

The CAP formula allowed for the sharing of institutional costs when residents were deemed to have social needs. It is, therefore, not surprising to note that during the early years of CAP's operation, many institutions which had previously been operated under provincial health or correctional auspices were placed under the auspices of provincial social service departments, thereby becoming eligible for cost-sharing. At the time, this process was, in fact, encouraged as a step in the right direction by federal officials.

The impact of such transfers of responsibility on provincial social service department expenditures and on the level of CAP contributions should be taken into account; obviously such transfers of responsibility did not constitute a real

TABLE 5

NUMBER OF BEDS FOR ADULTS IN HOMES FOR SPECIAL CARE RATED FOR COST-SHARING UNDER CANADA ASSISTANCE PLAN PER THOUSAND OF POPULATION 20 YEARS AND OVER, AND 65 YEARS AND OVER IN 1966, 1969, 1972, 1975, 1978, AND 1980

	1966		1969		1972		1975		1978		1980	
	20+	65+	20+	65+	20+	65+	20+	65+	20+	65+	20+	65+
Nfld.	3.4	28.0	4.4	37.1	5.8	43.1	8.3	70.3	8.4	69.5	8.0	63.4
P.E.I.	8.9	45.7	15.5	82.3	17.3	92.7	18.6	102.4	19.1	105.5	17.9	99.0
N.S.	4.7	29.7	7.6	49.4	10.7	69.1	11.5	75.1	13.6	86.8	13.5	83.7
N.B.	5.6	36.6	7.0	47.0	9.4	62.9	10.4	70.4	12.6	85.0	15.1	99.9
Que.	5.7	52.7	5.0	46.3	6.3	47.9	7.8	65.9	7.8	62.9	7.7	60.5
Ont.	5.7	41.7	8.6	64.8	10.4	77.0	12.9	96.2	12.8	91.8	13.1	90.5
Man.	7.9	50.8	8.5	53.8	9.7	61.0	13.1	82.1	13.5	81.1	13.8	79.8
Sask.	7.0	43.2	9.0	54.3	10.4	59.2	14.4	81.4	14.6	82.9	14.3	79.8
Alta.	9.1	71.7	10.0	80.0	11.5	92.3	14.3	115.7	14.2	121.7	13.2	112.2
B.C.	8.0	51.4	8.1	55.6	9.9	67.0	12.6	87.4	14.1	93.7	13.5	87.1
Yukon					7.2	195.0	22.3	662.5	19.0	361.4	19.0	316.2
N.W.T.							4.2	84.4	2.7	42.9	3.0	50.1
Canada	6.3	47.0	7.5	57.6	9.1	68.4	11.4	85.7	11.8	85.5	11.8	82.9

SOURCE: Canada Health and Welfare Canada, *Homes for Special Care*, various dates.

increase in the level of available services, but did mean that such facilities became eligible for cost-sharing. The benefits accruing to residents in these facilities through coming under provincial social service department auspices may also have been considerable.

The number of beds for adults numbered 72,409 in 1966, and had reached 192,565 in 1981. The ratio of adult beds per thousand of the population twenty years and older rose from 6.3 in 1966 to 11.8 in 1980. The ratio per thousand of the population sixty-five and older increased from 47.0 in 1966 to 82.9 in 1980. Table 5 shows the disaggregation of these ratios by provinces and territories.

Again, care must be taken when interpreting these and other findings regarding numbers of beds available. Provincial listings of facilities are not always fully up to date, and, in any case, the number of "listed" or "rated" beds cost-shared in each home does not always translate directly into either "available" beds or "occupied" beds.

Another important point of difference among the provinces is the proportions of homes which are operated by provincial or municipal authorities, by voluntary or charitable organizations, or by private individuals or companies. The very marked differences in these proportions from province to province probably reflect strikingly different social, economic, and/or political histories.

Table 6, which shows the distribution of adult homes for special care by auspices as of March 31, 1981, demonstrates that most homes for adults in Canada fall under private or profit-making auspices. Just over 19 percent fall under provincial and municipal auspices in both cases, leaving 23 percent of homes for adults under voluntary or charitable auspices. These national averages conceal important provincial differences. Quebec, for example, has virtually *no* facilities falling under voluntary auspices, whereas in Ontario 27 percent of adult facilities are operated by voluntary organizations.

Many other contrasts can be drawn. For example, 19 percent of Manitoba's facilities for adults are under provincial/municipal auspices, whereas 44 percent of the adult facilities are under such auspices in Saskatchewan.

Another variable relevant to both expenditures and quality of care is the size of a residential facility. Generally, residential care is expensive. Whether there are significant economies of scale to be gained by operating larger institutions is not clear. What is recognized is that the larger the institution, the more difficult it is to ensure personalized care and to avoid some of the depersonalizing aspects of institutional life. In 1981, about 30 percent of beds in homes for special care for adults were in facilities of over 200 beds. About 23 percent of beds were in facilities with between 50 to 99 beds, and another 23 percent were in 100 to 199-bed institutions. This type of distribution was typical for all provinces with Quebec, Manitoba, Saskatchewan, and British Columbia having slightly higher proportions in facilities in the 25–49 bed range than did the other provinces.

The Federal-Provincial Working Group identified the high cost of residential

TABLE 6

HOMES FOR SPECIAL CARE FOR ADULTS BY AUSPICES, MARCH 31, 1981

	Provincial Municipal		Voluntary Charitable		Proprietary (Private)		Total	
	No.	%	No.	%	No.	%	No.	%
Nfld.	4	4.4	21	23.3	65	72.3	90	100.0
P.E.I.	16	59.3	4	14.8	7	25.9	27	100.0
N.S.	30	15.5	45	23.3	118	61.2	193	100.0
N.B.	7	1.8	61	15.6	322	82.6	390	100.0
Que.	318	47.5	3	0.4	348	52.1	669	100.0
Ont.	119	8.9	363	27.3	850	63.8	1,332	100.0
Man.	29	19.3	90	60.0	31	20.7	150	100.0
Sask.	88	44.2	96	48.2	15	7.6	199	100.0
Alta.	152	50.5	74	24.6	75	24.9	301	100.0
B.C.	20	2.7	196	26.9	512	70.4	728	100.0
Yukon	4	57.1	3	42.9	—	—	7	100.0
N.W.T.	3	60.0	2	40.0	—	—	5	100.0
Canada	790	19.3	958	23.4	2,343	57.3	4,091	100.0

care as a major factor contributing to the rapid growth in social services expenditures in the late 1960s. A true picture of residential care expenditures is not easy to obtain, however, since once again accounting practices within and between provinces vary over time. Social assistance payments to residents may, for example, be shown either as an assistance expenditure or as a residential care expenditure. Finally, in some provinces municipalities pay a share of the costs.

Nonetheless, the available evidence suggests that adult institutional care expenditures have grown as a proportion of all social service expenditures, or as in a province like Prince Edward Island, have always been a major part of total expenditures. In recent years adult residential care has accounted for about 25 percent of provincial social service department expenditures with the range going from less than 20 percent to well over 30 percent.

Child Welfare

Canadian child welfare services really matured and came of age during the last twenty years in response to a series of important demographic and social changes, including the peaking of the "baby boom" in 1959, and a rapid growth in the number and proportion of illegitimate births in the 1960s. Provincial child welfare services and nongovernmental child and family agencies underwent drastic expansion and reorganization during this period, and federal cost-sharing of child welfare services by means of the 1966 Canada Assistance Plan contributed substantially to this growth. Here we discuss provincial comparisons on the dimensions of expenditures in child welfare, the number of children in care and provision of residential facilities.

Expenditures

Some of the definitional problems already mentioned in relation to residential and other programs have an impact on any attempt to assemble consistent series of child welfare expenditures at the provincial level. Because a large part of child welfare expenditures involves the physical maintenance of children in care, some expenditures are likely to appear as social assistance expenditures rather than as child welfare.

Table 7 identifies provincial child welfare expenditures per capita of population aged 0–19 over the period 1963–64 to 1980–81. Ranking order of spending by provinces suggests that for seven years between 1963–64 and 1980–81, Manitoba, British Columbia, Alberta, Quebec, and Ontario, in this order, have been the highest spending provinces per capita of the child population aged 0–19 years inclusive, followed by Newfoundland, Nova Scotia, Prince Edward Island, and Saskatchewan with equal average ranking, and New Brunswick.

In terms of actual per capita expenditures, the latest year for which all

TABLE 7

PROVINCIAL CHILD WELFARE EXPENDITURES (ADJUSTED)[a] PER CAPITA OF POPULATION AGED 0–19 YEARS INCLUSIVE (CONSTANT 1971 DOLLARS)

	1963–64	1966–67	1969–70	1972–73	1975–76	1978–79	1980–81
Nfld.	3.45	6.29	8.84	13.37	20.24	22.26	27.53
P.E.I.	4.96	7.45	10.00	13.88	9.45	13.64	10.30
N.S.	4.22	3.90	11.90	15.05	13.25	15.00	17.36
N.B.	1.80	4.07	n.a.	8.03	n.a.	10.26	n.a.
Que.[b]	2.72	19.88	37.26	10.47	15.68	27.68	31.09
Ont.	3.24	8.02	13.46	14.59	18.81	23.41	27.65
Man.	7.32	8.79	12.24	20.87	39.66	39.88	43.14
Sask.	6.05	8.23	6.61	11.77	12.71	14.00	17.94
Alta.	7.46	9.47	13.55	13.82	22.19	22.67	35.99
B.C.	8.33	15.31	23.58	26.08	18.69	20.91	30.76
Canada[b]	4.20	12.12	21.80[c]	14.42	18.69[c]	23.71	29.48[c]

[a]Proportionate share of administrative costs included in child welfare expenditures.
[b]Includes some anomalous figures for Quebec.
[c]Excludes New Brunswick.

provinces are represented, 1978–79 gives a slightly differing ranking order with Manitoba at the top, New Brunswick at the bottom, and British Columbia falling to sixth position. It may be noted here that Manitoba over the years has tended to increase the proportion of its children who are in residential facilities, whereas New Brunswick has tended to remain at a fairly low level.

Although the child welfare expenditure figures must be treated with some caution because of problems of interpretation in some provinces and because it has been necessary to allocate a proportionate burden of administration expenditures to them, nonetheless, the resulting figures do appear to represent in the main consistent series. Looking at total child welfare expenditures, we see that the growth rate since 1966 is much higher in some provinces than in others, as reflected in table 8.

Of provinces with consistent figures, the highest rate of growth in current dollars are Alberta (1,115.8 percent), Newfoundland (1066.1 percent), and Ontario (871.5 percent). The provinces with the lowest rates of growth are British Columbia (579.3 percent), Saskatchewan (462.1 percent), and Prince Edward Island (327.4 percent).

Generally, it can be said that the rate of increase in child welfare expenditure has not matched the rate of increase in total provincial social service department expenditures. A partial explanation for this slower rate of growth appears to lie in the fact that child welfare departments were in virtually all cases fully operational when the Canada Assistance Plan was introduced in 1966, so that the impact on staffing levels, though important, would not be as significant as for some other newer services, and existing residential facilities would simply continue to be used. At the same time, social assistance rates were improved sharply in the years after 1966, and salary levels for all types of staff also rose sharply, so that the impact of cost-sharing on total departmental spending would be greater than for child welfare services alone. Moreover, services such as child day care and homemakers were in most provinces developed only after 1966. Finally, the main demographic reason for increased demand for child welfare services, namely, number of illegitimate births, fell after 1970, and at the same time the total child population was also declining.

In 1980–81, Canada spent half a billion current dollars on child welfare services, of which the federal contribution under the Canada Assistance Plan was $285 million. In constant dollars, the rate of growth between 1966 and 1981 was about 150 percent. Going back to 1963–64 and excluding some anomalous figures for Quebec in 1966 and 1969, the rate of growth in constant dollars was about 600 percent.

NUMBER OF CHILDREN IN CARE

After 1959, the number of children admitted to care increased steadily throughout Canada until a peak was reached in the early 1970s. At this time, a high proportion of the children in care were illegitimate. After 1972, the

TABLE 8

PROVINCIAL CHILD WELFARE EXPENDITURES (ADJUSTED)[a] PERCENTAGES OF EXPENDITURES IN 1966–67 (CURRENT DOLLARS)

	Nfld.	P.E.I.	N.S.	N.B.	Que.	Ont.	Man.	Sask.	Alta.	B.C.
1963–64	49.4	60.6	100.6	41.1	11.9	34.1	72.5	65.6	68.9	44.8
1966–67	100.0	100.0	100.0	100.0	100.0	100.0	100.0	100.0	100.0	100.0
1969–70	161.0	149.0	338.0		205.2	195.9	137.1	88.6	167.9	185.6
1972–73	271.3	227.2	474.4	236.2	61.7	239.3	255.1	161.9	194.6	240.8
1975–76	543.5	206.1	549.4		117.4	414.0	636.4	221.4	425.5	240.7
1978–79	731.4	365.7	753.6	488.3	247.5	627.2	773.0	302.2	565.6	325.3
1980–81	1,066.1	327.4	1,020.7		321.6	871.5	971.9	462.1	1,115.8	579.3

[a]Proportionate share of administrative costs included in child welfare expenditures.

numbers and proportions of children in care at the end of each year fell somewhat, though not the number of admissions. Admissions to care have almost doubled between 1959 and 1977, and this increased level of activity appears to have been maintained in recent years, even though the size of the child population at large has declined.[6]

Marked differences exist among provinces in the percentage of children in care and these differences tend to persist as reflected in table 9. Quebec, for example, had twice the percentage of children in care that Newfoundland had in 1961–62, and almost three times the percentage in 1980–81. So much are these differences the case that one can talk of high provinces, Quebec, Alberta, and British Columbia, and low provinces, Ontario, Newfoundland, Prince Edward Island, and Saskatchewan.[7]

A complete explanation of why more children are in care in some provinces than in others is not possible here. Ontario and British Columbia, for example, have historically had highly developed delivery arrangements and so on, and yet the proportion of the child population in care in each province has remained different. A partial explanation may lie in the network of over fifty children's aid societies across Ontario compared with the clustering of service provision in and around Vancouver, and the distribution of services on a regional basis throughout the rest of British Columbia.

In fact, the mix of services provided appears to have some influence on whether children are in care or not. Newfoundland has only been able to regionalize its services on a systematic basis in the last fifteen years but still has a consistently low proportion of children in care. Underdeveloped accessibility and services may, therefore, afford a partial explanation for the low numbers of children in care in Newfoundland. But lower rates of illegitimacy and family dissolution may offer alternative explanations. As well, Newfoundland has made a direct attempt to tackle the problem of poverty affecting children by providing financial assistance to relatives caring for them.

The influence of poverty on the child welfare services is not usually discernible from the analysis of the available statistics. The presenting reasons for children being admitted to care tend instead to reflect the personal characteristics of parents or children. Illegitimacy and single parenthood affect a high proportion of children served, and this applies to many children not specifically relinquished for adoption but admitted to care for other reasons.

Larger family size also appears to be associated with children having contact with the child welfare services. For example, the number of children involved in protection/prevention cases in Ontario is consistently higher than the average number of children per family in the general population. But while the Quebec study, Operation 30,000[8] confirms this general finding concerning family size, the report qualifies it by noting that delinquents tend to come from large families, that protection cases come from families of average size, and that child abuse cases come from small families (small being one or two children, average three to five children, and large families six children or more). The Quebec study also notes that larger families tend to occur in rural areas.[9] In addition, the proportion of children in care who are orphans is higher in rural areas than in other parts of Quebec, between 5 and 10 percent compared with 4 percent for the whole province.[10] Finally, in the total Quebec child welfare population, 11 percent of children have a deceased father and 12 percent have a deceased mother. The Quebec data, therefore, build up a picture of general family vulnerability without dealing directly with the issue of low income.[11]

The Quebec data are comparable with the British Columbia data on reasons for admission.[12] Some 16 percent of children in care in Quebec are reported to have been abandoned compared to 8 percent of admissions in British Columbia in 1976–77; in the latter case, however, nearly 43 percent of admissions are said to be due to parent failure and/or neglect.

RESIDENTIAL CARE

Comparison of provincial developments in the residential or institutional care of children presents a number of definitional problems. For the purposes of the Canada Assistance Plan, child care institutions include the range of residential facilities usually found operating in conjunction with provincial child welfare programs such as receiving homes, group homes, and residences for the emotionally disturbed. They also include training schools for juveniles where these are supervised or operated by provincial departments of social services and the residents are placed therein under a child welfare authority.

There are, however, a number of residual problems. Foster homes and group homes may overlap in terms of size, but only the latter are designated as homes for special care for purposes of cost-sharing. There are also interface problems in the areas of corrections and mental health. In the case of the rehabilitation of young offenders, where programs have remained or fallen under the auspices of corrections, they cannot be cost-shared under CAP. Instead, since 1974 on an interim basis there have been funding agreements signed with a number of provinces (Ontario, New Brunswick, the Yukon Territory, Quebec, and British Columbia). Where programs for emotionally disturbed children clearly fall under mental health rather than child welfare auspices, they cannot be cost-shared by CAP. This latter factor goes some way towards explaining why Quebec has more residential provisions proportionately than does Ontario, since some facilities in Ontario fall under mental health auspices and are thus not cost-shared.

Table 10 identifies the number of beds rated for cost-sharing per thousand of population age 0–19 years over the period 1968 to 1980. If we take the latest year for which figures are available, that is, 1980–81, Ontario and British Columbia both have 2.4 rated (i.e., rated or approved for cost-sharing) beds per 1,000 of the population aged 0–19 years inclusive; New Brunswick has 2.2 rated beds and Newfoundland 2.6 rated beds. Alberta has 1.9 rated beds. There

TABLE 9

Children in Care of Child Welfare Services as a Percentage of All Children in Each Province, Territory, and Canada[a] Aged 0–14 Years Inclusive in 1961–62, 1971–72, 1976–77 to 1980–81

	1961–62	1966–67	1971–72	1976–77	1977–78	1978–79	1979–80	1980–81
Nfld.	0.51	0.79	0.91	0.75	0.69	0.71	0.77	0.77
P.E.I.	0.90	1.25	1.19	0.91	0.84	0.97	0.96	0.72
N.S.	1.20	1.52	1.74	1.42	1.35	1.31	1.27	1.23
N.B.	0.65	0.98	1.48	1.44	1.24	1.20	1.17	1.14
Que.	1.21	1.91	2.20	2.06	1.98	2.04	2.09	2.14
Ont.	0.70	0.75	0.74	0.63	0.64	0.69	0.72	0.68
Man.	0.85	1.25	1.70	1.54	1.39	1.42	1.33	1.49
Sask.	0.79	1.02	1.15	1.10	1.07	1.07	0.98	0.98
Alta.	1.00	1.17	1.56	2.14	2.07	2.42	2.04	1.94
B.C.	1.12	1.48	1.69	1.62	1.55	1.53	1.53	1.50
Yukon Terr.	n.a.	n.a.	n.a.	n.a.	3.05	3.18	3.17	2.63
N.W.T.	n.a.	n.a.	n.a.	n.a.	3.07	3.10	3.17	2.40
Canada	0.94	1.27	1.44	1.35	1.32	1.38	1.36	1.35

[a]Exclusive of Yukon Territory and North West Territories in 1961–62, 1966–67, and 1976–77.

TABLE 10

NUMBER OF RATED [a] BEDS IN CHILD CARE INSTITUTIONS PER THOUSAND OF POPULATION AGED 0–19 YEARS IN 1968, 1969, 1972, 1977, AND 1980

	1968	1969	1972	1977	1980
Nfld.	0.3	2.7	2.4	2.4	2.6
P.E.I.	1.6	1.8	1.8	1.0	1.3
N.S.	1.9	2.6	0.9	3.2	3.5
N.B.	0.7	1.0	1.8	1.9	2.2
Que.	5.4	4.4	6.2	7.5	7.4
Ont.	0.8	0.9	1.2	2.2	2.4
Man.	0.9	1.0	0.8	3.4	5.2
Sask.	0.3	0.4	0.6	0.8	0.9
Alta.	1.5	1.3	1.5	2.2	1.9
B.C.	0.7	1.1	1.7	2.8	2.4
Yukon Terr.			7.6	9.5	10.1
N.W.T.				8.6	9.6
Canada	2.2	2.1	2.7	3.7	3.8

SOURCE: Canada, Health and Welfare Canada, *Homes for Special Care,* various dates.
[a]Rated for cost-sharing as Homes for Special Care under the Canada Assistance Plan.

are, therefore, some marked similarities between provinces. At the same time, there are marked dissimilarities. Manitoba has 5.2 rated beds and Quebec 7.4 rated beds, whereas Saskatchewan has 0.9 rated beds. The mean Canadian figure in 1980–81 was 3.8.

Given these similarities and dissimilarities in the basic provision of residential spaces by provinces, it is not surprising that some provinces have much higher proportions of their in-care population living in residential facilities than do others. Again this is a characteristic which, with some exceptions, persists over time. In the period 1961–62 to 1976–77, Quebec's proportion living in such facilities actually fell from 58.2 to 31.5 percent of their in-care population, but still remained the highest of all the provinces. Newfoundland and Alberta have consistently had relatively high proportions in residential facilities, between 17 and 24 percent in the case of Newfoundland and 13 and 16 percent in the case of Alberta. The proportion has gradually risen in Manitoba and British Columbia. By contrast, Prince Edward Island, Nova Scotia, New Brunswick, and Saskatchewan have consistently low proportions in such care.

The above observations are generally borne out when provinces are ranked in terms of numbers of rated beds for cost-sharing, the percentage of children in care in residential facilities, and the percentage of the total child population aged 0–19 years inclusive in care, who are in residential facilities as reflected in table 11. The provinces with a high proportion of their in-care population in

TABLE 11

NUMBER OF CHILDREN LOCATED IN RESIDENTIAL INSTITUTIONS AND GROUP HOMES AS PERCENTAGE OF CHILDREN IN CARE BY PROVINCE IN 1961–62, 1966–67, 1971–72, AND 1976–77

	1961–62		1966–67		1971–72		1976–77	
	No.	% of Children in Care	No.	% of Children in Care	No.	% of Children in Care	No.	% of Children in Care
Nfld.	167	17.3	379	24.0	300	17.0	337	24.4
P.E.I.	34	10.1	10	2.1	13	7.7	12[b]	4.0
N.S.	168	5.5	194	5.0	140	3.3	167	5.4
N.B.	137	9.2	74	3.4	187[b]	6.2	209	7.6
Que.	13,152[a]	58.2	10,104	27.3	12,564	31.9	9,836	31.5
Ont.	1,582	11.3	1,548	9.4	2,234	13.7	2,952	22.8
Man.	100	3.9	325[b]	8.5	390[b]	8.0	939	23.4
Sask.	184[b]	7.4	228	6.9	291	9.0	162	6.0
Alta.	746	15.9	791	13.3	1,078	13.4	1,705	16.3
B.C.	375[b]	6.6	688	8.1	1,583	15.4	1,874	19.8
Total	16,545	28.8	13,701	17.2	18,783	20.6	18,193	23.2
Percentage of 0–19-year age group		2.17		1.63		2.22		2.22

[a]Includes institutions for unmarried mothers.
[b]Estimate.

residential facilities tend to rank highest in terms of such children as a proportion of the child population and in terms of spending levels.

Finally, there has been a measure of consistency in terms of the proportion of the total child population aged 0–19 years living in residential care. In the four years 1961–62, 1966–67, 1971–72, and 1976–77 the numbers per 1000 have been 2.17, 1.63, 2.22, and 2.22 respectively. Because of numbers, Quebec has been the predominant influence in this consistency, though their numbers of children in such care fell from 13,152 in 1961–62 to 9,836 in 1976–77.

The availability of residential facilities obviously has some influence on whether they are used or not. Although Quebec has made serious efforts to reduce its use of residential institutions, they remain a large part of its available placement resources. The Homes for Special Care figures show an increase in the number of residential places available for children in Canada but some decline in average size of the homes. These trends have some relevance to current interest in deinstitutionalization, but the available information suggests the need or, and continued reliance on, a diversified range of placement facilities.

Although it is possible to draw comparisons between provinces with regard to child welfare services, this should only be done with great caution. The history, legislation, and structure of provincial services differ. Nonetheless, provincial child welfare services have been subject to similar social, legal, and demographic influences and have responded in similar ways. The provinces have also all received cost-sharing under the Canada Assistance Plan since 1966, and have all increased their spending in real terms on child welfare services, even though the rates of growth have differed.

Trends in Departmental Employment Levels

A reading of provincial annual reports for the late 1960s indicates that the infusion of additional funding from the Canada Assistance Plan contributions permitted many provincial social service departments and the agencies they supported to recruit more staff, and more particularly, more trained staff. There was also an expansion of both services and activities. This rate of growth was maintained throughout the period 1966, 1972, and 1978. Table 12 provides a comparison of rates of growth in provincial and territorial social service department expenditures, number of salary earners, and cost of salaries between 1966, 1972, and 1978. The number of salary earners doubled between 1966 and 1972, and by 1978 was three times the level in 1966.

When we juxtapose the provincial social service department expenditure figures with Statistics Canada quarterly figures for the number of provincial government employees in the social welfare sector in 1966, 1972, and 1978, as on table 13, some interesting trends emerge. While total provincial government expenditures rose by 555 percent in this period, social service department

TABLE 12

COMPARISON OF RATES OF GROWTH IN PROVINCIAL AND TERRITORIAL SOCIAL SERVICE DEPARTMENT EXPENDITURES, NUMBER OF SALARY EARNERS, AND COST OF SALARIES, 1966, 1972, AND 1978 (CURRENT DOLLARS)

	Total S.S. Dept. Expenditures			Increase in Number of Salary Earners			Increase in Cost of Salaries		
	1966	1972	1978	1966	1972	1978	1966	1972	1978
Nfld.	100.0	195.5	400.9	100.0	187.3	358.0	100.0	320.5	1,258.2
P.E.I.	100.0	152.6	381.1	100.0	218.4	287.3	100.0	420.3	1,271.1
N.S.	100.0	408.5	1,156.6	100.0	188.9	163.9	100.0	320.4	484.4
N.B.	100.0	367.4	1,069.5	100.0	331.6	410.3	100.0	505.4	1,205.4
Que.	100.0	300.1	811.8	100.0	275.0	292.4	100.0	448.2	970.9
Ont.	100.0	414.2	1,208.0	100.0	178.6	561.0	100.0	286.6	1,634.5
Man.	100.0	301.8	535.8	100.0	122.6	217.8	100.0	203.6	659.3
Sask.	100.0	224.9	977.6	100.0	96.7	136.4	100.0	152.6	463.6
Alta.	100.0	283.5	694.2	100.0	161.5	326.9	100.0	276.4	1,098.5
B.C.	100.0	236.6	769.8	100.0	n.a.	n.a.	100.0	n.a.	n.a.
N.W.T. and Yukon	100.0	601.9	1,437.3	100.0	910.0	1,615.0	100.0	1,486.5	3,578.2
Canada	100.0	305.8	846.4	100.0	200.2	317.0	100.0	325.4	1,032.2

SOURCES: Provincial and territorial public accounts, and Statistics Canada, *Employees of Provincial Governments*, Cat. 72-077 Quarterly, July–September 1966, July–September 1972, and July–September 1978.

TABLE 13

NUMBER OF SALARY EARNERS AND GROSS SALARIES IN PROVINCIAL AND TERRITORIAL WELFARE SERVICES IN THE QUARTERLY PERIODS ENDING SEPTEMBER 30, 1966, 1972, AND 1978, COMPARED WITH TOTAL QUARTERLY PROVINCIAL AND TERRITORIAL GOVERNMENT NUMBER OF SALARY EARNERS AND TOTAL QUARTERLY EXPENDITURES, AND PERCENTAGE RATES OF GROWTH IN 1966, 1972, AND 1978 ($ '000s)

	September 30, 1966				September 30, 1972				September 30, 1978			
	No.	%	$	%	No.	%	$	%	No.	%	$	%
Nfld.	553	100.0	462.5	100.0	1,036.0	187.3	1,482.3	320.5	1,980.0	358.0	5,819.1	1,258.2
P.E.I.	228	100.0	149.9	100.0	498.0	218.4	630.1	420.3	655.0	287.3	1,905.4	1,271.1
N.S.	288	100.0	353.5	100.0	544.0	188.9	1,132.5	320.4	472.0	163.9	1,712.4	484.4
N.B.	155	100.0	198.8	100.0	514.0	331.6	1,004.7	505.4	636.0	410.3	2,396.4	1,205.4
Que	2,240	100.0	2,411.2	100.0	6,161.0	275.0	10,805.9	448.2	6,549.0	292.4	23,411.4	970.9
Ont.	1,070	100.0	1,518.8	100.0	1,911.0	178.6	4,353.6	286.6	6,003.0	561.0	24,828.1	1,634.5
Man.	495	100.0	618.4	100.0	607.0	122.6	1,259.0	203.6	1,078.0	217.8	4,077.2	659.3
Sask.	982	100.0	1,155.5	100.0	950.0	96.7	1,763.0	152.6	1,339.0	136.4	5,356.5	463.6
Alta.	841	100.0	907.9	100.0	1,358.0	161.5	2,509.6	276.4	2,749.0	326.9	9,973.6	1,098.5
B.C.[a]												
N.W.T.	20		31.2		137.0		342.3		232.0		757.1	
Yukon					45.0		121.5		91.0		359.3	
Canada	6,872	100.0	7,807.7	100.0	13,761.0	200.2	25,404.5	325.4	21,784.0	317.0	80,592.3	1,032.2
Proportion of total no. of earners		5.0				7.0				7.5		
Proportion of total government spending				4.5				6.4				7.1

Total quarterly expenditures

July–September 1966 Government Total	%	July–September 1972 Government Total	%	July–September 1978 Government Total	%
$174,351.6	100.0	$394,939.3	226.5	$1,142,241.2	655.1

SOURCE: Statistics Canada, *Provincial Government Employment*, Cat. 72-007, various dates.

[a]No salary data for British Columbia.

expenditures rose 746 percent. In turn, while the number of salary earners in the social welfare sector rose by 217 percent, their salaries rose by 932 percent in current dollars. Social service salaries rose at a faster rate than social service expenditures as a whole in this period. It must be noted, however, that social service sector salary increases were only as high as, or were slightly below, increases in provincial salaries generally.

There is no easy way to determine whether the quantity or quality of service improved as a result of improved staffing levels and/or improved qualifications. A full answer to this question would require extremely reliable and detailed information—more than is available from ordinary public records.[13]

Generally, there is prima facie evidence that the combination of higher qualifications and more staff has at least provided the prerequisites for better services. On the other hand, Howard Glennerster has noted the tendency for "people-intensive" services such as education, health, and personal social services to suffer from what economists call the "relative price effect," namely, that since a large component of social services is attributable to personnel costs and because it is difficult to measure productivity, the growth of expenditures appears to exceed increases in productivity.[14] At the same time, demands for services may have risen along with the expectations of the general public. In fact, what constitutes demand and what supply may not be determined very easily, since increased staffing levels appear to lead to more clients being served, for example, in the case of preventive child welfare services, and in turn higher numbers of children may be admitted to care. But though caseloads may have fallen generally, further reductions may still be desirable both from an administrative and social work point of view.

Sharing in Prosperity

While there has been congruence between social service expenditures and increasing prosperity for some provinces, for others there is a lack of congruence. This is reflected in the social service share of total provincial government spending which fluctuated throughout the period under review, as indicated by table 14.

The fluctuations were the most dramatic in Newfoundland, where the social service share declined from 20.4 percent in 1963–64 to 9.9 percent in 1981–82. However, as a share of Newfoundland's domestic product, social service department spending remained relatively stable, increasing from 3.6 percent in 1963–64 to 4.2 percent in 1975–76, and returning to 3.6 percent by 1981–82. This is a reflection, among other things, of increased governmental spending in areas other than social assistance and personal social services.

Only Prince Edward Island had social service spending approaching that of Newfoundland as a proportion of domestic product in 1963–64, 2.2 percent. This rose to 3.9 percent in 1966–67 and 4.3 percent in 1981–82. All other

TABLE 14

PROVINCIAL SOCIAL SERVICE DEPARTMENT EXPENDITURES AS PERCENTAGE OF TOTAL PROVINCIAL GOVERNMENT EXPENDITURES BETWEEN 1963–64 AND 1981–82

	1963–64	1966–67	1969–70	1972–73	1975–76	1978–79	1981–82
Nfld.	20.4	17.1	12.2	9.4	9.5	8.4	9.9
P.E.I.	11.8	16.3	12.6	9.5	10.8	10.0	10.9
N.S.	8.6	6.8	4.5	8.0	8.8	8.8	8.8
N.B.	9.4	7.6	7.2	9.4	12.3	12.2	10.0
Que.	15.1	13.2	14.9	14.4	14.7	14.7	14.7
Ont.	7.0	7.0	6.9	6.5	8.3	8.0	9.0
Man.	14.4	10.3	11.8	16.0	10.3	9.8	10.0
Sask.	8.7	7.0	6.2	8.7	11.8	11.6	11.8
Alta.	10.9	9.4	7.5	12.8	9.2	9.6	11.4
B.C.	8.6	10.0	9.0	11.2	14.1	12.5	12.6
Yukon	4.9	4.7	6.3	4.2	5.3	4.5	5.0
N.W.T.	7.4	10.6	7.8	6.7	7.3	8.2	7.8
Total	10.9	10.1	9.8	10.3	11.9	10.9	11.6

TABLE 15

Provincial Social Service Department Expenditures as a Percentage of Provincial Gross Domestic Product and Gross National Product, 1963–64 to 1981–82

	1963–64	1966–67	1969–70	1972–73	1975–76	1978–79	1981–82
Nfld.	3.6	3.5	4.0	4.1	4.2	3.8	3.6
P.E.I.	2.2	3.9	3.4	3.4	4.3	3.9	4.3
N.S.	0.8	0.7	0.7	0.5	2.1	2.2	2.5
N.B.	1.3	1.2	1.7	2.4	3.4	3.3	2.9
Que.	1.1	1.5	1.7	2.8	3.2	3.5	3.8
Ont.	0.3	0.4	0.6	0.9	1.3	1.4	1.4
Man.	0.9	1.1	1.1	2.1	1.6	1.7	1.9
Sask.	0.7	0.7	0.7	1.2	2.0	2.0	2.0
Alta.	1.0	1.0	1.1	1.6	1.3	1.2	1.7
B.C.	0.7	1.1	1.2	1.5	2.5	2.0	2.0
Yukon and N.W.T.	0.9	1.1	2.1	3.3	3.3	3.1	2.8
Total provincial social service expenditures as percentage of GNP	0.8	0.9	1.3	1.7	2.2	2.1	2.3

provinces increased their social services share of their respective domestic products, but stayed fairly static as a proportion of governmental spending. With the exception of Quebec, which accounts for 14.7 percent of governmental spending, and British Columbia with 12.6 percent, the other provinces are similar in their proportions of government spending with a range of 8.8 percent to 11.8 percent.

By and large, therefore, social service departments have shared in the growing prosperity of their provinces but have not significantly changed their relative importance within overall governmental spending. Table 15 shows provincial social service department expenditures as a percentage of gross provincial and gross national product over the period 1963–64 to 1981–82. Total provincial social service department spending rose from 0.8 percent of gross national product to 2.3 percent in 1981–82. Given the increase in the types and range of programs, and given increases in staffing and salary levels, it is likely that provincial departments have played more of an income maintenance than a redistributive role with respect to social assistance recipients. The latter have shared in growing prosperity, but their relative position is likely to have remained the same.

As stated earlier, there were valid pressures for growth in social service department expenditures throughout the period under review. Consequently, some programs within departments have grown at a faster rate than others. Analysis of long-term spending trends appears to make possible the setting of priorities and goals in the social services, as in other areas.

Conclusion

Comparisons of aggregate expenditure figures require an awareness of the circumstances in which spending has occurred. In this study, persistent differences have become apparent in levels of social service expenditures and in types of facilities. Provincial departments have developed or expanded social programs at different points in time, affecting both absolute spending levels and rates of growth. Demand for services differs from province to province, as do the availability of resources. With such complexity, caution in interpretation is needed. But comparative analysis within Canada, as without, appears useful if Canadians are to make informed decisions about the social services they require.

NOTES

1. See, for example, Working Party on Social Services, *Interim Report* (October 1974); Canada, House of Commons, *Report of the Parliamentary Task Force on Federal-Provincial Fiscal Arrangements, Fiscal Federalism in Canada* (Ottawa, August 1981); and Derek P. J. Hum, *Federalism and the Poor: A Review of the Canada Assistance Plan* (Toronto: Ontario Economic Council, 1983).

2. Federal Provincial Working Group, *On the Costs of Welfare Programs*, Final Report to the Federal-Provincial Conference of Ministers of Welfare (Ottawa, January 1971).

3. Quebec did not sign a cost-sharing agreement with the federal government, but made use of the opting-out provisions of the Established Programs (Interim Arrangements) Act, and received a four-point income tax abatement in place of conditional grants. In other respects, Quebec has operated as other provinces have under the Canada Assistance Plan. This factor should be borne in mind in the present discussion, but we are primarily concerned here with actual expenditures of the provincial departments, rather than simply with the question of federal transfers.

4. In Nova Scotia the provincial government pays not less than 75 percent of municipal social assistance costs and 66.6 percent of costs of maintaining residents in municipal homes for special care. The province pays the full cost of maintaining wards who are children of unmarried mothers, and shares the cost of all other children in care on an equal basis with the municipalities. In Ontario, municipalities contribute 20 percent of short-term general welfare assistance and of the cost of child welfare services.

5. See, for example, Bleddyn Davies, *Social Needs and Resources in Local Services* (London: Michael Joseph, 1968); Bleddyn Davies, Andrew Barton, and Ian McMillan, *Variations in Children's Services Among British Urban Authorities: A Causal Analysis*, Occasional Papers on Social Administration No. 45 (London: G. Bell and Sons, 1972); Bleddyn Davies and Michael Reddin, *Universality, Selectivity and Effectiveness in Social Policy* (London: Heinemann, 1978); A. C. Beddington and Bleddyn Davies, "Territorial Need Indicators: A New Approach," pts. 1 and 2, *Journal of Social Policy* 9, no. 2 (April 1980); 9, no. 4 (October 1980).

6. H. Philip Hepworth, *Foster Care and Adoption in Canada* (Ottawa: Canadian Council on Social Development, 1980), p. 55.

7. The Yukon Territory and the Northwest Territories also have high proportions of their child population in care, but are generally omitted from discussion here due to the fact they serve a predominantly native population, and native children are proportionately overrepresented in the child welfare population in Canada, and special logistical problems apply to the delivery of personal social services in the north.

8. Quebec, Ministère des affaires sociales, *Operation 30000*, rapport final (Octobre 1979).

9. Ibid., p. 110.

10. Ibid., annexe statistique, tableaux A-49, A-50.

11. Ibid., tableaux B-13-1, B-13-2.

12. Hepworth, p. 59.

13. Graham Riches, *Spending is Choosing: Restraint and Growth in Saskatchewan's Personal Social Services, 1966–1977*, vol. 2, reference tables (Regina, Social Administration Research Unit, Faculty of Social Work, University of Regina, 1979), regarding problems of obtaining reliable staffing figures in Saskatchewan.

14. See Howard Glennerster, *Social Service Budgets and Social Policy: British and American Experience* (New York: Barnes and Noble Books, 1975); P. M. Rees and F. P. Thompson, "The Relative Price Effect in Public Expenditure: Its Nature and Method of Calculation," *Statistical News* (Central Statistical Office) 18 (August 1972); Frank Gould and Barbara Roweth, "Public Spending and Social Policy: The United Kingdom, 1950–1977," *Journal of Social Policy* 9, no. 3 (July 1980): 337–57.

Chapter Nine

Social Welfare Development in Alberta: The Federal-Provincial Interplay

RICHARD B. SPLANE

This chapter deals with the development of social welfare in Alberta in the 1960s and is primarily a case study of the relationship of the Canada Assistance Plan (CAP) to the provincial programs that were to become wholly or partly shareable under the plan. It is hoped that the inquiry will shed some light on the nature of federal-provincial relationships in the development of the Canadian welfare state. Did the leadership come from the federal level, as a number of writers have suggested? Has it been cooperative or competitive; harmonious or combative? Was it based on shared or divergent objectives? Were the relationships wholly determined by the broad policies of the two levels of government or were they substantially affected by individual ministers and by individuals and groups sharing common points of view within the federal and provincial bureaucracies? And can useful generalizations be made about this array of complex questions on the basis of a study of a few programs within a single decade?

These questions are considered here through an examination of the views expressed by Dr. Leslie Bella, who, in her extensive writings on Alberta's social welfare development in the 1960s,[1] has taken issue with other writers on the questions of federal versus provincial leadership. She suggests that her analysis provides a needed corrective to the studies of a number of Canadian political scientists—Smiley, Simeon, Dupre, Bryden, and Dyck—whose "analyses of the development of the welfare state in Canada give the leading role to the federal government."[2] More specifically she asserts that "federal initiatives were not . . . a major causal variable influencing the consolidation and expansion of Alberta's welfare state in the 1960s."[3]

This chapter questions Dr. Bella's conclusions in respect to the relationship of the development of the Canada Assistance Plan to the development of provincial welfare programs in the 1960s. By reference to a federal-provincial program not dealt with by Dr. Bella and by some generalized commentary on relationships respecting program development in the years after the 1960s, her views on the nature and locus of leadership respecting social programs are also questioned.

In referring to a number of Dr. Bella's findings and viewpoints, the author writes, at times, in the first person. This is because Dr. Bella in three of the works cited above refers to me as one of the federal officials centrally involved in the development of CAP.

Before one can understand the factors affecting Alberta's social welfare programs in the 1960s, one needs to know something of their earlier development.

Social Welfare in Alberta before 1960

Before the 1960s Alberta's record in the field of social welfare was notably and at times scandalously poor. Since 1935, the province had been governed by the Social Credit party. The party had come to power in the depth of the economic depression under the charismatic leadership of William Aberhart who had been a school principal and evangelical radio broadcaster. As party leader and premier, William Aberhart combined a radical theory of monetary policy, which could not be implemented at the provincial level, with conservatism in other policy areas. His views and that of his spiritual heir and political successor, Ernest Manning, respecting social welfare may have been affected by their religious faith, which could be described as prophetic fundamentalism.

Whatever the cause, Alberta's growth in prosperity during the 1940s and 1950s and its progress in a number of aspects of its social, educational, and cultural life was not matched in social welfare. Scandals arising from its handling of child welfare in the mid-1940s and involving an internationally publicized inquiry conducted in defiance of the provincial government by Charlotte Whitton[4] did little to change the policies of the government. Throughout the twenty-five years from 1935 to 1969, Alberta remained out of harmony with the social welfare thinking in the western world exemplified, for example, by the reforms of the Roosevelt era in the United States; the Beveridge plan for a welfare state in Britain; the federal postwar reconstruction proposals of 1945 in Canada; the social welfare developments in the neighbouring provinces of British Columbia and Saskatchewan; and the policy statements and advocacy of agencies in the voluntary sector, notably the Canadian Welfare Council (now the Canadian Council on Social Development) and the Canadian Association of Social Workers.

As late as the mid-1950s, the provincial Department of Welfare remained small and administered its categorical assistance and other programs largely from Edmonton. In 1955 it had only 145 staff members, none of whom were professional social workers. The municipalities, with meagre provincial cost-sharing arrangements, were called upon to provide almost all of such social services as were provided as well as social assistance. In many small municipalities, social assistance was granted by town clerks who were apt to be "both arbitrary and punitive"—a view expressed by two provincial officials who later became deputy ministers.[5]

The New Bureaucracy

As the decade of the 1950s was ending, there were few indications of change in the declared positions of the provincial cabinet on social welfare questions. Important changes, however, were occurring in the next level of policy making in the structure of government—the bureaucracy. Here a new group of officials were moving into senior positions in the Department of Public Welfare. The advent of this new leadership was made possible through the closely spaced retirement of the officials who had, from much earlier times, occupied the six or seven senior posts in the department.

In discussing the important bureaucratic developments that were to follow, I will be drawing on data in Dr. Bella's thesis, my own working relationships with the officials involved, and my recent communications with two of them, Duncan Rogers and William McFarland.

The latter was the first social worker to be appointed by the department, an event which occurred in 1958 and was an early indication of some melting in the government's attitude toward the profession, which was still (and incorrectly) identified with Charlotte Whitton.[6] He was a graduate of the School of Social Work of the University of British Columbia and his appointment as deputy superintendent of child welfare brought a new philosophy and new methods to the administration of services for children. An earlier appointment was that of John Ward who, although not previously in the social welfare field, readily identified with it and helped to open the department to broader influences and relationships. He was a participant in a plan worked out with Professor William Dixon, director of the University of British Columbia's School of Social Work, through which senior administrators from the Alberta department were admitted to the school for an academic year of education and training, irrespective of the level of their academic preparation. (There was no school of social work in Alberta until much later.) John Ward was one of the initial group of officials to benefit from this arrangement. Two others were Kenneth Motherwell and John Smith, who were later to provide leadership in the areas of income security and personal and community social services.

The person whose appointment as deputy minister in 1960 was to be of immeasurable importance in the policy and program changes of the next several years was Duncan Rogers. Rogers was the son of a United Church clergyman and had grown up in small Alberta towns. He recalls that during his boyhood in Carstairs, a town north of Calgary, he saw countless numbers of unemployed and homeless men riding the railroad boxcars and sometimes coming to the manse for food and help. After service in the Royal Canadian Air Force, the completion of a degree in education, and a number of years in banking—largely in Alberta's own regional banking outlets, known as Treasury Branches—he sought and obtained a transfer to the Department of Public Welfare. In that setting he believed he would have opportunities to develop programs that would meet the human needs that had been so manifestly neglected in the depression of the 1930s and were still not being effectively addressed.

For four years the position he held combined the duties of departmental accountant and director of personnel. This gave him a knowledge of all aspects of the department's work without being identified with the administration of its specific programs. It was during this period, before his appointment as deputy minister, that Duncan Rogers was influenced by the separate visits to Edmonton of two outstanding leaders in the voluntary sector of the social welfare field: R. E. G. Davis, executive director of the Canadian Welfare Council, and Norman Cragg, executive secretary of the Public Welfare Division of the council.

The visit of Norman Cragg was to be of notable importance.[7] Cragg was an Alberta-born social worker who was shortly to leave the council for an important assignment abroad before returning to succeed me in Health and Welfare Canada as director of unemployment assistance in 1965 and to become the first director of the Canada Assistance Plan. His visit to Edmonton in the late 1950s was for public discussion of the public assistance proposals that were part of the council's 1958 *Policy Statement on Social Security*. What he had to say about both the process by which the proposals were developed and the actions they called for were of special interest to Duncan Rogers. The process had involved members of the federal, provincial, and municipal network of the CWC's Public Welfare Division. Norman Cragg, as its executive secretary, had been joined for the development process by F. R. (Fred) MacKinnon who had been seconded to the CWC for this purpose by the Nova Scotia government. Fred MacKinnon, also a social worker, was to become one of the most influential provincial deputy ministers during the development of CAP and on through the sixties and seventies when he also performed various roles in the voluntary sector.

In the process of developing the council's proposals, Cragg and MacKinnon had been in close touch with officials at all levels in the Department of National Health and Welfare, notably the deputy minister, George Davidson, the director of the Research Division, Joseph Willard, and other members of that division, myself included.

Development of the Canada Assistance Plan

The outcome of this process were the proposals that caught Duncan Rogers's interest as he heard them discussed by Norman Cragg. In essence, they took as their starting-point the Unemployment Assistance Act, which had been passed in 1956 and amended in 1957, seeing it as a measure which pointed the way to a restructuring of the public assistance system in Canada. The proposals envisaged further legislation which would bring within the Unemployment Assistance Act—or a broader measure to supplant it—the shared cost categorical assistance programs for the aged, blind, and disabled as well as purely provincial categorical programs, notably mothers' allowances. The proposed integrated measure would replace the means test approach of the categorical assistance programs with the more flexible needs test approach that was demonstrating its value under some parts of the Unemployment Assistance Act.

Duncan Rogers found these proposals to be in harmony with his own assessment of the problems of public assistance and his ideas as deputy minister continued to centre upon them. I learned this in my first visit to Edmonton as director of unemployment assistance in 1960—a visit I extended for the purpose of exploring more fully with him and his colleagues the province's utilization of the existing federal-provincial programs and the prospects for a new integrated public assistance program which would also include vocational rehabilitation.

As a native Albertan who had left the province in the late 1930s (for study in Eastern Canada followed by service in the RCAF and further studies in economics, history, and social work at the London School of Economics and the University of Toronto), I had observed with concern Alberta's resistance to contemporary approaches to social welfare and the slow pace of its social welfare development. It was, therefore, with particular pleasure that I learned at first hand of the changes that were occurring in my home province. The cordial relationships established during this visit were immeasurably strengthened over the years. In the period leading to the enactment of CAP, exchanges of ideas, consultations on program issues, and collaborative planning sessions on the development of the proposed new legislation were too numerous to chronicle. They involved myself, my deputy minister, Joseph Willard, consultants and administrators in my own branch, notably Ronald Draper, D. J. Byrne, William Dyson, and latterly, Norman Cragg, and members of other branches, including the Research Division.

The close relationship of federal officials and Alberta officials during the lead-up to the Canada Assistance Plan, however, was not in any way unique. Similar relationships existed with officials in the other provinces. What was notable about Alberta was that Duncan Rogers was able to interpret the case for the restructuring of public assistance to his colleagues, to significant groups in the community and most importantly, to his first two ministers—R. D. Jorgenson and Leonard Halmrast. Their support for the evolving elements of

CAP was strong and consistent. Halmrast's position statements and his letters to federal ministers were of considerable importance in the arenas of political decision making in the mid-1960s.

Accounts of the development of the Canada Assistance Plan have appeared elsewhere[8] and accordingly only certain aspects of that developmental process require discussion here. A point to be emphasized has already been suggested: the process would primarily emerge from the policy lines associated with the Unemployment Assistance Act. Both the strengths and the defects of that measure contributed to its being the fulcrum for the integration of public assistance and the launching pad for the federal government in the action it was taking on welfare services—the welfare services component of CAP—complementary to the initiative it had already taken in 1958 on hospital and diagnostic services.

When George Davidson discussed with me my role as the first full-time director of unemployment assistance, he predicted that I would be involved as much or more in the development of a new program as I would in the administration of the existing one. Joseph Willard, when he succeeded George Davidson as deputy minister in 1960, was even more committed to that view. Within a few months he secured ministerial authority for the first step in generating new policy within the bureaucracy, namely the setting up of an interdepartmental committee. This Committee on General Welfare Assistance had the essential representation from the Department of Finance (then clearly the most powerful voice in government) and from other interested departments. I was appointed chairman and the secretary was Ronald Draper, a colleague with academic training in public administration who later became widely respected in the provinces for his administrative acumen and who, on secondment from Health and Welfare Canada, was to undertake brief assignments in a number of provincial welfare departments.

The existence of a formalized process of policy revision and reform materially affected my relationships and those of my colleagues in the Unemployment Assistance Division with the provinces. It became understood and accepted that the two objectives of the division were to encourage the optimum utilization of the existing act and to amend it substantially or replace it as soon as the opportunity arose to do so.

What was clear to seasoned provincial officials and became well appreciated by Duncan Rogers and his senior colleagues in Alberta was that their part—as officials—in bringing about policy changes in the public assistance field was crucial. As Dr. Bella noted in her thesis, there is little support from the public for improving general welfare assistance programs. Political aspirants and office holders find it easier to attack such programs and those who are said to be abusing them than to seek ways of strengthening them. Only when officials, with support from others in the social welfare field, succeed both in countering the stereotypes about welfare recipients and in insistently presenting evidence on the real costs of meagre and demeaning public assistance is the ground laid for legislative change. Even then the ministers and legislators are likely to insist that any improvements in social welfare services be accompanied by measures to encourage or enforce employment. Developing social assistance and welfare service proposals that would gain the support, first of welfare ministers and then of their cabinet colleagues, was the task faced in common by federal and provincial officials in the early 1960s.

Dr. Bella's thesis recounts the process of ministerial and cabinet conversion that was undertaken in Alberta. With variations, similar processes were occurring in the other provinces. In some there was considerable concern about the opposition that the integration of public assistance programs would encounter from those who were eligible or expected to be eligible for one of the categorical assistance measures. Although the trend was toward the integrated needs-tested approach and although the provinces had the option to phase out their old age assistance, blind persons' and disabled persons' allowance case loads and to receive cost sharing under the Unemployment Assistance Act, no province was prepared to go far in that direction until there was new federal legislation that made explicit provision for integration.

At the federal level the obstacles to the adoption of a new federal-provincial initiative involving public assistance and welfare services were formidable. The social policy priorities of the political parties were retirement insurance and medicare. Quebec, in the exhilaration of the Quiet Revolution, was proclaiming its determination to be fully in charge of its social programs. The Liberal party, then in opposition, responded to this mood within its principal power base by resolving when returned to office to attach an opting-out formula to all future shared-cost programs.

Various earlier accounts of how the Canada Assistance Plan emerged from so unpromising an environment have traced the political events within the three minority governments of the early and mid-1960s; have assessed the importance of the War on Poverty and the part played by its highly placed proponent, Tom Kent; have referred to the significant role the interim opting-out legislation played in providing the Quebec government with a face-saving means of participating fully in the new federal-provincial program while appearing not to; and have portrayed the social trends of the 1960s and the demands they generated for a wider range of publicly supported human services than had been contemplated in earlier decades.

In my own earlier account of the development of the Canada Assistance Plan,[9] I emphasized two points in addition to those touched on above. One had to do with the role of the late Joseph Willard. It was Dr. Willard who succeeded in having the public assistance question dealt with as complementary to the development of the new social insurance program, the Canada Pension Plan. Once a proposal for new public assistance legislation could gain acceptance as a major question for policy consideration in federal-provincial conferences, he anticipated that provincial support for nothing less than the Canadian Welfare Council's 1958 proposals would emerge and gain strong support. This proved to be the case. The provinces not only opted for the type of integration that had been proposed by the CWC but called for moving beyond the institutional welfare services covered under the Unemployment Assistance Act to non-institutional service. By the time the developmental process was complete, the plan embraced integrated social assistance and also extended to as broad a range of personal and community social services as federal and provincial officials, working together, could devise.

A second point I stressed was that the battle that was fought to secure the Canada Assistance Plan was not between federal and provincial ministers and officials. It was a battle between opposing forces with differing priorities within the federal government. In looking back at the successful outcome of the operation conducted by the minister and officials of the Department of National Health and Welfare, I made the following comment: "In the case of the Canada Assistance Plan, victory was achieved over formidable opposition when, as a culmination of prolonged and intense work at the official level, supporting forces in the anti-poverty programme of the Privy Council Office were brought into an alliance which also included provincial ministers and officials."[10]

The Question of National Standards

In the work from which the above quotation is drawn my remarks about the opposition encountered within the federal government were general. A more specific comment is appropriate now because of statements made at different times, and with some emphasis, by Dr. Bella. These were that federal welfare officials wanted the Canada Assistance Plan to contain "a universal standard of adequacy in welfare programs across Canada"[11] and "requirements for national standards."[12] Dr. Bella also stated, in the notes accompanying her article in *Canadian Public Administration*, that these provisions were removed from the draft CAP legislation as a concession to Quebec and that the removal was to meet the wishes of all the provinces.[13]

My recollection concerning the national standards question is that CAP contains all the specific standards that were ever regarded by federal officials as being practicable. But "standards" was both a term and a concept that we sought to avoid. No serious consideration was given to "a universal standard of adequacy in welfare programs across Canada," for two reasons. First, because it would have been impossible to formulate in specific terms and, second, because it would have violated the principle that the terms and conditions of assistance are for the provinces to decide.

What federal welfare officials and their minister and ultimately Parliament wanted the plan to do were the following: to have the provinces provide social assistance, based on a needs test, to all persons in need; to have the items of basic and special needs defined broadly; to encourage the development and utilization of community and personal social services; to ensure that appeal machinery was provided so that applicants and recipients had the right to appeal against administrative decisions; to require that length of residence in a province not be made a condition for the receipt of assistance; to strengthen the administration of social assistance and welfare service programs; to provide the basis for an information system by requiring the exchange of administrative and program data; to share in the operation of work activity projects for persons with limited work skills; and, above all, to encourage the prevention of dependency through the optimum utilization of these several components of the plan.

The element that was lost from the plan in the final stages of its last submission to the cabinet may well have been referred to as "national standards." What it was, however, was a provision for annual reviews of the administrative and program operation of the plan, province by province. Such a provision had existed in some of the earlier categorical assistance legislation. As CAP was being developed an annual review provision was regarded by federal welfare officials as offering a continuation of the type of creative federal-provincial consultation that had characterized the development of the plan. Having administered the Unemployment Act, which had no such provision, and which lacked any internal evidence of its social purposes, I was one of those who wanted to see an annual review provision in the Canada Assistance Plan. I, personally, had heard of no objection to it from the provinces and was distressed both by its eleventh-hour removal from the draft legislation and by the manner of the removal—which took place while Dr. Willard was absent and when no time remained to argue, at the ministerial level, for a reversal of the action. But having won the big battles for the elements of CAP outlined above, the departmental officials in Health and Welfare Canada did not grieve long over the removal of this provision in the final internal skirmish of a long and hard-fought battle.

The Competitive Metaphor

This record of an episode in the closing stages of the policy process of CAP'S development within the federal system is the only part of the story of that development, as I have just recounted it, that was not available to Dr. Bella in her research on this subject. Her selection and interpretation of available data, however, resulted in a quite different CAP chronicle than the one I have presented. In her account, the provinces, and particularly Alberta, are pictured as being the source of the ideas that ultimately prevailed, with the federal government having to make numerous concessions which added to or subtracted from whatever policy positions it had in mind at a given point in the developmental process. Dr. Bella uses various metaphors to enliven her account, employing the leadership concept in a way that suggests that leadership has a win/lose connotation. In more than one context she uses a high-stakes card-game analogy, referring to the provinces as "holding the top card."

To illustrate provincial leadership, Dr. Bella chose to refer to a Rogers-Splane exchange of correspondence in September 1965.[14] This was a time when Duncan Rogers and his colleagues were developing a program to strengthen the province's community and personal social services and when CAP was moving toward its enactment the following year. By the spring of 1965, after a major change in direction, the policy lines of the provincial measure that was to become the Preventive Social Services Act (PSS) had secured ministerial approval and Duncan Rogers was seeking to elicit the crucially important municipal support needed for its implementation. Dr. Bella quotes him as beginning a meeting with municipal officials in April 1965 with the following words: "The problem I have is that under CAP, Alberta will gain or recover, or not have to spend, approximately $10 million. What are we going to do with it? I'd like you to tell me. Specifically, I am interested in using this money to prevent people from having to get in to the welfare situation."[15]

The Rogers-Splane exchange of letters to which Dr. Bella drew attention includes a letter from Duncan Rogers to me dated September 22, 1965, in which he expressed the hope that PSS expenditures would prove to be shareable under CAP. He recognized that since neither act had been passed, no firm decisions were possible. He felt that by then his government was quite strongly committed to the PSS concept and went on to remark that "the matter of sharing will not be a deciding factor in whether or not the Province undertakes such a program." He added that "we are going to have to sell the program on its own merits and will sort out the matter of sharing afterwards."

Dr. Bella regards this letter as providing noteworthy support for her provincial leadership hypothesis, commenting that "This extract again shows that Alberta persisted in designing legislation broader in terms of reference than that of Ottawa and 'leadership' (at least in the case of Alberta) was not with the federal government."[16]

The tenuous nature of this conclusion, based as it was on slight if not contradictory evidence, led me to look more closely at the entire basis of Dr. Bella's study as outlined in her doctoral thesis. In the thesis she describes the two approaches she employed, the initial one being a "comparison of spending on social services by the two levels of government in the sixties . . . through visual inspection of the relation between spending in Ottawa and Alberta." In elaborating on this approach, Dr. Bella explains that "If spending in Alberta 'takes off' before that of Ottawa, then the province can be said to be leading. If on the other hand rapid increases in Alberta follow a change in the rate of increase of spending in Ottawa, then the federal government can be said to be leading."[17]

The results of this analysis were not, by Dr. Bella's own testimony, particularly conclusive. Not surprisingly, Alberta's welfare expenditures began to increase in the late 1950s because of the various measures taken in the Department of Public Welfare through the impetus of the new group of senior officials. Noting that "during the decade of the sixties, the general increase in health and welfare spending for both levels of government was between 300% and 400%," Dr. Bella remarks that this was not helpful on the leadership question but that semi-logarithmic graphs using the same data indicated that "federal initiatives do not appear to have influenced the pace of reform in Alberta."[18] She qualifies this, however, in stating that "spending as a measure of policy omits the purpose of that policy; there is no causal chain linking independent and dependent variables, and therefore there is no assurance of the direction of the relationship."[19]

This is, nonetheless, the quantitative basis for the conclusions she reached concerning provincial versus federal leadership in social programs.

Dr. Bella's second approach "involves the analysis of the context in which the initiatives were introduced in Ottawa and in Edmonton, to identify the influence of one level of government on the other."[20] As will be evident from the foregoing discussion, Dr. Bella's analysis of the factors affecting the various shared-cost programs in the period and the interpretation she places on them differ markedly from mine and from those of Dr. Rand Dyck.

Contrasting Federal-Provincial Relationships

In differing with Dr. Bella on the nature of the federal-provincial relationship that characterized the development of the Canada Assistance Plan, I do not contend that the amity and cooperation that I have suggested were present in this instance were typical of the relationship of the two levels of government in respect to all other programs.

Had Dr. Bella's inquiries, for example, extended beyond public assistance and welfare services programs to federal-provincial health programs, she would have found a classic example of a drama in which "the top card" simile and the various confrontational metaphors she used in respect to the development of CAP would have been quite appropriate. This is not the place to recount, in any detail, the saga of Alberta and nation-wide medicare. In its simplest terms, however, the Government of Alberta strenuously opposed the principle of public medical care as proposed by the Hall Royal Commission in 1964 and incorporated in federal legislation in 1966. Alberta was supported in its opposition by two powerful allies, the Canadian Medical Association and the Canadian Health Insurance Association, which had collaborated with the province in establishing an insurance company consortium. When the federal government, confident that it had strong public support, pressed forward with the implementation of the medicare program, Alberta signed its agreement with the federal government on July 1, 1969, but registered its strong protest. The province's health minister, who had been battling "socialized health and medical care" for more than a decade, resigned in bitterness from his post.[21]

Developments since the 1960s

That two such contrasting scenarios as those relating to CAP and medicare could be played out in the same decade, suggests that ten years is too short a period from which to draw useful conclusions about federal-provincial relationships on social programs. There may, however, be merit in briefly scanning subsequent developments by way either of discerning that there has been an underlying consistency in the approaches that have been followed or, alternatively, of establishing that broader and more sustained research is needed on how the two levels of government deal with each other in this important field.

Such a brief review of the period quickly establishes that there were no further examples in succeeding years of the level of harmony and cooperation that characterized the development of the Canada Assistance Plan. There was, however, a period following the election of the Conservative government in 1971 when Alberta played an active part in intergovernmental activities affecting social policy. This extended through the early stages of the Federal-Provincial Review of Social Security which began in 1973. Alberta played a creditable role in this collective endeavour to rethink and restructure Canada's social security system. Duncan Rogers, for example, served as chairman of the review's Task Force on Social Services. In addition, Bruce Rawson, the senior deputy minister of the Ministry of Social Services and Community Health, made a substantial contribution to the intensive deliberations on the income support and supplementation strategies of the review.

There seemed to be favourable omens for good relations between the two levels of government when Bruce Rawson was recruited to major administrative and policy roles in the federal government and his position in Alberta was filled by Stanley Mansbridge, a management mandarin from Ottawa. But even if that exchange had created a basis for continued harmony of relationships at the official level, other far more weighty and clearly negative factors were the emerging determinants at the ministerial and prime ministerial levels. From the mid-1970s and into the 1980s there was extreme tension and conflict between the federal and provincial governments over energy policy and the federal proposal for an entrenched charter of rights and freedoms within a patriated constitution. The most dramatic manifestation of the conflict was Alberta's action in reducing and threatening to cut off oil supplies to Eastern Canada.

So serious a deterioration of intergovernmental relationships could not fail to influence discussions on lesser issues. One of these was the proposal for a new shared-cost federal-provincial social services program. This had been agreed to by all provinces in 1975 but it lost provincial support and was withdrawn in 1978. An element in Alberta's approach to the matter appears to have been the highly favourable financial position Alberta enjoyed from oil revenues in the late 1970s. Whereas the incentive to secure revenues from federal shared-cost programs had been a vitally important factor through most of Alberta's history, such programs no longer held financial inducements for the province. Indeed, because of Alberta's high per capita income and the operation of the country's fiscal arrangements, a new nation-wide shared-cost program would take money from the province rather than adding to its revenues.

A second issue causing friction between the two governments was the province's initiation of a work for welfare scheme which appeared to be in violation of the Canada Assistance Plan if not of the Charter of Human Rights. The issue receded as the scheme itself dwindled in size and visibility but the scheme's initiation together with other actions of the provincial ministers in the social policy portfolios both relating to social programs and to the deployment of senior personnel seemed idiosyncratic, out of harmony with modern concepts of social welfare, and somewhat reminiscent of the mood and practices of the Alberta of the 1940s and 1950s.

A third and continuing issue was Alberta's adoption of user fees for hospital services and its failure to prevent extra billing by physicians. Because these practices in Alberta, and some other provinces, threatened Canada's national health insurance system, the Liberal government (1980–84) sought to eliminate them through having Parliament enact new legislation, the Canada Health Act. This shared-cost measure, enacted in June 1984 by a unanimous vote in the House of Commons, authorizes the federal government to withhold from the payments otherwise due to a province an amount equal to the sum of the hospital user charges and extra billing by physicians that were permitted to be made within the province. By November 1984 Alberta had not agreed to conform to these provisions of the act and the stage seemed to be set for a replay of the medicare shoot-out scenario of the late 1960s. The Progressive Conservative government elected in September 1984, with its commitment to improved federal-provincial relations, may, however, find means to carry out the terms of the federal act in some less confrontational manner.

Conclusion

The foregoing case study of the relationships between the implementation of the Canada Assistance Plan and certain provincial welfare programs, the reference to the medicare imbroglio, and the scanning of relationships between Ottawa and Alberta since the 1960s provide no easy answers to the questions posed at the beginning of the chapter. What is revealed is the presence of intermingled issues of great complexity involving the constitution, fiscal arrangements, human rights, the most vulnerable groups in the population, and special interest groups—including the medical profession and other powerful forces promoting various forms of privatization. Given the presence of issues of this character and magnitude, it seems clear that both specialized and broadly based studies of Alberta's relationships with the federal government in the field of social policy are needed before valid conclusions can be made about them. Meanwhile, caution in regard to sweeping generalizations is advised.

NOTES

1. Leslie Bella, "The Politics of the Right-Wing 'Welfare State'" (Ph.D. thesis, University of Alberta, 1981); Leslie Bella, "The Canada Assistance Plan," *The Social Worker* 45 (Summer 1977): 86–92; Leslie Bella, "The Goal Effectiveness of Alberta's Preventive Social Service Program," *Canadian Public Policy* 8 (Spring 1982): 143–55; Leslie Bella, "The Provincial Role in the Canadian Welfare State: The Influence of Provincial Social Policy Initiatives on the Design of the Canada Assistance Plan," *Canadian Public Administration* 22 (Fall 1979): 439–52.

2. Bella, "Politics of the 'Welfare State'," pp. 149–50.

3. Bella, "Provincial Role," p. 439.

4. Charlotte Whitton, *Welfare in Alberta: The Report of a Study* (Edmonton: Imperial Order Daughters of the Empire, Alberta Chapter, 1947).

5. Bella, "Politics of the 'Welfare State'," p. 13.

6. Although a charter member of the Canadian Association of Social Workers, Charlotte Whitton had no formal social work education. By the time of the Alberta inquiry she had allowed her membership in the association to lapse and was regarded as being at odds with the profession on a number of issues.

7. Duncan Rogers to Richard Splane, 15 June 1982 (correspondence in the author's possession).

8. Rand Dyck, "Poverty and Policy Making in the Sixties" (Ph.D. thesis, Queen's University, 1973); Rand Dyck, "The Canada Assistance Plan: The Ultimate in Cooperative Federalism," *Canadian Public Administration* (Winter 1976): 567–602; Richard Simeon, *Federal-Provincial Diplomacy: The Making of Recent Policy in Canada* (Toronto: University of Toronto Press, 1972); Richard Splane, "Social Policy Making in the Government of Canada: Reflections of a Reformist Bureaucrat," in *Canadian Social Policy* (Waterloo: Wilfrid Laurier University Press, 1978), ed. Shankar A. Yelaja, pp. 209–26.

9. Splane, "Social Policy Making."

10. Ibid., p. 214.

11. Bella, "Politics of the 'Welfare State'," p. 149.

12. Bella, "Provincial Role," p. 447.

13. Ibid., pp. 447n21 and 452n30.

14. Bella, "Politics of the 'Welfare State'," p. 146.

15. Ibid., p. 117.

16. Ibid., p. 146.
17. Ibid., p. 8.
18. Ibid., p. 133.
19. Ibid., pp. 133–34.
20. Ibid., p. 8.
21. Malcolm G. Taylor, *Health Insurance and Canadian Public Policy: The Seven Decisions that Created the Canadian Health Insurance System* (Montreal: McGill-Queen's University Press and the Institute of Public Administration of Canada, 1978), p. 376.